Due Return Date Date	Due Return Date Date

THE ETHICAL IDEALISM OF MATTHEW ARNOLD

UNIVERSITY OF TORONTO DEPARTMENT OF ENGLISH

Studies and Texts, No. 7

WILLIAM ROBBINS

The Ethical Idealism
of
Matthew Arnold

A STUDY OF THE NATURE AND SOURCES

OF HIS MORAL AND RELIGIOUS IDEAS

UNIVERSITY OF TORONTO PRESS

1959

PR
4024
R6
1959

Contents

v

Preface

To the purist, the title of this book may seem to beg the question. Indeed, the student of literature who rashly selects a tool from the philosopher's working kit is liable to find it turning in his hand to display a disconcertingly sharp edge. So a friend of mine found when, in conversation with a professor of philosophy, he offered what seemed to him, and to me, a sound comment on the relation of will to reason in human conduct. 'As you are no doubt aware,' the man of philosophy replied suavely, 'that is an epistemological sophistication.' My friend paled, and the rest was silence.

It would probably have been of little comfort to my frustrated friend to recall Matthew Arnold's mock humility in the face of an even weightier rebuke from Frederic Harrison, that he was lacking in 'a philosophy with coherent, interdependent, subordinate, and derivative principles'. For Arnold showed both a controversial adroitness and a peculiar pleasure in dealing with criticism of this kind. Moreover, he was undeniably vulnerable in his freely admitted lack of system and in his airy trespassing on the terminological preserves of the philosopher and the theologian. In claiming for Arnold the name of ethical idealist, then, it is necessary to say that the term expresses the bent of his moral nature and philosophic mind; it does not classify, or embalm, his opinions in a technically impeccable phrase.

Perhaps no major writer has given more openings to his critics than Arnold, or offered so clear a warning on the dangers of habitual irony. From his own day to ours, his deprecation of his speculative talents and his references to himself as a mere amateur have been seized on, repeated, and elaborated, by his enemies with avidity, by his friends with regret. There are two main reasons for this urge to 'seethe the kid in its mother's milk'. One is his unqualified confidence in pronouncements on matters of religion and morality, following hard upon his disavowals of specialized scholarly equipment. The other is his loose and literary use of words treated with scholastic precision in theological and philosophical studies. As the charge of insincerity could never be brought against him, his religious views have been regularly assailed as shallow, incompetent, or presumptuous, and frequently defended by a line of argument which asks us to condone wrong-headedness for the sake of true-heartedness.

There have not been wanting critics and scholars to give Arnold serious consideration in the fields where his detractors have found him utterly lacking. Pfleiderer, for example, has described him as an ethical idealist in the line of Fichte, and A. C. McGiffert has compared him with Ritschl. But there seems little point in matching Pfleiderer against J. M. Robertson, or in trying to compensate for F. H. Bradley's attack with a quotation from McGiffert. Nor could one construct an Arnoldian 'philosophy' on such *obiter dicta* as Professor Lowry's reasonable but guarded statement that Arnold 'probably knew more philosophy than he is generally given credit for', and Professor Barzun's cool concession that 'Compared with some of the religious enthusiasts of today . . . Matthew Arnold would be accounted a precisian.' It is more to the point to examine what he had to say, and why he felt he had to say it, in the light of his reading, his life and times, and his considerable influence. When this is done, the conviction emerges that in a broadly human context, and Arnold was primarily concerned with what he called the 'human problem', there is no happier term to apply to him than ethical idealist.

On the large scale of complete critical biography, this service of re-assessment has been performed for Arnold the man and writer by Lionel Trilling. In fairness of judgment, shrewdness of insight, and fullness of illustration and information, Professor Trilling's book is superior to any other work on Arnold. But it is becoming difficult to deal adequately with the whole of Arnold in one book, as we become increasingly aware through experience of the challenge to the modern age in his effort to see life steadily and see it whole. With a clearer view of the Victorians, and a more balanced estimate than prevailed in the first quarter of this century, the opinion grows that Arnold was in many ways the most modern of them. References to him, on the whole respectful in tone, have been increasing in articles and reviews, and studies of particular aspects of his work and life are likely to be the rule rather than the exception. One such is the late E. K. Brown's provocative thesis that a conflict amounting to a psychological fracture runs through Arnold's character and achievement. Certainly we have only to compare Trilling's vastly enlarged frame of reference with Sherman's simple though just evaluation to see the change that has taken place. Nor is it merely that we

know more; it is rather that Arnold the religious humanist, the
ethical idealist, challenges that increased knowledge even as he
challenged the knowledge of his own day.

Arnold did not understand all the difficulties and frustrations
of the modern age, nor did he achieve any comprehensive solu-
tion, or speak with a prophet's voice. Newman and Mill were
more logical, Carlyle and Tennyson more oracular. His signi-
ficance is that he was uniquely aware of the need to harmonize
the lessons and values of the past with the modern temper and
responsibilities. When Carlyle thunders for the fortieth time, 'Do
something!' Arnold murmurs 'coals to Newcastle', and asks
quietly, 'Do what? To what end?' When Newman condemns the
liberal and sceptical modern intellect and finds the only salvation
in a revivified mediæval faith, Arnold tells us that Newman has
adopted a solution that is 'for the educated man today, speaking
frankly, impossible'. When the sonorous music of *In Memoriam*
has closed on a note of ecstasy, and the poet has appealed to his
thrilled readers to believe where they cannot prove, Arnold
remarks that 'Tennyson is, after all, somewhat deficient in
intellectual power'.

Arnold's function is to remind enthusiasts and extremists of
the Aristotelian golden mean, to reject obscurantism on behalf of
man's instinct for expansion and change, to rebuke innovation
in the name of painfully acquired wisdom, to check fanaticism
and blind materialism by reminders of the spiritual needs of man,
to help us live by that happy fusion of powers he calls 'the
imaginative reason'. He offers, not a rounded and coherent
philosophy, but rather a set of humanistic ideals which stress the
need for balance and a sane perspective. At a time when reason
tells us that the direction in which we are going is more important
than the rate at which we go, a matter indeed of survival, his ideas
are at least as cogent as they were in his own day. He prophesied
that he was likely to have his turn; it is rather that what he had to
say has continuing relevance, that many of his attitudes and
insights operate in a larger dimension of time than that represented
by the Victorian age.

The increased awareness of Arnold as a modern, not merely
a Victorian writer, has carried with it an occasional admission
that even his religious essays are not the 'Dead Sea fruit' that
Herbert Paul regretted. They were to Arnold an essential part
of his criticism of life, a part he wished to be remembered by, and

a part containing, in his opinion, some of the best prose he wrote. There is room for more than one study of this body of his work, if its nature and bearing are to be adequately recognized. A scholar with full equipment and insight will in time issue the 'definitive' study; this book meanwhile attempts some examination of Arnold's ideas, their sources in his reading and environment, their relation to currents of thought and belief in his own day, and their relevance to some of the currents still moving within the main stream.

A word to the reader on the form of the book may not be amiss. The last chapter is in a sense an epilogue, an essay touching on certain aspects of the contemporary scene. A reader unfamiliar with Arnold's religious writings might prefer to move from chapter III to chapter VIII, leaving until later those chapters, IV to VII inclusive, which investigate in detail the nature and sources of his main religious and ethical ideas. Admittedly, the notes at the back bulk rather large. Along with the textual references, a good deal of supplementary material, whether supporting evidence or pertinent comment, has been relegated to these notes.

It is pleasant to recall the stimulus towards Arnold studies given me by the late G. G. Sedgewick, rare spirit and beloved teacher at the University of British Columbia; the doctoral thesis on Arnold's religious thought begun at the University of Toronto under the guidance of E. K. Brown, whose untimely death was a conspicuous loss to scholarship in English literature; the continued assistance and encouragement from Professor A. S. P. Woodhouse, of the University of Toronto. Any merit this study may show must reflect the inspiration of these minds and the standards of scholarship they set; any failure to respond to that inspiration or to meet those standards can reflect only my own limitations. To the grant of a scholarship from the Royal Society of Canada, and to the grant, by the President and Board of Governors of the University of British Columbia, of a leave of absence on generous terms, I owe the opportunity to spend a year in London, using the facilities of the British Museum reading room to bring into book form my study of Arnold. To the Humanities Research Council of Canada and the Publications Fund of the University of Toronto Press, I am indebted for assistance towards publication; to their anonymous readers, to the Editorial Department of the University of Toronto Press, and to my friend and colleague Edmund

Morrison, I am indebted for helpful and judicious criticism.
Where faults persist it is not for lack of good advice and a dis-
cerning eye. Finally, to the alertness, patience, and interest of my
wife, Margaret Robbins, in reading and typing the manuscript
and in compiling the Index, I owe the completion of the book
within a reasonable period of time.

W. R.

1. BACKGROUND AND CONTENT

CHAPTER I

The Old and the New:
A Survey of the Years 1860–1880

Religion he knows, and physical science he knows, but the immense work between the two, which is for literature to accomplish, he knows nothing of. . . . On the one hand, he was full of the great future for physical science, and begging the University to make up her mind to it, and to resign much of her literary studies; on the other hand, he was full, almost defiantly full, of counsels and resolves for retaining and upholding the old ecclesiastical and dogmatic form of religion. From a juxtaposition of this kind nothing but shocks and collisions can come.

> Letter of Arnold referring to a
> speech by Lord Salisbury at Oxford,
> June, 1870

The Liberalism which gives a colour to society now, is very different from that character of thought which bore the name thirty or forty years ago. Now it is scarcely a party; it is the educated lay world.

> J. H. NEWMAN, *Apologia Pro Vita Sua*

WRITERS on controversial topics are only too prone to see the years of their own involvement as epoch-making, especially when religious issues are in question. Yet there are good grounds for accepting contemporary views of the 1860's and 1870's in England as a time of crisis in religion. It is true that the storms building up to those decades appear to have abated by 1880. In 1881 Arnold echoed Newman's comment, quoted above, by writing to his faithful French correspondent, M. Fonanès: 'Religious disputes . . . still attract great attention, and create passions and parties; but certainly they have not the significance which they once had. The moral is that whoever treats religion, religious discussions, questions of churches and sects, as absorbing, is not in vital sympathy with the movement of men's minds at present. . . . The great centre-current of our time is a *lay* current.'[1] And G. M. Young tells us in *Victorian England* that by the time Oxford scholars had settled documents of the faith with German thoroughness, they gave them to a generation interested 'neither in the faith nor in the documents';

3

even 'by 1880 the electorate had other things to take sides on' than quarrels over ritual and rubric.

This very indifferentism, however, or this satiety, was itself a reaction to a period when the quarrelling had been loud and fierce; this great 'lay current', increasingly secular and sociological, was fed by streams of thought that flowed freely through channels cleared out or widened during the sixties and seventies. For it was then that increasing ritualistic 'excesses' committed by Anglican priests in the name of catholic tradition, and the ultramontanism crowned by the new dogma of papal infallibility in 1870, filled the pages of journals with warning and prophecy, or with contemptuous dismissals which failed to hide the alarm of the Protestant and patriot. Huxley was vigorously and effectively popularizing the ideas of physical science with his lectures on theory and method, while Tyndall drew on himself the full range of theological attack with his Belfast Address of 1874, in which he announced that 'we claim, and we shall wrest from theology, the entire domain of cosmological theory'. In 1872 Arnold wrote to M. Fontanès that though much had been accomplished in liberalizing religion, 'il n'est pas assez pour familiariser les esprits avec l'idée . . . d'une véritable révolution à accomplir dans leur croyances religieuses'; in 1873 he told the same correspondent that *Literature and Dogma* was already, in one month from publication, in its third edition, a popularity owing entirely to its subject matter, for in general 'tout ce qui vient de moi s'écoule très lentement'.

Here, then, were three great issues that the ordinary reader could follow, enlivened as they were by legal prosecutions, Acts of Parliament, and public debate both witty and acrimonious. He may not have cared where a priest stood while officiating at the communion table, but he was responsive to clamour against Romish tendencies and renewed cries of 'No Popery!' He may not have followed the arguments of biblical scholars, but he could follow Jowett and Arnold when they stated that the Bible was to be read like any other book, as literature. He may not have seen all that the fascinating lecturer Huxley saw in a piece of chalk, but he could hardly miss the drama and eloquence of the clash between the exponents of evolutionary and materialistic theories on the one hand, and on the other the defenders of the supernatural and of creation by divine fiat. No doubt, as M. B. Reckitt suggests in calling this period 'the climax of Victorianism', the commercial prosperity and general expansion around 1870 left the educated reader freer to observe and take sides in the Ritualist controversy and the debate on the relations of Church and State. And it must be noted that not all clergy were depressed or alarmed. There was, for example, the Reverend Francis Kilvert, whose *Diary* reveals a happy blend of Anglican piety, pagan satisfactions, and conscientious good works, a sort of primrose *via media* on which even the straying rationalist or Romanist is met with friendly converse.

Cheerful optimism or serene tolerance, however, were hardly the distinguishing notes of the controversies over biblical criticism, Ritualist practices, and the claims of physical science. The first two conflicts are now of mainly antiquarian interest to that 'educated lay world' recognized by Newman and Arnold, and the lines of the third have been re-drawn many times. But in the years around 1870 the amount of space given to all three by newspapers and periodicals, and the violence of the partisanship, suggest that there was still excitement for the general reader as well as a feeling of urgency in the devout and the informed. The champions of physical science were marching in step with the liberal and rationalist exponents of scientific biblical criticism, and the claims of orthodoxy and tradition were being countered with claims equally vigorous and much more confident. Orthodox religion was on the defensive, and the impression given by the verbal exchanges of extremists is one of utterly irreconcilable differences. To W. K. Clifford, Christianity was 'that awful plague which has destroyed two civilizations, and but barely failed to slay such promise of good as is now struggling to live amongst men'.[2] The Church and ecclesiasticism fared, if possible, even worse. Nor were the militantly orthodox inferior in invective. When Mill's *Three Essays on Religion* was issued posthumously in 1874, the *Church Herald* offered a touching obituary:

Mr J. Stuart Mill, who has just gone to his account, would have been a remarkable writer of English if his innate self-consciousness and abounding self-confidence had not made him a notorious literary prig. . . . His death is no loss to anybody, for he was a rank but amiable infidel, and a most dangerous person. The sooner those 'lights of thought' who agree with him go to the same place, the better it will be for both Church and State.[3]

These extremes will serve to show the degree of acrimonious bitterness with which the fight was carried on. But there were

B

the reconcilers, of whom Matthew Arnold was one. His effort in this direction will be the subject of the next chapter; at the head of this chapter is his recognition of the opposing forces, and of the curious fact that they could exist unreconciled in a single impercipient intelligence.

In 1870, Disraeli noted the current 'disturbance of mind' and 'ascendant materialism'. They were caused, 'Firstly, by the powerful assault on the divinity of Semitic literature by the Germans; and secondly, by recent discoveries of science, which are hastily supposed to be inconsistent with our long-received convictions as to the relations between the Creator and the created.'[4] This cool recognition of the situation was hardly enough for Gladstone, who became a self-appointed and unsuccessful apologist for menaced Christianity, to the extent of engaging in a quixotic defence of the Mosaic cosmogony. In 1872 he attacked the 'noxious crop' of rationalist writings come to his attention that year, specifically, the *First Principles* of Spencer, *Der alte und der neue Glaube* by Strauss, and Winwood Reade's *Martyrdom of Man*, and concluded eloquently: 'It is not only the Christian Church, or only the Holy Scripture, or only Christianity, which is attacked. The disposition is boldly proclaimed to deal with root and branch, and to snap utterly the ties which, under the still venerable name of Religion, unite man with the unseen world, and lighten the struggles and the woes of life by the hope of a better land.'[5]

Leaving oratorical flights to one side, we may turn to one who was both temperate and tolerant, learned and imaginative, for an acute summing-up of the crucial issue. No one was better qualified than Benjamin Jowett to indicate the position of the moderate and thoughtful man who was equally impatient of cocksure materialism and obscurantist orthodoxy. Himself a sincere churchman, a powerful cultural and religious influence upon young men at Oxford, and a contributor to *Essays and Reviews*, which had outraged the orthodox in 1860, Jowett could be expected to express in representative terms the point of view of the thinking man who accepted the findings of science, but not their application to every sphere of man's life. In 1873, he expressed surprise at Strauss's basing his *Der alte und der neue Glaube* upon Darwinism, which Jowett considered 'inadequate' rather than untrue, and concluded with this question: 'Are we to be sunk in materialism and sensualism, feebly rising into a sort of senti-

mentalism, because Strauss and others have shown that the
Gospels partake of the character of other ancient writings, or
because Darwin has imagined a theory by which one species may
pass into another?' [6] One response to this rhetorical question was
Matthew Arnold's reinterpretation of the Bible and Christianity
in an effort to establish their unique claim to permanence as
moral and spiritual guides, independent of the discoveries of
physical science and the destructive results of historical and
rational criticism.

To many, the distinguishing feature of these years was the
triumph of liberalism in thought, which made it apparent that the
stubborn traditionalist was fighting a battle in some respects
already lost. Bishops like Wilberforce and statesmen like Gladstone
were confronted with an intellectual world in which heresies and
defections could no longer, as with earlier isolated figures like
Shelley and Blanco White, be viewed as 'the sad aberration of
exceptional spirits, partly unstrung by their very sensitiveness
to pain and evil', but must be recognized as reflecting 'the con-
sidered conviction of cool thinkers, ripe students, men unbroken
by sorrow, and perfectly determined to adjust their lives to their
logical conclusions'.[7] If a bias is detected here, we may obtain
corroborative evidence from Newman's diagnosis in the *Apologia*,
where his own attitude was clear enough in his prophetic fear of
'a bottomless liberalism of thought'. It was not Liberalism as 'the
badge of a theological school', he went on. 'At present it is
nothing else than that deep, plausible scepticism, . . . the develop-
ment of human reason, as practically exercised by the natural
man.' The great change which had taken place over a period of
'thirty or forty years' was apparent to other observers besides
Newman and Arnold, but the majority of orthodox clergymen, like
Bishop Wilberforce, and lay defenders, like Gladstone, went on
stoutly defending outworks and blockhouses long since by-passed
by the enemy.

The most unfortunate element in the situation, from the
point of view of liberal and scholarly theologians, was the rigid
emphasis on conformity, no matter how unintelligent. Pfleiderer
refers to the 'moral terrorism' and 'intellectual tyranny' which
earlier attempts at elasticity of thought had encountered.[8]
Andrew D. White tells us that there was 'a cynical aphorism'
current at the time on the subject of preferment, to the effect that
'He may hold anything who will hold his tongue.' [9] Westcott, while

still a master at Harrow, admitted in 1861, 'It is acknowledged by all that men of high intellectual culture have for some years shrunk from taking Orders.'[10] And Mark Pattison, in an essay in 1863 on 'Learning in the Church of England', declared, 'The High Church clergyman carries with him into everything he does a fatal stereotype of theological opinion. Trained not to employ his reason in his theology, he never thinks of employing it in any other direction.'[11]

Even allowing for the bitterness doubtless felt by Pattison at the hostile reception accorded to *Essays and Reviews*, by continental standards a very mild venture into rationalist criticism, the consensus of opinion points to a condition of intellectual timidity in the Church. Jowett was both dismayed and pessimistic. In 1861 he had prophesied that 'In a few years there will be no religion among young men, *unless religion is shown to be consistent with criticism.*'[12] In 1870 his worst fears were being realized. 'People have no fixed principles and no education in the higher sense, and all sorts of Ritualisms and Spiritualisms and Aestheticisms take their place (just at this moment the Aesthetic seems to have got a curious hold at Oxford).'[13] We see here, among other possibilities, the influence of Ruskin and the later development of the Oxford Movement; but the important implication is that able men could not find satisfaction within the Church for both their emotional and spiritual needs *and* their critical intelligences.

As a result of this stubborn opposition to the scientific spirit and to new ideas, biblical criticism in England lagged far behind the position which it had attained on the Continent (another aphorism current at the time stated that while Germany had a theology and no Church, England had a Church and no theology). Not that advocates of critical methods had been wanting in England even in the earlier part of the century. With Coleridge and Thomas Arnold as influential pioneers, the critical and historical study of the Bible had also found exponents in men like Whately, Thirlwall, Julius Hare, Milman, and Maurice. In 1835 (the year of Strauss's *Leben Jesu* in Germany) Dr Arnold had suggested to Julius Hare that one of the main purposes of a proposed 'theological review' should be 'To make some beginnings of Biblical Criticism, which, as far as relates to the Old Testament, is in England almost non-existent.'[14] But Dr Arnold, who regarded the Tübingen school with abhorrence for their radical views, was himself regarded as a dangerous radical in England. Liberal theologians, denounced and opposed by fellow-churchmen at every turn, and themselves fearful of the utilitarian philosophers and secular rationalists, made their lonely contributions in a sporadic and non-systematic way. The curiously individualist position of the religious critic in England is clearly shown by the vigorous attack on Bishop Colenso by both Matthew Arnold and Maurice, when this liberal theologian published in 1862 his critical examination of the Pentateuch, a study fully in line with corresponding work done on the Continent. The divergences of aim and method from their own were genuine and distinct, at least in the opinion of the attackers, but to most contemporary and subsequent critics this violent attack by a brother 'rationalist' like Arnold was irrational in the extreme.

Nothing serves better to show the temper of the times with respect to the Higher Criticism than the Colenso case, which to a modern reader has all the elements of the higher comedy. Driven to a fresh perusal of the sacred text by the puzzled questions of intelligent Zulus, the mathematically trained Bishop of Natal found himself unable, in all honesty, to go on accepting and defending conflicts in dates, scientific impossibilities, and arithmetical discrepancies that outraged common sense. His candour compelled him to publish the result of his study in 1862, in *The Pentateuch and the Book of Joshua Critically Examined*. As a result of the outcry against the book, Colenso was deposed by his metropolitan, Bishop Gray of Cape Town. This action met with episcopal approval in England, but was later declared null and void by a judicial committee of the Privy Council, on the grounds that Bishop Gray had exceeded his authority. Bishop Gray went so far in his defiance of the government as to have the Rev. W. K. Macrorie consecrated as bishop to replace Colenso. On their joint departure to South Africa they compared themselves to Paul setting out on his missionary journey, a piece of 'extravagant rant' which inspired in *The Times* of October 8, 1868, a description of Gray's High Church sympathizers as 'a society for propagating Bishops in foreign parts'. By March of 1869 vehemence had replaced satire. *The Times* spoke of 'civil war' in Natal, stressed the illegality of Macrorie's appointment as worse than Colenso's opinions, and warned that a distaste for being dragged into 'the squabbles of the clergy' might make the government sympathetic to propaganda for the disestablishment of the Church of England.

Meanwhile Colenso continued his researches, which ran to

seven parts by 1879. The first part was issued in a people's edition in 1865, and attack and defence flowed from the press in a stream represented by nine columns of entries in the British Museum catalogue. The titles include *Moses or the Zulu?* and *Confessions of a Missionary*; there were vindications of Noah's Ark, of the Pentateuch, and of Bishop Colenso. Bishop Tait wrote to Colenso's brother-in-law, the Bishop of Labuan, asking what was wrong with the offender. The reply was: 'Mathematical notions and western ways of viewing things have plainly led him astray. He says, in short, that he can believe in a miracle, but he cannot believe in a bad sum.' [15] Surely, said Canon Liddon in reproaching Dean Stanley for his liberal sympathies, he had not cast his lot with 'men like Colenso, who are labouring to destroy and blot out the faith of Jesus Christ from the hearts of the people'.[16] Bishop Lee of Manchester said that 'the very nearest and dearest of our con-solations are taken from us when one line of that sacred volume, on which we base everything, is said to be unfaithful or untrust-worthy'.[17] Since the Bishop of Natal had said this of many lines, Lee could find 'no language befitting a gentleman and a Christian which he could use in his condemnation'. Colenso's reply was to ask the Bishop of Manchester whether he rested his faith and hopes on the eleventh chapter of Leviticus, where 'the hare is not to be eaten, because he cheweth the cud, but divideth not the hoof'.

It was the shock of this puerile exchange, the saintly and generous Maurice admitted, that turned his indignation away from Colenso to its proper object, the narrow-minded literalness that would base the religious spirit, and especially the Christian faith, on physically demonstrable fact rather than on moral truth. No wonder that an 'old official at a certain University' remarked, 'I have listened for forty years to the sermons at St ———'s, and thank God! I am a Christian still.' Yet though Maurice, in *The Claims of the Bible and Science*, defended Colenso's integrity, he felt strongly the danger attached to such rationalistic exegesis being regarded as essential to faith, when faith in a loving God was itself essential to the Christian life. 'In what respect', he asked, 'are we likely to be the wiser or the better for these questions being thrust on the attention of the laity in every country town, before their moral and spiritual import has been duly considered and recognized?' This, as we shall see in the next chapter, was exactly the position of Arnold, who stated that Colenso's book reposed on 'a total misconception of the essential elements of the religious problem' and was both supererogatory and mischievous. Such has not been the consensus of scholarly opinion, and though there is a flavour of absurdity about some of Colenso's arithmetical tests, the value and originality of his work were stressed at the time by Abraham Kuenen. Coming from Arnold such criticism, understandable enough as a protest from disturbed orthodoxy, could be attributed only to an inner conflict of values, in which the radical critic seeking truth at all costs was at least temporarily submerged by the conservative moralist alarmed by the cost of truth.

One clue to the combination of intellectual timidity and critical confusion marking the religious thought of the age, and the consequent time lag in speculative development, is furnished by Pfleiderer, who points to the lack of a philosophical or meta-physical basis of any solidity for nineteenth-century formal theology in England. This, of course, is in striking contrast to Germany, where the teachings of the 'Romantic' philosophers, particularly of Hegel, had been used with great effect to supply system and direction to the speculative efforts of theologians. Pfleiderer finds even a work as good as Martineau's *Study of Religion* lacking in 'a closer analysis of the psychological nature of religion, and particularly a more thorough examination of the historical development of the religious consciousness of mankind'.[18] And W. O. Raymond, in a survey of the Higher Criticism in England during the nineteenth century, concludes that the typical attitude of the English mind to questions of philosophy and religion is marked by 'individualism, subjectivity, lack of systematic develop-ment, absence of radicalism'.[19] These qualities are not necessarily weaknesses; even if they are regarded as characteristic marks of the English mind at any time rather than of the English mind in the nineteenth century, they may, as well as their opposites, make effective contributions to thought and criticism. But they are seen in exaggerated form in the period and field under dis-cussion, and that at a time when a united though flexible front was required if religion was to absorb the best of modern thought without yielding any really vital ground.

If strictly defensive tactics and the eloquence of fear were the main response to the application of scientific methods to historical studies of the Bible, there was another area in which the forces of orthodoxy took a vigorous initiative. The story of the Oxford

Movement, which developed into High Church Anglicanism or Anglo-Catholicism, has been told often enough, with emphasis upon the guiding genius of Newman and Pusey and upon the influence of the Romantic Revival, reflecting the passion for history and tradition and the exalting of mystery and the life of the spirit over mere fact and empirical reasoning. What concerns us here is the special character of the movement. As revealed both by the Tractarian phase and, after Newman's conversion to Rome, by the development of Ritualism, it was an assertion of ecclesiastical and priestly Christianity against the power of the State and against individualistic Protestantism. It based its beliefs and its claims upon the apostolic succession and the sacramental powers, especially those centring on the Eucharist— indeed, it would not be inaccurate to say that the distinguishing features of the movement from that day to this have been the sacerdotal and the sacramental.

The nominal start of the movement, the suppression of ten Irish bishoprics by the government, provoking Keble's 'National Apostasy' sermon in 1833, was irrational as a focus of resentment for the dedicated few at Oxford. These superfluous bishoprics were as great a scandal as absentee landlordism. The group at Oxford had themselves spoken against the 'lethargy and corruption' of the eighteenth-century church, against pluralism and apathy and absenteeism, with great vigour. But whereas the Evangelicals, the later Low Church party, had sought to justify the Church of England to God and man by enthusiastic labours in the vineyard, the future Anglo-Catholics believed the Church could save her soul only by asserting her independence of the State and her divine destiny. A few abuses, especially if consecrated by mediæval precedent, were nothing compared with the need for a ringing declaration and clear definition of the Church's historical witness and doctrinal position. Failure to speak out had assisted the disintegrating powers of Protestant sectarianism and rational liberalism, and had encouraged the increasing subservience of Church to State since the Reformation. The way to bring about a rebirth of the true Church in England was to reaffirm the notes of catholicity and continuity, with the place of prime importance given to the doctrine of the apostolic succession. 'The Church as it is now,' declared Thomas Arnold, 'no power on earth can save.' With this Cassandran warning the Oxford group agreed, save that to them Arnold represented the liberal and

Erastian Protestantism that played into the hands of the enemy, while to him these 'Newmanite' and 'Romanizing' reactionaries were that 'great Antichristian apostasy' which 'had for its root the tenet of "a priestly government transmitted by a mystical succession from the Apostles".' [20]

Both the strength and the weakness of the movement, and of its later development, arose from its uncompromising hostility to the main stream of modern thought. To a secular belief in progress these men opposed the concept of eternal and unchanging order; to a growing scientific materialism they opposed a belief in a supreme spiritual reality; to a liberal individualism they opposed a conservative preference for authority and obedience; to the worldly power of the State struggling to cope with the clashing interests of its citizens, they opposed the unworldly power of the Church binding the souls of its people in corporate worship and offering regenerative grace through the divine sacramental channels. Resting their claims upon a profound study of the early Church Fathers and upon unbroken tradition, they were less shaken by the historical criticism of the Bible than were the Evangelicals, whose faith was based in a doctrine of 'plenary inspiration'. Their sincerity and devotion were as marked as their ecclesiastical learning, with the result that their sermons and articles attracted much attention in an age 'destitute of faith but terrified of scepticism'. They could appeal to the sense of novelty with the old that was again new, to the sense of awe and reverence with their intense belief that the sacrificial mystery was the centre of the Christian life. Finally, they spoke out as a restorative force, seeking to bring the Church of England back to an earlier level of dignity and power, and to claim for her the true notes of catholicity and antiquity forfeited in the 'corruption' of the Roman Church.

Yet for all the ability and devotedness of the men of the movement, the main positive result was not to change the nature of the Church of England as a whole, which in effect was what they desired, but to stimulate to renewed life and activity every section of that Church. To some observers the proud certainty seemed like exclusive arrogance. Indeed, when Newman remarked after an opinion of Dr Arnold's was repeated to him, 'But is *he* a Christian?' not all his suave explanations could erase the impression that his first utterance contained his real thought. To others, as H. L. Stewart tells us, there was a lack of reality in the questions about the niceties of the Nicene creed that obsessed the

Tractarians, in the days of Chartism and *Hard Times* and the *Song of the Shirt*. It was men like Maurice and Kingsley who made proper application of texts on the meek and the suffering: 'They too thought that England was apostate—not so much, however, because heresy was appearing, as because humanity was vanishing; not so much because men were missing the finer implications of "Triune Godhead" as because they were despising the obvious implications of Christian brotherhood.' [21] But what really turned most Englishmen within and without the Church against the movement itself was the 'Romanizing' tendency, clear enough by the date of *Tract XC*[22] and confirmed by Newman's conversion in 1845. William G. Ward and others had already gone over to Rome, and the trickle continued afterwards, but the I-told-you-so prophets had their real triumph when Newman's course became as clear to himself as it had been to his more suspicious critics.

The defections to Rome took on sinister meaning to some observers when the Pope restored a Roman Catholic hierarchy in England in 1850, with the convert Wiseman, later to become a Cardinal, as the first Archbishop of Westminster. Nor were the fears that inspired the outcry of alarmists at these external signs entirely absent from the minds of the judicious and tolerant, especially if they attended to the confident claims of some English Roman Catholics. In 1860 Cardinal Wiseman obtained permission from the Pope to establish 'an Academia of the Catholic Religion affiliated to that in Rome'. The papers read there from 1861 on, published in 1865 in three volumes as *Essays in Religion and Literature*, contained some inflammable material, in particular, the addresses of Dr Manning, later Archbishop and Cardinal. In 1864, with a glance at the Church of England being torn apart by Rationalist and Romanist, he said, 'We need only gather our sheaves into the garner.' Young men were falling away from the 'incoherent and untenable' Anglican formularies, and the rationalism inherent in resting Christianity upon scripture alone was gathering head. In his 1866 inaugural address, his main theme was the rapid advance of Catholicism in the Anglican communion, and his certainty that the Roman Catholic Church would gain by any Anglican attack on Protestantism.

Fear of a restored Roman Catholicism helps to explain the uproar in the sixties and seventies over Ritualism, that passionate concern for the externals of worship which developed out of the Oxford Movement, and which continued until extreme Anglo-

Catholicism was, and is, separated from Rome only by the doctrine of papal supremacy. When Newman gave up his attempt to find in Anglicanism the true Catholic faith and followed both his logic and his emotions to Rome, the intellectual and doctrinal fervour which had inspired the Tracts was soon subordinated to an enthusiasm for the badges and signs of Catholic worship. Incense, altar lights, coloured vestments, the elevation of the Host, genuflection, auricular confession, a revived monasticism, adoration of the consecrated elements as containing the Real Objective Presence—such practices were 'purifying' restorations to the Ritualists and dangerous innovations to their critics. The Ritualists were quite clear on what they were doing, and why, as a statement by Littledale shows:

It may be argued that good and vigorous preaching will fill the cravings of the congregations, and make the employment of material stimuli superfluous, if not mischievous. But good preaching is among the rarest of good things. . . . If good actors were common, the adventitious aid of scenery and properties would be comparatively unimportant, because the harmonious action of all the persons of the drama would be sufficient to create an illusion able to rivet the attention of the spectators. But as the great majority of actors are mere sticks, . . . managers have constantly been compelled to make a gorgeous spectacle their main attraction. . . . Hence a lesson may be learnt . . . from the stage, for it is an axiom in liturgiology that no public worship is really deserving of its name unless it be histrionic.[23]

It would be hard to say whether this frank passage was more offensive to the nineteenth-century Evangelical for its analogy, or to the nineteenth-century rationalist for its implied view of human intelligence. Commenting on the whole tenor of *The Church and the World,* from which this excerpt was taken, the *Quarterly Review* believed that the 'splendid accessories' school was bound to lose in its attempt to do to the Prayer Book what Newman had done to the Thirty-nine Articles. Newman's 'noble mind' took him to Rome, but he left behind him 'the evil heritage of a sophistry that has been troubling us ever since'. *The Times* reviewer made a strong attack on this same collection of essays for its arrogance and general Romish direction; indeed the pages of *The Times* from 1865 to 1875 are a good index to the amount of disturbance the Ritualist High Churchmen caused. Scornful of 'rubrical antics' which to Newman himself were 'gilt and gingerbread', the reviewers remark on 'these annual epidemics of clerical excitement'. Yet the tone continually changes from sarcasm to alarm as the writers contemplate the evils of a drift to Rome *via* Ritualism, a loss of the Protestant strain fundamental to the Reformation, and a break-up of authority within the Church of England itself. Dean Henry Alford admitted that 'To the superficial observer the Church of England is casting off her moorings, and drifting back to Romanism.' [24] Not only to superficial or partisan observers was this apparent. So detached a rationalist as George Eliot told the future Earl of Oxford and Asquith in '1873 or 1874' that he would live 'to see a great renascence of religion among thoughtful people', and in reply to his question as to which church would benefit, named the Roman Catholic Church. [25]

The threat to the authority of the Church, and consequently of the State, was, however, the real and continuing issue. What the Church was facing was in effect a rebellion on the right, a yearning to restore the complete Catholic tradition. This was difficult to deal with, for many of the 'innovations' in worship merely presented in exaggerated form the elements of catholicity and apostolicity that the Church was bound to maintain against the dissolving tendencies of dissent and liberalism. Compromise and moderation in these matters, as presented in her own rubrics and in her earlier simpler worship, were essential to her continuance as a national, comprehensive, and established Church. Yet by this very compromise and moderation, involving acquiescence in decisions by judicial committees of the Privy Council, she was to the more rigid High Churchmen selling her soul into Erastian bondage and maintaining the anomaly and impiety of secular control in spiritual affairs.

Besides the fear of a Church shattered by internal dissensions, there was the second and graver fear, to which *The Times* gave frequent expression. Coming on top of the protracted and futile opposition to the spirit of free inquiry, what could be achieved by this bickering over 'obsolete garments', 'mediæval attitudes', and doctrinal points impossible to settle, save a growing alienation of the onlookers, a hostile judgment upon the Church as an archaic institution unable to adjust its ideas to social change and scientific advance? 'The millions of this country', *The Times* said in August, 1868, 'will eventually govern it, and the Church need fear nothing so long as it stands with them.' But it could be a national Church only if it represented the nation's 'religious beliefs' and 'moral sentiment'. This would not be the outcome if congregations were repelled by ceremonials and forms that deliberately repudiated the Reformation. In November of 1866 *The Times* had warned of 'a growing dislike of the Church', a weariness and indifference of cultivated persons towards Church questions: 'Men of intelligence hold themselves apart from the futile disputes, the narrow ecclesiasticism, the frivolous tastes of the clergy.'

Such a statement carries its own bias, ignoring the honesty and spiritual depth of men like Keble, whose Anglo-Catholicism was very far from being bound up with ritualistic detail. Lamenting in 1865 the Bishop of London's effort to have a Royal Commission deal in part with the proposed Prayer Book revision, Keble finds it suicidal for the Church to allow such continued interference with her own affairs, for the liberalism of the day, 'not so much irreligious as anti-dogmatic', would play one Church party against another to get rid of 'all distinct and exclusive teaching'. If Churchmen join Erastians and Dissenters in urging government action, where will changes stop? Keble warns that a one-sided anti-Catholic policy will develop, ultimately 'displacing those who are called Tractarians or the like' and overthrowing 'the sort of equilibrium which for many years has providentially existed among us'.[26] Behind Keble's fear is a hope of 're-union among Christians'. For him, naturally, the name of Christian is doctrinally defined: 'Of all doctrines, that of the Eucharistical Sacrifice is the one on which, in the eyes both of East and West, our Catholicity would appear most questionable. A hair's breadth more of wavering ... would seem ... an entire forfeiture of our position.' The anxiety here is for something more than liturgical or ritual Catholicism. Yet to the 'cultivated persons' of *The Times* article, and still more to their descendants aware of what the study of comparative religion has done to a belief in the divine and unique symbolism of the Eucharist, even Keble's stand on the central and transcendent mystery would have its share of intellectual futility and mediæval obsolescence.

On this note we may turn to consider the third great issue, the one of steadily increasing import—the dissolving effect of scientific method and discovery upon the old authorities and beliefs. The sceptical forces operating in the other two areas drew from the methods of scientific research the questions applied with such damaging effect to the authenticity, historicity, or uniqueness of creed, scripture, and sacrament. But the proponents of physical science were, after all, critical of ancient documents or practices only in so far as these were used as authorities to condemn or deny their findings. The theories being confidently and vigorously propounded in the sixties and seventies were establishing a view of the earth and of man completely at variance with the views of orthodoxy based on scripture and tradition. Not that the scientific theories were new, but the supporting evidence had become irresistible to any impartial mind. The authority for the opposing traditional beliefs was increasingly regarded as meaningless *in the context of physical science*, whatever value it might continue to have as moral parable, religious history, and poetic or symbolic myth.

How swift had been the advance is seen by a glance back at 1844. Although Lyell's *Principles of Geology* had already made some impact, the *Vestiges of the Natural History of Creation* was published anonymously in that year, and indeed the authorship of Robert Chambers was not revealed until 1884, thirteen years after his death. The need for caution is clear from the fact that a scientifically acceptable definition of species in 1844 was that of Philip Gosse in *An Introduction to Zoology*. They were 'those distinct forms which are believed to have proceeded direct from the creating hand of God', passed down 'through all succeeding generations without loss and without confusion'.[27] Few dared challenge this statement, J. Y. Simpson tells us, and most believed it. Yet in thirty years the pious and puritan Gosse, devoted student of Nature though he was, had become something of an oddity in the world of science. Darwin had followed Lyell; biology had joined with geology, and with physics and chemistry, in finding man, as well as his total environment, explainable by purely natural laws of birth, growth, and decay, of order and of change. It is worth repeating Tyndall's challenge: 'We claim, and we shall wrest from theology, the entire domain of cosmological theory.'

Two aspects of the conflict filled the period with the smoke and noise of battle. One was the passionate outcry of those, already noted in the discussion of the Colenso case, whose religious faith was founded on 'the impregnable rock of Holy Scripture', to the extent that every word and line was regarded as historically and scientifically true. 'The intolerance and obscurantism of a large section of religious opinion', says E. L. Woodward, 'was in open contrast with the exact methods of scientific investigation, and the attitude of the Church towards biblical criticism seemed to shut out any hope of reconciling religion and science.' [28] But even these fanatical literalists could not long retain Moses as official geologist, nor cry down the evidence for the evolutionary development of man. To such a theologian as F. D. Maurice, their fears of Darwin and Huxley were unworthy, as were the charges that 'these opinions must lead to materialism and atheism'. His considered statement showed where, rather than on textual accuracy or on the analogies and reasoning of 'natural religion', the religious mind should take its stand:

A man who accepts the Scriptures of the Old and New Testament, and not Paley's 'Natural Theology', as his Bible; . . . who starts with the belief in God as his Father, has no right to cherish those apprehensions, or to indulge in those insinuations. Claiming for man a place *above* nature—a direct relation to God through a Mediator—a mansion in a house which is eternal in the heavens—he cannot be anxious about the place which man may be found to hold *in* nature. . . . We want only free room and courage to tell men that they are made in God's image, and that He seeks to raise them to that image. [29]

Here was one answer that could be made, and that increasingly came to be made—in effect, that the truths of religion and the truths of physical science moved on different planes. Another response was indicated by the prolific and learned, if erratic, F. W. Newman. Himself a free-thinker and believer in scientific inquiry (a most illuminating study of the nineteenth century could be centred on the conflicting minds and careers of the Newman brothers), he called for a severer logic, for stricter notions of proof, in religious matters. The sceptic (etymologically an *inquirer*) puts the whole supernatural element in the Gospels on the level of delusion and hearsay. The improbable carries 'no moral weight', and 'the true foundation of religion is ethics, not history'. We have a rich heritage, says Newman, but for ethical truth we need ethical proof; for historical facts we need historical witness. And the latter is acceptable only when 'overwhelming evidence satisfies well-informed minds of the most opposite character'. When the sceptic is answered, the bigot disappears, and religion is reconciled with truth on the same foundation as science. In this brief pamphlet Newman even manages a glance forward at the growing science of comparative religion: 'Instead of moralizing over Mormon incredulity, we ought to see in it, as in a mirror, how Christianity was built up.' [30]

The main strategy of the orthodox before the advancing forces

of physical science, however, was neither the flight to the strato-
sphere of F. D. Maurice, nor the fifth-column welcome of F. W.
Newman. It was rather a re-enactment on the intellectual level of
the Charge of the Light Brigade, against the forces of the new
'barbarism', with a reckless zeal and a net result that recall the
Laureate's most memorable lines. Hence came the 'shocks and
collisions' of a heated controversy whose one-sided nature was
rapidly becoming clear. In 1871 Tylor's *Primitive Culture*, as
Woodward tells us, in applying Darwin's method to anthropology
was 'the precursor of a new school of thought which educated men
could not ignore and appeals to traditional authority could not
suppress'.[31] Yet a typical response is that of the *Quarterly Review*
article, 'Tylor and Lubbock', in which five books by these famous
scholars, published from 1865 to 1870, are considered as a whole.
These anthropological researchers, the reviewer maintains, *despite
themselves* support the dualistic hypothesis of an impassable gulf,
a difference in *kind* not degree, between man and the highest of
brutes. Why? Because they find universal use of language, morals,
and religion, because they find retrogression as well as progress
among tribes or peoples, and most important, because they have
failed utterly to produce evidence of a transitional group or phase.
They have acknowledged the 'missing link'. These findings of
'ethnology and archæology', the reviewer triumphantly con-
cludes, tend to show the inadequacy of the Darwinian theory of
evolution, and the need for the only explanatory factor—'the
action of a DIVINE MIND as the direct and immediate originator
and cause of the existence of its created image, the mind of man'.[32]
We may be grateful to them, however, and even to Darwin, whose
theory of the origin of man furnishes a *reductio ad absurdum* in a
world where man is 'ordained observer, historian and master'.

The dogmas and presuppositions which dominate this naïvely
confident review are clear, and the review as a whole reminds us
how important it is, in considering the relations of religion and
science, to distinguish the mid-Victorian phase of the conflict from
later developments. How much a set of assumptions will reflect
an age is pleasantly illustrated by an evidence of (æsthetic)
retrogression found by the reviewer in Lubbock's reports. It is
'remarkable that . . . in the Stone period we find very fair drawings
of animals, yet . . . throughout that of Bronze . . . ornamentation is
confined to various combinations of straight and curved lines and
geometrical patterns'.

The second aspect of the conflict was of deeper and more lasting significance than differing views of creation. It is clear in Maurice's transcendent idealism, and in the comments of the *Quarterly* reviewer who declared that the whole question of a transition from animal to human nature involved processes and essential principles that move us into the domain of philosophy and psychology (we again see the earlier phase of the conflict in the assumption that such a move necessarily takes us out of the realm of the mechanical and merely natural). The concern for a spiritual view of life against a growing, and at times aggressive, materialism was the cause of many dramatic encounters and declarations: of Disraeli's announcing that he was on the side of the angels, of Carlyle's rebuff to a greeting from Huxley, of Huxley's triumphing over Bishop Wilberforce, in knowledge and in manners, in public debate. The part of Tyndall's Belfast address which precipitated the debate with Martineau was not the flamboyant challenge quoted earlier. It was a speculation tentatively expressed, as befitted a scientific speaker. In following the insight of mind into molecular matter beyond microscopic revelation to the eye, Tyndall saw 'a necessity engendered by Science' that might justify crossing 'the boundary of the experimental evidence' and finding in matter 'the promise and potency of all terrestrial life'.[33] But, he conceded, experimental proof for spontaneous generation was not yet satisfactory.

This statement drew upon Tyndall what he called 'a storm of opprobrium', and what one of his critics referred to as a 'chorus of dissent'. Ignoring the opprobrium, of which the *Dublin Review* offered an example, we may notice a specimen of dissent in the Anglican (Evangelical) *Christian Observer*. The writer refutes Tyndall by stating that if God *had* intended evolution of form into form, and of intelligence out of matter, He would have said so. Why did the huge extinct animals, with their strength and armour fitting them for 'success in the battle of life', not survive as the fittest? The wisdom of God had prepared the earth for man by the extinction of those monsters. Evolution as a theory, then, is 'totally at fault here' and is defeated 'on scientific principles alone'.[34]

Had all the replies been of this calibre, Tyndall would hardly have bothered to take up the question again, though Huxley might well have sighed and girded his loins for another bout of popular scientific lectures. But among the replies was an opening address at Manchester New College, London, in October of 1874,

c

by Principal James Martineau, entitled 'Religion as Affected by Modern Materialism'. Tyndall had already written his 'Apology for the Belfast Address' to deal with his noisier critics; now he showed his sense of a more formidable antagonist in the liberal, philosophical, and learned Martineau by publishing 'The Rev. James Martineau and the Belfast Address'. Martineau answered this attack on his position with a long and carefully considered article in the *Contemporary Review*, later published in book form as *Modern Materialism: Its Attitude towards Theology*. In the courteous exchanges of these two outstanding figures, the real question at issue between the scientist and the theologian is made clear: Is knowledge possible in areas of experience to which the scientific method has not been, and perhaps cannot be, applied?

At the conclusion of his Belfast Address, Tyndall had said that there was much that was important besides understanding—namely feeling—in poetry, art, and religion. Scientifically grotesque and even dangerous as such experiences may have been at times, it would be wise to 'recognize them as the forms of a force, mischievous if permitted to intrude on the region of objective *knowledge*, over which it holds no command, but capable of adding, in the region of *poetry* and *emotion*, inward completeness and dignity to man'.[35] It was this distinction that Martineau challenged. The assumptions behind man's religious positions, he said, were 'beyond the contradiction, because not within the logical range, of the natural sciences'.[36] Yet for their 'ethical power', these positions were 'absolutely dependent on their objective truth'. (We may see here, incidentally, in the use of 'knowledge' by the one speaker and 'truth' by the other, the never-the-twain-shall-meet quality common to most such debates.) Tyndall had taxed him with letting his assumptions remain as such. But 'in every reasoned discourse assumptions have their proper place, as well as proofs; and the right selection of propositions to stand in the one position or the other depends on the speaker's thesis and the hearer's needs'. Again the shifting plane of the discussion is obvious, Martineau's last four words containing a postulate that Tyndall would find irrelevant. The assumption that Martineau himself found essential to man's ethical being had been clearly put in an early study, 'Present Influences on Present Theology'. Having summed up the mid-century influences as the ecclesiastical (Newman), the philosophical (Coleridge to Maurice), and the literary (Carlyle), Martineau concluded: 'Even for truth of *representation*, and infinitely more for faithfulness of character and action, a distinctive reverence for man as *more than natural*, as the abode of God in a sense quite false of clouds and stars, as intrusted with himself that he may surrender to a higher —is indispensable.' [37]

It is interesting to see how near these men approach, in spite of their disagreement on the limits and nature of the knowable. Tyndall states bluntly that the main point of difference, as he sees it, is that religion is a matter of feeling to him, while Martineau insists on knowledge. 'When I attempt to give the Power which I see manifested in the Universe an objective form, personal or otherwise,' says Tyndall, 'it slips away from me, declining all intellectual manipulation.' [38] What Martineau claims as knowledge is only a subjective emotion or need. There *is* a formative power, a *unity of life* from the inorganic to man, and perhaps this is a part or function of a 'Higher Life'. 'I resist no such idea,' he goes on, 'as long as it is not dogmatically imposed. Left for the human mind freely to operate upon, the idea has ethical vitality.' But matter itself is the mystery, for we cannot answer the question —how are physical facts *connected with* states of consciousness? How is the transition effected? The question we ask about this inherent potency is not, who put the power there, but, what is the power? All we know is what the senses, aided by science, tell us. To some men the 'dry light' of intellect is enough; others are stimulated by the mystery: 'What is really needed is the lifting power of an ideal element in human life.' Granted free play to this, then 'purer and mightier' minds will emerge, because of 'their deeper knowledge of matter and their more faithful conformity to its laws'.

In his critique of Tyndall's position, Martineau picks up Tyndall's charge that he had been misquoted as saying that materialism *explains* everything. Very well then, says Martineau, our scientist is inconsistent. For to assume a bond of union between facts, or lines of succession, is to set up a hypothesis *explaining* the second by the first, that is, to set up a higher conception from which deductions can be made of 'both sets of previously separate facts'. Atomic materialism is just such a hypothesis (or assumption), and the law of the conservation of energy is 'only an Ideal of the Reason', however indispensable as a goal and guide for empirical research. Now if there is this Power that Tyndall talks about, why not go a step further and see in it a man-like (spiritual) force rather than a brute-like (material) force? 'The similitude to man means no more and goes no further than the supremacy of intellectual insight and moral ends over every inferior alternative.' [39] Why not attribute thought, the highest of human exercises, to this Power that has already been to some extent personified? Why not identify the collective energies with the Divine Will? We press into nature in hopes of finding what is beyond nature, and it is odd of the scientist to try to limit determinate causation, when the whole of his effort shows the co-existence of conscious aim and purpose with it: 'If there were only mind-excluding force in nature, how could there arise a force-resisting mind in him?' Teleology and causality are one, says Martineau; mechanical necessity is but the persistence of purpose: 'The inexorability of nature is but the faithfulness of God, the maintenance of those unswerving habits in the universe, without which it could train no mind and school no character.' [40]

Though Martineau is an unorthodox theologian, a philosophic Unitarian, it is striking to find so close an approach. The scientist admits 'the lifting power of an ideal element', which draws its ethical vitality from a profound study of matter; the theologian explains the laws of nature as identical with the ethical force that derives from the idea of God. The difference would seem to be one of words. Yet Martineau finally insists on a distinction that lifts the ethical idea into the religious sphere. That immanent *life* of Tyndall's he will continue to call the Causal Will. For the higher or ideal life will be ethically sterile, he believes, unless it is thought of as transcendent Mind and Will, 'infinitely Wise and Good and Holy'. How else can the 'higher' mean moral and intellectual sublimity? As Divine Causality it harmonizes with Reason; as 'Perfect Reason and Righteous Will' it can be the object of religious faith. Martineau is keenly aware that the truth he postulates as indispensable to the ethical nature of man is very different from the 'objective knowledge' of Tyndall, even when the latter achieves his knowledge by the working hypothesis of a 'formative Power'. But he is not in the least disturbed by this. 'I am profoundly conscious', he says, 'how strong is the set of the *Zeit-Geist* against me'—that is, that rational questions can only be asked in the realm of the natural sciences—yet it is but 'a mere pulsation of the *Ewigkeits-geist* that never sweeps by'.

There were other, and in the long run perhaps deeper, conflicts than those we have been considering, involving a reshaping of the

very forms and frames of thought. The *Zeitgeist* that Martineau
rebuked in the name of the Eternal Spirit was compelling the
Victorian to learn to live with change, and stirring his pulse to
a rapid beat and his mood to a Utopian optimism by the mere
excitement of pace. In an essay entitled 'Realisable Ideals', W. R.
Greg said in 1872, 'We *remember* light as it was in the days of
Solomon, we *see* it as Drummond and Faraday have made it.' [41]
Surely the mental and moral force that has shaped our modern
locomotion and communication from the material world can be
fired with enthusiasm for Humanity and bring us nearer to the
ideal State: 'Thought has not yet grown feebler than electricity
and gases in moulding the destinies of man.' [42] Deeper again than
this sense of temporal progress was the shifting of the whole frame
of thought, under the influence of scientific theory and discovery,
from being to becoming, with so much of continuing and painful
adjustment. 'The age was learning,' G. M. Young tells us, 'but it
had not mastered, the lesson that truth lies not in the statement
but in the process; it had a childlike craving for certitude, as if the
natural end of every refuted dogma was to be replaced by another
dogma.' [43]

Sometimes, too, the issues discussed expressed themselves
dramatically in the clash of generations, as we see in *Father and
Son*, where Edmund Gosse describes as 'harsh and void and
negative', as 'sterile and cruel', the 'stringent piety' of the
Evangelical religion so satisfying and necessary to his father, that
odd combination of devoted zoologist and devout fundamentalist.
More moving than this clash of a strong father and stronger son is
the story of the weaker and more sensitive Hale White in the
anonymously published *Autobiography of Mark Rutherford*. It is the
story of many who carried on a fruitless search in the intellectual
backwaters of the age. He is prepared for the Ministry at a
Dissenting college, where 'German' is only a vague term of
reproach, where systematic theology consists of a Calvinistic
manual setting forth the whole scheme of redemption, useless
'in repressing one solitary evil inclination', and where talks are
never upon religion as 'affecting the soul, but upon it as something
subsidiary to chapels, "causes", deacons, and the like'. Nor does
he find the Unitarians any better, priding themselves on intel-
lectual superiority, orthodox save that the exercises they delight
in are 'demonstrations of the unity of God from texts in the Bible,
and polemics against tritheism'. Between the repellent nature of

typical congregations and the remorseless attacks of the rationalist Mardon, Rutherford is left to grope his own painful way to some kind of belief. His need is for friendship, for love. One hundred years earlier he could have 'transferred this burning longing to the unseen God', but 'it was mere cheating of myself and a mockery to think about love for the only God whom I knew—the forces which maintained the universe'.

Of our three great issues of the time, which gave off so much heat for the amount of light, the first two for many people now have vitality mainly as they relate to the third. The theological and scriptural, as witnesses to the life of the spirit and as sanctions for the morality of man, have increasingly been viewed in the light of the psychological, sociological, and anthropological, which in turn have increasingly tended to assimilate the aims and methods of the physical sciences. Certainly biblical criticism was losing its hold on the general educated reader when Jowett could write to Mrs Humphrey Ward in 1892, 'I seldom . . . talk on religious subjects. It seems to me that the world is growing rather tired of German criticism, having got out of it nearly all that it is capable of giving.' [44] And when Modernism, to name the school freely accepting the results of critical inquiry, developed a left wing within Anglo-Catholicism itself, as expressed in writing from *Lux Mundi* in 1889 to *Essays Catholic and Critical* in 1926, the lack of general protest prompted this comment in the *Encyclopædia Britannica's* article on 'the Church of England': 'It is probably the case that the change is more due to decline of interest in such controversies than to the spread of more modern views.'

We come back to the third great area of controversy, to the debate between Tyndall and Martineau, between the new philosophy that again 'called all in doubt' and the religion that had thought at least some positions secure. The problems raised about the nature of the cosmos, the nature of man, the nature of experience, have constantly changed their form—it may be interesting to hazard a few comments about the simpler of them in a final chapter on later developments. The scientist has become the religious philosopher in men like Whitehead; the theologian C. E. Raven has immersed himself in the study of science (Martineau, indeed, took great delight in quoting Clerk Maxwell against Tyndall, to the effect that metaphysical speculation was no thing of the past, that 'the discussion of the categories of existence' continued to fascinate every fresh mind). And the dualistic or twofold view of truth appears again in our 'neo-scholastics' to annoy Miss Kathleen Nott as much as it annoyed Tyndall when used by Maurice or Martineau.

It is time to remind ourselves of the quotation from Arnold at the head of this chapter, pointing out both the nature of the main conflict and the need for a reconciling influence. The sceptic and the agnostic took over the 'ethical trenchancy of the Evangelicals', says G. M. Young, and became equally dogmatic on the subject of scientific integrity. It was for literature, for the humanistic spirit, to apply itself to the all-important task of reconciling differences and dissolving antagonisms that were seldom rational and never profitable. J. H. Muirhead tells us that a new attitude was becoming apparent among the younger men of the fifties and sixties, owing partly to the teaching of Carlyle, Emerson, Tennyson, Browning, and Matthew Arnold:

There was an increasing number of those who were prepared neither to sacrifice the reality of the experience represented by morality, art, religion, to what appeared to be the demand of positive science for a rigidly naturalistic world nor to allow that the vindication of that reality depended on the maintenance of doctrines resting on other foundations than the witness of the spirit of man himself.[45]

Here is a description of the position occupied by many men, so easily obscured for us in the dust kicked up around 1870 by the battling extremists. The ethical yet humanistic idealism indicated in Muirhead's analysis is close enough to Arnold's own position, or at least to his intention, to introduce the examination of his religious ideas.

CHAPTER II

The Religious Thought of Matthew Arnold

I do hope that what influence I have may be of use in the
troubled times which I see are before us as a healing and recon-
ciling influence, and it is this which makes me glad to find—what
I find more and more—that I have influence.
                                          Letter of June 25, 1870

When I see the conviction of the ablest and most serious men
round me that a great change must come, a great plunge must
be taken, I think it well, I must say, instead of simply dilating,
as both the religious and the anti-religious world are fond of
doing, on the plunge's utterness, tremendousness, and awful-
ness, to show mankind that it need not be in terror and despair,
that everything essential to its progress stands firm and
unchanged.
                                    Letter of November, 1874

WHEN Matthew Arnold effected the inevitable transition
from culture to religion, from attempts to make 'reason and
the will of God prevail' to definitions and interpretations of the
'will of God', he succeeded, characteristically, both in avoiding
the extremes and in antagonizing the extremists. The orthodox
Christian was naturally suspicious of a man who set out to rescue
religion from 'the extravagances theologians have taught people
to utter', while the militant rationalist was outraged at being
told that, compared with Professor Clifford, Moody and Sankey
were 'masters of the philosophy of history'. Catholics were
bluntly if euphoniously warned that Catholicism was 'fatally
losing itself in the multiplication of dogmas, Mariolatry, and
miracle-mongering', and Puritans were expected to take sweetly
and lightly the assertion that there was 'more of Jesus in St
Theresa's little finger than in John Knox's whole body'. The
British and Foreign School Society was derided for its motto,
'The Bible, the whole Bible, and nothing but the Bible'; yet
Bishop Colenso was taken severely to task for publishing his
detailed critical findings on the errors and contradictions in the
Pentateuch. It would not, in fact, have been surprising had an-
other Kingsley come forward with a pamphlet—'What, then,
does Mr Arnold mean?' To break this hypothetical query down
into a number of more pertinent questions, and to answer them

from Arnold's own statements, will serve as an introduction to Arnold's main ideas.

What was the situation as Arnold saw it? In 1882 he wrote to Sir Mountstuart Grant Duff:

The central fact of the situation always remains for me this: that whereas the basis of things amidst all chance and change has even in Europe generally been for ever so long supernatural Christianity, and far more so in England than in Europe generally, this basis is certainly going—amidst the full consciousness of the continentals that it is going, and amidst the provincial unconsciousness of the English that it is going.[1]

This was the general development, revealing the operation of the *Zeitgeist*. Was it marked by any special features? 'The special feature of our times' was to Arnold the fact that '*the masses* are losing the Bible and its religion. At the Renascence, many cultivated wits lost it. . . . But now it is *the people* which is getting detached from the Bible.' [2] How did Arnold feel about this? First, that the general tendency was inevitable. The spirit of the age was killing belief in miracles as surely as it had killed belief in witchcraft. Secondly, that the moral influence and spiritual consolation of religion must be retained, since 'religion is the solidest of realities, and Christianity the greatest and happiest stroke ever yet made for human perfection'.[3] How did Arnold propose to slough the obsolete and retain the vitally true? 'Dissolvents', he answered, 'of the old European system of dominant ideas and facts we must all be, all of us who have any power of working; what we have to study is that we may not be acrid dissolvents of it.' [4] Applied to religion, what did this mean? That merely to destroy 'the illusions of Popular Christianity' was indefensible: 'when it is done, the whole work of again cementing the alliance between the imagination and conduct remains to be effected'.[5] To destroy belief in miracles and to sweep out metaphysical cobwebs was necessary, but the positive task remained. What was this positive task? It was to 'ease a severe transition, to diminish violent shocks and bitter pain', to have done with 'all this negative, unfruitful business, and to get to religion again;—to the use of the Bible upon new grounds which shall be secure'.[6] To whom was Arnold speaking? To 'men of free and active minds, who, though they may be profoundly dissatisfied with the received theology, are yet interested in religion and more or less acquainted with the Bible'.[7]

Finally, what was the ultimate aim of Arnold's campaign on behalf of the Bible and religion? A renovated Christianity, a transformed and genuinely comprehensive Church, capable of satisfying man's need for conduct with a moral teaching founded on the vital and permanent truths in the Scriptures, his imagination with the rich poetic symbolism of tradition, and his intelligence with a fruitful and enlightened religious thought based on a recognition of 'the Socratic interdependence of knowledge and virtue'. Perhaps the fullest statement of this vision was made in 1878, in the essay 'Irish Catholicism and British Liberalism':

I persist in thinking that the prevailing form for the Christianity of the future will be the form of Catholicism; but a Catholicism purged, opening itself to the light and air, having the consciousness of its own poetry, freed from its sacerdotal despotism and freed from its pseudo-scientific apparatus of superannuated dogma. Its forms will be retained, as symbolizing with the force and charm of poetry a few cardinal facts and ideas, simple indeed, but indispensable and inexhaustible, and on which our race could lay hold only by materializing them.[8]

It is easy to see why Arnold regarded his writing as 'conservative and religious' as well as 'critical', and himself as a 'reconciling' influence. It is equally easy to see why he antagonized both the orthodox and the radical. If some of this hostility was caused by the ambivalence of Arnold's thought, some of it was the expression of puzzled irritation. His ideas in the main might be ethical, humanistic, and naturalistic, but the vocabulary, references and emotional overtones of traditional religion were retained (explicitly and designedly). This is apparent in the last and most effective summary made by Arnold of the essentials of his ethico-psychological position in matters of religion, offered in the essay 'A Comment on Christmas':

Therefore, when we are asked: What really is Christmas, and what does it celebrate? we answer: The birthday of Jesus. But what, then, is the miracle of the Incarnation? A homage to the virtue of pureness, and to the manifestation of this virtue in Jesus. What is Lent, and the miracle of the temptation? A homage to the virtue of self-control and to the manifestation of this virtue in Jesus. What does Easter celebrate? Jesus victorious over death by dying. By dying how? Dying to re-live. To re-live in Paradise, in another world? No, in this. But if in this, what is the kingdom of God? The ideal society of the future. Then what is immortality? To live in the eternal order, which never dies. What is salvation by Jesus Christ? The attainment of this immortality. Through what means? Through faith in Jesus, and appropriation of his method, secret and temper.[9]

The 'natural supernaturalism' of this Arnoldian catechism reveals a usage of terms which, in spite of their religious associations, to Arnold have primarily moral and social and psychological values.

The key to Arnold's religious thought lies in his use of the words *experience* and *verifiable*. Add to these the words *natural, fact, scientific*, and *psychological*, and the critical apparatus with which Arnold explores the area of religion is revealed, together with a sense of the pitfalls which await the user of this apparatus who speaks from the library rather than from the laboratory. Modern science, Arnold says, inspires the demand for verification. But it is not to nature and the laboratory that Arnold turns when he condemns rational systems of thought deduced from 'truths' established *a priori*—it is to maturing human knowledge, and to a lowest common denominator of experience established by the verdict of history. This makes for an amœboid and diversified attack; it also begs a great many questions, questions which Arnold's critics were prompt to ask.

When the logical conclusion of Schopenhauer's pessimism is contrasted with the grounds for joy in the teachings of Jesus, we *feel* (the extent to which Arnold uses this verb is significant) that the *fact* is with Jesus, and that Schopenhauer utters a paradox. The superiority of good conduct over bad is a matter of experience, and the objectified verdict of experience is equated with that of science: 'The miserable sense of sin from unrighteousness, the joyful witness of a good conscience from righteousness . . . are facts of human nature and can be verified by science.'[10] An equally sound basis is claimed for the traditional sources of morality and religion: 'The truth and grandeur of the Old Testament most comes out experimentally—so it is with Christianity.'[11] Finally, the preservation of these sources depends upon their being established as a fact: 'Has or has not Christianity, in fact, the same want of natural truth as our traditional religion? Of questions about religion, it may be said to be at the present time, for a serious man, the only important one.'[12] By clearing away the rank theological growths of dogma, miracles, and metaphysics, by letting the 'maximum of intelligence play freely around stock notions', Arnold proposes to get religion back on a psychologically verifiable basis.

Nowhere is Arnold's experiential emphasis more apparent than in his reinterpretation of the Pauline message, when he tries to show the Dissenting sects that their lack of sweetness and light is ultimately based in an unsound theology. 'We have seen', he says, 'how Puritanism seems to come by its religion in the first instance theologically and from authority; Paul by his, on the other hand, psychologically and from experience.' [13] Having done battle for the ideas embodied in such terms as election, predestination, imputed righteousness, and justification, Puritans have proceeded to hold to these notions mechanically and with separatist fierceness, even to confuse them with religion itself. Arnold pays tribute to Calvin's seriousness and Wesley's lovely piety, but he condemns these two main sources of English Puritanism for the controversial rigidity of the Calvinist emphasis on predestination and the Wesleyan obsession with justification through faith:

As a religious teacher, Wesley is to be judged by his doctrine; and his doctrine, like the Calvinistic scheme, rests with all its weight on the assertion of certain minutely described proceedings on God's part, independent of us, our experience, and our will; and leads its recipients to look, in religion, not so much for an arduous progress on their own part, and the exercise of their activity, as for strokes of magic, and what may be called a sensational character.[14]

Calvinism and Methodism, appealing to man's fears and hopes respectively, erred in deriving their religion from doctrinal authority, and Arnold suggests three reasons for the failure to understand Paul. First, the translation of the basic Epistle to the Romans is biased owing to the extent that the minds of the translators were filled with the doctrines of election and predestination. Secondly, Paul orientalized. He spoke in vivid metaphorical terms peculiar to a language which made no distinction between words used scientifically and words used poetically. Thirdly, he judaized. He made arbitrary use of the Old Testament as a sort of talisman, and in doing so was merely faithful to the genius of his time and race. A judicious examination, by an impartial and cultivated mind, is necessary in order to separate the permanent truth of Paul's utterances from the figures of Jewish theology, and the subsequent doctrinal petrifications.

Paul began within the sphere of reality and experience, a scientific sphere, where the moral law is the greatest fact. With the unique Jewish consciousness of the reality of sin and the necessity for righteousness, he bore witness to the inner conflict. Of course he referred to the fall of Adam, but this is rhetorical illustration, for Paul derived his sense of sin from experience and not from Genesis. 'I see', he said, 'a law in my members fighting against the law of my mind.' To develop the dogma of original sin from this experience is to ignore the primary elements in the experience itself, which are personal and psychological. Hebraically aware of an external master-impulse, in Arnold's famous definition the 'Eternal not ourselves that makes for righteousness', Paul naturally gave the name of God to this controlling power, as the Hebrews had always done. His sense of uplift at finding himself in harmony with the moral order he proceeded to express in terms of the elect and the reprobate, of predestination and the will of God. But the primary thing, to Arnold, is the feeling of peace and spiritual well-being at the triumph of the higher rational self over the lower animal self, not the literal interpretation emerging in a stock theological image like that of the clay and the potter. And even here Paul's judaizing is less significant than his original power of insight, which leads him on to say that 'God is the saviour of all men, especially of those that believe', a statement which flatly contradicts the Calvinist doctrine of election. Here Paul passes from the sphere of moral insight, where his experience is akin to that of pagan thinkers from Socrates and Plato to Epictetus and Marcus Aurelius, to the sphere of moral practice, or religion, where the Bible and Christianity make their unique contribution. The 'morbid and subjective brooding' of the Puritan, absorbed in the contemplation of sin, is not present in Paul, to whom 'sin is not a monster to be mused on, but an impotence to be got rid of'.

This response of the master-impulse in himself to the 'Eternal not ourselves which makes for righteousness' is one great discovery of Paul. The other is the emphasis on the solidarity of mankind, the Christian idea that all men are brothers and that our neighbours are but an extension of ourselves. Here, where an emotional effort reinforces the moral one, sympathy and imaginative insight carry us into the sphere of religion, which Arnold defines as 'morality touched with emotion'. And this sense of solidarity, Arnold claims, is another *fact* of human nature.

There is, of course, something mystical about this larger sphere. To pass beyond the essentially rational and objective facts of sin and conduct requires in us a special capacity receptive of influences and sympathies. But this too is a simple fact of human experience. Arnold cites our pleasure in a spring day, and our falling in love, as examples of emotional responses to situations which we do not manufacture, in which we are essentially passive, and out of which we derive buoyancy, animation, and confidence. In its finest form this becomes the 'power that worketh in us'; Paul's religious strength lies in his moving freely between this rather mystical world of sympathy and influence and the rational world of moral choice, so combining the 'power in us' with reason and conscience.

What enabled Paul to pass to this larger sphere was the example of Jesus. He spoke of Jesus as the Messiah, having been bred up in the Messianic lore of the Jewish doctors, but his primary emphasis, to Arnold, was upon the fulfilment of God's righteousness through Christ, who exemplified 'the law of the spirit' with such incomparable splendour that in loving and following him 'the struggling stream of duty . . . was suddenly reinforced by the immense tidal wave of sympathy and emotion. To this new and potent influence Paul gave the name of faith.' [15] Faith, then, becomes a fidelity to the felt but unseen, through identification with Christ. Here we have the age-old crux of religious discussion: How is this identification achieved? How does faith work? Not by accepting of covenants, in the fashion of Puritanism, but by dying with Christ, that is, by subjugating all base and selfish impulses. Reason recognizes these impulses; faith controls them. We achieve a degree of self-conquest in attachment to a child or a friend. How much more do we achieve by devotion to the great exemplar of virtue, the personification of the moral order that is God's will! This attachment, history shows, is peculiarly Christ's. Based in the affections, it thereby communicates itself, and the element of solidarity enters.

The 'dying to sin', as Christ died to the selfish impulse in men, results in our rising to a higher spiritual life within the sphere of our visible earthly existence.[16] Here Arnold carries his critical reinterpretation on to deal with the remaining doctrine of imputed righteousness and the miracle of the resurrection. To Paul Christ's death was not a substitution, a sacrificial atonement, but a reconciling sacrifice. As the just man suffers not on his own account, but for us, that is, through our stupid misunderstanding and persecution of him, so Christ died to the base lower self in man. Hence he becomes the supreme example of reconcilement with God—in practical terms, of harmony with the moral order. If this is not clear to our reason, grace—that is, the emotion of love for the great exemplar, working on that inner capacity by which we are passively receptive to sympathies and influences—may enter in. So we rise to a higher life, by virtue of this psychological process which to Arnold is faith, and we achieve a sense of 'justification'.

While Paul naturally 'orientalized' the process under the figures of blood, atonement, suffering, and propitiation, the whole central idea of identification with Christ through dying with him became a spiritualized concept. This is equally true of the resurrection. Paul inevitably held the idea from its physical and miraculous side, as naturally as the gentle and intelligent Sir Matthew Hale, breathing the intellectual air of the seventeenth century, held to the current notions about witchcraft. But Paul's originality lay in his conceiving of the resurrection from its practical and moral side. Death, in this sense, is being submerged by sin and the flesh, life is the visible victory of the higher self. Popular theology, characteristically missing the primary and original elements, and seizing on the secondary and derivative, commits here the major blunder, which is to Arnold, 'the fixing the attention on the past miracle of Christ's physical resurrection, and losing sight of the continuing miracle of the Christian's spiritual resurrection'.[17]

This purblind treatment of the central idea in Christianity is to Arnold representative of the theological mishandling of religion. By mistaking metaphor for fact, by weaving theories from language and failing to distinguish and hold fast to the embedded ideas, both popular and learned theology find themselves in the nineteenth century in an intellectual position which is indefensible. Jesus came to 'restore the intuition' to the Pharisaic and mechanically dogmatizing Hebrews. Our 'materializing' theology must realize that on intellectual grounds it cannot cope with modern science and the *Zeitgeist*. The one thing needful is to 'restore the intuition', to proclaim clearly and constantly those permanent and psychologically verifiable truths which are fundamental to the Bible and Christianity, and indispensable to the moral and spiritual welfare of man. By resigning their futile claims to dogmatic authority, by emphasizing the few essentials of Christianity and retaining its rich symbolism in an admittedly poetic sense, the men of religion will be able to achieve and maintain a really valid authority over the moral being and imagination of both the masses and the cultivated minority.

Arnold states in one memorable figure that popular religion, with its emphasis on dogma, miracle and metaphysical proof rather than on the moral nature of man, has been made to stand on its apex rather than its base. Christianity, he says, can be put into no set of formulas or commandments. It is a risky thing to associate eternal truths with passing intellectual forms; inevitably the secondary and primary become confused. 'To popular opinion everywhere, religion is proved by miracles. . . . Yet how much more safe is it, as well as more fruitful, to look for the main confirmation of a religion in its intrinsic correspondence with urgent wants of human nature, in its profound necessity.'[18] The dogmatic insistence on such insubstantial evidence as miracles is really a thwarting of Christianity. Developed in primitive times, formed by a habit of mind, and based on inadequate knowledge, the Messianic *Aberglaube* of the Old Testament was passed on quite naturally to the compilers of the New, and reapplied in modified form to the life of Jesus, together with the fresh legends and miracles which grew up around the Messiah.

As the personal influence of Jesus faded, the 'extra-belief' grew stronger. First we got the Apostles' Creed, the *popular* science of Christianity. As Christianity spread, the 'Aryan' genius for metaphysics worked over this material, and the result was the Nicene Creed, or *learned* science of Christianity. But metaphysicians could and did quarrel, and the victorious party, ruffled by fighting, set forth the dogmatic formulation of Christianity in ever more insistent and uncompromising terms. The outcome was the Athanasian Creed, 'learned science with a strong dash of vindictive temper'. Now, says Arnold, it is quite possible (to a man of culture) and highly desirable to cut back through these and later dogmatic formulations and discover the true Bible-dogma. And what is this but the simple and verifiable truths of historical human experience?

It cannot be too carefully borne in mind that the real 'essence of Holy Scripture', its saving truth, is not such criticism at all as the so-called orthodox dogma attempts, and attempts unsuccessfully. No, the real essence of Scripture is a much simpler matter. It is, for the Old Testament: *To him that ordereth his conversation right shall be shown the salvation of God!*—and, for the New Testament: *Follow Jesus!* This is Bible-dogma, as opposed to the dogma of our formularies. On this Bible-dogma if Churches were founded, and to preach this Bible-dogma if ministers were ordained, Churches and ministers would have all the dogma to which the Bible attaches eternal life. Plain and precise enough it is, in all conscience; with the advantage of being precisely *right*, whereas the dogma of our formularies is precisely *wrong*. And if anyone finds it too simple, let him remember that its hardness is practical, not speculative. It is a rule of *conduct*; let him act it, and he will find it hard enough.[19]

Such formulations as the Catholic Mass and the Protestant covenant of the blood of Christ are 'rude and blind criticisms', helpful to conduct at first, but bound to wilt in the breath of a later and more scientific *Zeitgeist*. Arnold quotes approvingly from Amiel: 'Pious fiction is still fiction. Truth has superior rights. The world must adapt itself to truth, not truth to the world. Copernicus upset the astronomy of the Middle Age; so much the worse for the astronomy. The Everlasting Gospel is revolutionizing the Churches; what does it matter?' [20] Nor is it only to the 'rude and blind criticisms' that the spirit of Christ is alien. All attempts to prove what cannot be proved, to claim infallibility for creeds, institutions, and systems of thought, to base the religious life upon any but the simplest foundation of verifiable human experience—all these are alien to the moral and spiritual life offered us in Christ, and exemplified by him. Nowhere does Arnold state the contrast more effectively than in his essay on Tolstoi:

Moral life is the gift of God, is God, and this true life, this union with God to which we aspire, we reach through Jesus. We reach it through union with Jesus and by adopting his life. This doctrine is proved true for us by the life in God, to be acquired through Jesus, being what our nature feels after and moves to, by the warning of misery if we are severed from it, the sanction of happiness if we find it. Of the access for *us*, at any rate, to the spirit of life, us who are born in Christendom, are in touch, conscious or unconscious, with Christianity, this is the true account. Questions over which the churches spend so much labour and time—questions about the Trinity, about the godhead of Christ, about the procession of the Holy Ghost, are not vital; what is vital is the doctrine of access to the spirit of life through Jesus.[21]

D

To restore the original intuition of Jesus in all its brightness, to bring back the real, experimental Christianity in place of the later 'extravaganza', we must penetrate the false proofs based on the attractive *Aberglaube* built up around Jesus, and come again at the internal evidence, as revealed in what Arnold calls the 'line' of Jesus. This is particularly important because of the power of dissolution possessed by this psychological 'line', a power which can be turned in a later age against the stubborn materializing of theological 'facts', just as Jesus used it to dissolve the 'facts' of his own period.

Jesus, says Arnold, was the Messiah Israel needed, though not the one they expected. Faced with the task of harmonizing the ideal of the Anointed Prince, expected by the Hebrews, with the concept of the Servant of God, which he was, Jesus, accustomed to the notions and imagery of his time, naturally expounded his message to some extent in terms of the popular *Aberglaube,* using as poetry the Messianic texts from Daniel which his disciples used literally. He did not change the object of man's life, righteousness. He clarified it, and pointed the way to its realization. He reapplied emotion to conduct, and added, most significantly, the sanction of happiness. Interested only in the individual, not in a Church or scheme of doctrine, he made clear, by precept and example, the threefold process by which salvation could be achieved.

First, in Arnold's analysis, is the *method*. This is inwardness, not merely repentance, but a change of the inner man. It is Socrates' 'Know thyself!' operating exclusively in the sphere of morals and religion, and expressed by the word conscience. Secondly, we have the *secret*. This is renouncement, as Paul discovered, the dying to the world and the lower self, by which we rise to that higher moral self and achieve a spiritual resurrection in this life. The method finds what righteousness is; the secret shows how to achieve it. Peace, joy, in fact life, are added to the stern duty of following the conscience, and the sanction is happiness. Arnold suggests that a possible name for the whole process would be psycho-physiology, but since Jesus appeals to experience and not theory, and since a doctrine is to him 'an intuition and a practical rule', the technical term is better avoided. Thirdly, there is the *temper*, the *epieikeia* of Jesus. This makes for perfect balance, for the preventing of an excess of either the method or the secret, and is fully seen only in Jesus himself. Protestantism has the method but too little of the secret; Catholicism has the secret but too little of the method: neither has the *epieikeia*. It is not discovered in institutions, only in individuals. The method by itself produces the political Dissenter; the secret by itself gives us the Flagellant. The best examples of the balance, the temper of sweet reasonableness characteristic of Jesus, is not furnished us by the great doctors of the Church but by such men as St Francis, the 'unknown author of the *Imitation*', and the mystic Tauler. None equals Jesus, though some may come near him. The whole process can be expressed in human terms, and contemplated as a human ideal, but only if we cease to regard Jesus as one aspect of a metaphysical Trinity, and look upon him as the complete and perfect example of the virtues he sought to inculcate, divine because of his unique harmony with the Eternal order that makes for righteousness.

This stress upon the psychologically verifiable in Christianity, this separation of the 'reasonable' Jesus from the thaumaturgical one, prepares us for Arnold's idea of God as 'nothing but a deeply-moved way of saying *conduct, or righteousness*'. This is the God of experience, as opposed to the God of miracles or the God of metaphysics. We shall see how Arnold proceeds, from what are to him irreducible and minimal facts of experience, to build up his definitions of God and religion.

The basic facts from which Arnold starts are the nature and aim of morality. Morality, he says, 'represents for everybody a thoroughly definite and ascertained idea:—the idea of human conduct regulated in a certain manner. Everybody, again, understands distinctly enough what is meant by man's perfection:—his reaching the best which his powers and circumstances allow him to reach.' [22] Not only is conduct so understood, but it is felt by everybody to be the most important thing in human experience, taking up at least three-fourths of life. Nations and men have been wrecked through inattention to conduct. Human nature as we know it really began with the fixing of moral habits, with such 'culture-conquests' as those embodied in the fifth and seventh commandments. In time these primitive controls were replaced by a heightened feeling regarding a course of action proved superior by generations of men. The note of the Eternal now enters, and morality assumes an authority greater than that of repetitious experience. The better way to live is felt to be a moral law; and the emotional attitude adopted towards this authority is what we call religion. Religion, then, has *conduct* for its object, not some metaphysical abstraction, and we today have the vast cumulative experience of the race to show us that we under-estimate conduct at our peril.

At this point a question emerges. Even granting the virtual equation of religion and morality, and the overwhelming im-portance of conduct, why turn to Israel for light? Why cling to the Bible? Because, says Arnold, the Jews were the only race completely possessed by the idea that righteousness saves, that to conduct belongs happiness. It is their unceasing testimony to the efficacy and grandeur of the power making for righteousness which renders their literature of enduring worth. As morality grew out of simple self-control, so religion grew out of morality, and at this later stage we find Israel hymning the praises of an Eternal that is the object, not only of faith, but of experience. Revelation is the heightened experience, the intuition, of the eternal master-impulse making for righteousness. In this sense the Bible is revealed religion. But man is naturally anthropomorphic, nowhere more than in tribal and patriarchal Israel. Hence by a natural development this great power for righteousness, proved by our experience the one way to a higher spiritual life, becomes invested with human qualities on a supernatural scale, and is even addressed as Father.

With the play of human emotions around this object of consciousness, the Old Testament *Aberglaube* of legend and miracle developed. Of course the contrast between the ideal and the actual, the spectacle of triumphant wickedness and miserable virtue, caused an imperfect people to project the promised happi-ness into a future life. The *Aberglaube* grew until even the teaching of Jesus had to be couched in its terms, with his true message discernible only in parables and in single maxims and sayings. But through it all runs the evidential and practical insistence on conduct, or righteousness, an idea as basic to the New Testament as to the Old. The test for retention today is again experience. 'Try it and see', says Arnold. Try a course in Greeley, Franklin, Bentham, and Spencer, and a course in the Bible. See for your-selves which makes more for righteousness, for that sense of happiness based on firm conviction, and expressive of harmony with what the experience of man has shown to be an eternal moral law.

One of the criticisms advanced against this pragmatic test was that Arnold had forsaken Hellenism for Hebraism, had reversed the stand taken in *Culture and Anarchy*. Such criticism missed the obvious fact that religion was an integral part of culture, as Arnold saw it. His definitions of culture, embracing reason and the will of God as the marks of that perfection which is man's goal, reveal clearly that the Hellenistic emphasis aimed at the English Philistine was not intended to be made at the expense of religion. Arnold's religious writings were a deepening and modification of his crusade for culture, not a retreat from Greece to Israel. The touchstone method used in his literary criticism comes into play, to distinguish between mere morality and that which is 'morality touched with emotion', or religion.

'Hold off from sensuality,' says Cicero; 'for, if you have given yourself up to it, you will find yourself unable to think of anything else.' That is morality. 'Blessed are the pure in heart,' says Jesus Christ, 'for they shall see God.' That is religion. 'We all want to live honestly, but cannot', says the Greek maxim-maker. That is morality. 'O wretched man that I am, who shall deliver me from the body of this death!' says St Paul. That is religion. . . . 'Live as you were meant to live!' is morality. 'Lay hold on eternal life!' is religion.[23]

Hebraism and Christianity, then, have that heightened insight and feeling about morality which constitutes religion. And in spite of men like Plato and Sophocles, from whom he gives examples of a genuinely religious attitude, Arnold insists that the intensity of experience in this most important phase of life belongs rather to Israel and the Bible. The glory of Greece is her superb development of the one-fourth of life which is the sphere of science and the arts. This sphere is important. Through inattention to or distortion of this one-fourth we get such dismal things as hymns, Puritan theology, and the whole over-emphasis upon doing which is the object of attack in *Culture and Anarchy*. But the sphere of conduct remains the more important. Through over-attention to the one-fourth Greece perished, the Renascence went astray, and France, Arnold implies, faces ultimate disaster. Israel too failed, through 'under-fidelity' to the three-fourths, but their imperishable distinction is that they experienced with unique intensity the relatively greater importance of the sphere of conduct and left us the supreme record of it. To Arnold the moral law is an absolute outside ourselves, towards which our experience moves, and Israel's wisdom consisted not in their personifying of this law, but in their exaltation of it: 'As well imagine a man with a sense for sculpture not cultivating it by the help of the remains

of Greek art, or a man with a sense for poetry not cultivating it
by the help of Homer and Shakespeare, as a man with a sense for
conduct not cultivating it by the help of the Bible!' [24]

The arithmetical quibbling with which Arnold speculates
upon whether conduct should make four-fifths, or even five-sixths
of life, and then settles for three-fourths, merely serves to catch
the reader. In a late essay, he says good-humouredly that perhaps
conduct is not three-fourths of life, but that 'conduct is, at any
rate, a very considerable part of life', and that to ignore this fact
involves cultural regression of the gravest sort. That Arnold's
outlook embraces a thoroughly secular humanism is clear from
his admission that perhaps in time science and art will adequately
motivate right conduct. He makes his own tremendous claim for
poetry as a spiritual stay in a future which has turned its back on
traditional religion. He formulates, with the 'total' man in mind,
his final definition of God as 'the stream of tendency by which all
things fulfil the law of their being', hardly a definition which even
the most advanced 'liberal' would consider a concession to
orthodoxy. But for all this, he says, we are not yet ripe, any more
than Greece was when she perished through over-attention to the
one-fourth. We are not likely ever to achieve that ripeness. The
instinct for self-preservation will still lead us to the Bible, where
'the righteousness that maketh for life' is most tellingly revealed,
and where we may discover for ourselves the peace and joy and
happiness which, as psychological sanctions for right living,
place Jesus Christ above Epictetus and Marcus Aurelius as a
moral and religious teacher.

To find grounds which are true, which are verifiable by
experience, is the motivation of Arnold's search. His own defini-
tion of God, as 'the Eternal that makes for righteousness', he
believes will correspond to our experience as it did to that of
Israel. This is the 'scientific' definition. All above this is poetry;
we discount the miracles, legends, and anthropomorphism,
because we know that here is the language of feeling as used by
Israel. But there must be a distinction between language used
poetically and language used scientifically, and when learned men
proceed to offer as scientific truth what cannot, by its very
nature, be verified, we are justified in seeking something more
primary and real. All the debate about causation, substance and
design; about God as a person, a thing, a moral Governor; about
the existence and relations of the Trinity—all this is very impres-

sive as an exercise in metaphysics, but tells us nothing that can be verified in our experience.

Arnold does not condemn this intellectual systematizing in itself; he condemns it because it pretends to speak scientifically and with authority on unverifiable matters. Israel personified God; it did not predicate personality. But learned theology, with 'an insane licence of affirmation', speaks of God as familiarly as if he were a man in the next street, of the relations of the Trinity as if they were three Lord Shaftesburys. The sinlessness of Christ is deduced in the way of dogma, from his divinity, whereas Paul, following the way of experience, arrived at a feeling of Christ's divinity from his sinlessness. Since experience is relative, the argument from design is weakened by the limitations of human knowledge. The terms 'perfect' and 'infinite' simply express a greater degree of these attributes than we can know in nature; to use them with a sense of exact attributes is misleading. Neither the God of miracles nor the God of metaphysics can support religion when we demand verification. What we have to fall back on is the God of experience, revealed to us simply as the operation of a mortal law, and so revealed to discerning pagans as well as to men like St Paul. Because of the relative nature of this awareness, the appeal to experience is itself relative to the insight and equipment of those who experience. Hence we find Arnold crediting Israel with a response, to 'the Eternal not ourselves', and a testimony, to the fact that salvation comes through obedience to the moral law, unequalled by any other race or age. The value of the individual response he describes, as we might expect, in cultural terms which govern the validity of any critical approach to religion: 'The worth of what a man thinks about God and the objects of religion depends on what the man *is*; and what the man *is*, depends on his having more or less reached the measure of a perfect and total man.' [25]

Of this relative and subjective judgment, which yet claimed to establish objective verification, many people naturally said, 'Very well, but why retain the name of God for something which, divested of intellectual and supernatural attributes, is merely a moral experience emotionally heightened?' Arnold gives his answer in terms of the imagination. We can obtain a meaning for 'God' from the philologist, who tells us that it comes from a common root word meaning 'Shining' or 'Brilliant', which may suggest a genesis in the worship of the life-giving Sun. But this offers nothing more than a philological derivation to set against metaphysical affirmations. We must take the word at a later stage, when it has become associated with an Eternal Power outside man, the object of poetical and approximate language, of awe and reverence. It deserves retention for two reasons: it is the rich symbol of man's imaginative reaching out for a reality higher than himself, and it is at the same time a way of communicating an experimental fact, the historical witness to the supreme moral revelation.

To seek to discard, like some philosophers, the name of God and to substitute for it such a name as the Unknowable, will seem to a plain man, surely, ridiculous. For *God*,—the name which has so engaged all men's feelings,—is at the same time by its very derivation a positive name, expressing that which is the most blessed of boons to man, Light; whereas *Unknowable* is a name merely negative. And no man could ever have cared anything about God in so far as he is simply unknowable. 'The Unknowable is our refuge and strength, a very present help in trouble', is what would occur to no man to think or say. Men cared about God for the sake of what they knew about him, not of what they did not. And they knew about him that he was the Eternal not ourselves that makes for righteousness, and as such they gave him that name for what gives light and warmth, *God*. It adds, indeed, to our awe of God that although we are able to know of him what so greatly concerns us, we know of him nothing more; but simply to be able to know nothing of him could beget in us no awe whatever.[26]

With the God of personality and the God of metaphysics disposed of on the grounds that they are not verifiable in experience, it becomes clear that, to Arnold, Israel was *unconsciously* deifying a natural moral law. Consciously, of course, they invoked a 'magnified and non-natural man', spoke in theurgical and thaumaturgical terms, and in their imaginative attempts at communication of experience laid the basis for both the mechanical and materializing theology of the Puritans, and the intellectual gymnastics of the Bishops of Winchester and Gloucester. But the vital matter is the witness to the moral law. We must read the Bible not as systematic theologians, nor as men of merely physical science, but as men of culture, allowing the 'total' mind to play freely around the ideas and images, interpreting the important three-fourths by the aid of the indispensable one-fourth. Had theologians used this approach—

they would have seen the fallacy of confounding the obscurity attach-
ing to the idea of God,—that vast *not ourselves* which transcends us,—
with the obscurity attaching to the idea of their Trinity, a confused
metaphysical speculation which puzzles us. The one, they would have
perceived, is the obscurity of a fog. And fog, they would have known,
has no proper place in our conceptions of God; since whatever our
minds *can* possess of God they know clearly, for no man, as Goethe
says, possesses what he does not understand; but they can possess of
Him but a very little. All this our dogmatic theologians would have
known, if they had had more science and more literature. And there-
fore, simple as the Bible and conduct are, still culture seems to be
required for them,—required to prevent our mis-handling and sophis-
ticating them.[27]

The same insistence on a combination of culture and common
sense is apparent when Arnold discusses the products of modern
biblical scholarship. The two main obstacles to a sound criticism
of the Bible and of religion are (1) the bias of the orthodox
theologian towards supporting traditional theology and (2) the
'vigorous and rigorous' theorizing of those critics, notably
German scholars, who have become engrossed in the problems of
investigation and minutiæ of research. The first group is to be
condemned for its lack of a 'free play of the mind' and its remote-
ness from the modern spirit, the second for the negative and
mechanical nature of its approach to a subject which calls for
imagination and a sense of proportion. The ideal equipment for a
writer on matters pertaining to religion Arnold finds exemplified
in Joubert: 'Penetration in these matters is valueless without
soul, and soul is valueless without penetration; both of these are
delicate qualities, and even in those who have them, easily
lost.' [28] What Arnold means here by 'soul' is variously expressed
elsewhere as insight, imagination, a feeling for essentials, above
all, as *tact*. While the British theologian suffers from an 'atrophy'
of the critical organ, the German scholar suffers a 'hypertrophy'
of it, and for all his learning is conspicuously lacking in 'tact'.
Perhaps what Arnold describes as the main element of the modern
spirit wherever it is found, the *imaginative reason*, best suggests the
fusion of qualities which he thinks imperative for fruitful critical
insight and interpretation.
     This demand for a positive attitude in religious criticism,
which leads Arnold to attack the 'cold negations' of the Tübingen
school as strongly as he did the 'insane licence of affirmation'

practised by orthodox theologians, reflects in part a principle of accommodation to the intellectual level and emotional needs of the many, a principle sanctioned in criticism for Arnold when the subject under consideration is one so vital to human well-being as religion. Nowhere is this clearer than in his first full-dress venture into the field in 1863, comparing Bishop Colenso's criticism of the Pentateuch and Dean Stanley's book on the Jewish Church. Criticism is inevitable by virtue of the operation of the *Zeitgeist*: 'Intellectual ideas are not the essence of the religious life; still the religious life connects itself, as I have said, with certain intellectual ideas, and all intellectual ideas follow a development independent of the religious life.' [29] This changing intellectual approach need not affect the essential truth. In Homeric criticism, the changing theories of authorship left unimpaired the beauty and truth of the poetry for the imagination. Now the reconciliation is not easy: 'It is one of the hardest tasks in the world to make new intellectual ideas harmonize truly with the religious life, to place them in their right light for that life.' But the reconciliation is possible, needful, and perfectly compatible with a free spirit of inquiry.

For the presence of this positive aim Arnold praises Stanley. 'Here is a clergyman, who, looking at the Bible, sees its contents in their right proportion, and gives to each matter its due prominence. Here is an inquirer, who, treating Scripture history with a perfectly free spirit—falsifying nothing, sophisticating nothing —treats it so that his freedom leaves the sacred power of that history inviolate.' Again, 'I praise his book for the very reason for which some critics find fault with it—for not giving prominence, in speaking of the Bible, to matters with which the real virtue of the Bible is not bound up.' For the absence of this positive aim Arnold blames Colenso: 'I censure his book, because while it impresses strongly on the reader that "the Pentateuch is not to be read as an authentic narrative", it so entirely fails to make him feel that it is "a narrative full of divine instruction in morals and religion".' It is not the 'born thinkers' who need the reconciliation effected for them. Like Spinoza, 'let them think in peace, these sublime solitaries'. It is the mass of mankind, including nearly all the educated minority, for whom intellectual ideas must be blended with the religious life. The contemporary situation, and the duty of the reformer in that situation, are summed up:

THE RELIGIOUS THOUGHT OF MATTHEW ARNOLD 47

Protestantism has formed the notion that every syllable and letter of the Bible is the direct utterance of the Most High. The critical ideas of our century are forcing Protestantism away from this proposition, untrue like the proposition that the Pope is infallible: but the religious reformer is not he who rivets our minds upon the untruth of this proposition, who bewilders the religious life by insisting on the intellectual blunder of which it has been guilty in entertaining it; he is the man who makes us feel the future which undoubtedly exists for the religious life in the absence of it.[30]

In the article on 'The Bishop and the Philosopher', Colenso suffers still more by comparison with Spinoza. Arnold insists that such books as Colenso's, which may affect general culture, must come before the tribunal of literary criticism. This tribunal asks three questions of the book: Does it edify the uninformed? Does it further instruct the informed? Does it have pretensions, but really do neither? The arithmetical demonstrations of Colenso certainly do not inform the instructed, says Arnold, since they add nothing to what is already assumed by scholars regarding the unhistoricity of the Pentateuch. Certainly they do not edify the many. As for informing the unenlightened, that is a fallacy. Arnold agrees with 'Plato, Spinoza and Newman' that 'old moral ideas leaven and humanize the multitude; new intellectual ideas filter slowly down to them from the thinking few'. Not the doctrines of the Reformation touched the many, says Arnold, but its 'moral truth'. Spinoza himself set out 'reluctantly' in the *Tractatus Theologico-Politicus* to inform the instructed, and suceeded, by virtue of his emphasis on the essentials of religion and by his brief dismissal of 'verbal matters' which occupy Colenso, in achieving the highest kind of edification. He produced a positive work which answers the questions of culture and literary criticism satisfactorily. 'If the English clergy must err,' says Arnold finally, 'let them learn from this outcast of Israel to err nobly! Along with the weak trifling of the Bishop of Natal, let it be lawful to cast into the huge cauldron, out of which the new world is to be born, the strong thought of Spinoza!' [31]

The 'appeal to experience' central in Arnold's religious criticism would appear to be an appeal to the experience of the discerning few. When Arnold posits culture and common sense as necessary equipment for interpreting the Bible, we may rephrase it as 'the common sense of the cultured minority', who will save the Bible 'for the masses'. Because Jesus was so far above the

heads of his reporters, literary criticism is necessary to disentangle
what Jesus really said from what they set down afterwards.
The experience of books, of the way in which men express them-
selves, is necessary to interpret the real experience of men in a
given situation, particularly when the feelings are so deeply
engaged as they are in religion.

In this endeavour, which has for its aim the retention of
religion and the edifying of the many, the work of the Tübingen
critics and men like them is inadequate. For their 'collecting,
editing, and illustrating' Arnold has nothing but praise, at
least when exhibited in the work of a man like Baur, but their
fanciful hypotheses and yearnings for system and symmetry are as
barren of vital truth as the obstructionist tactics of the tradi-
tionalists. To the untrained reader's 'practical hold on the Bible
they conduce nothing, but rather divert from it; and yet they
are often really further from the truth, all the while, than even
the traditional view which they profess to annihilate'.[32] This
negative emphasis represents a great danger, a danger which
Arnold sums up for us in his *Last Essays on Church and Religion*:

> Meanwhile the day will most certainly arrive, when the great body
> of liberal opinion in this country will adhere to the first half of the
> doctrine of Continental liberals;—will admit that traditionary religion
> is utterly untenable. And the danger is, that from the habits of their
> minds, and from seeing the thing treated as certain, and from hearing
> nothing urged against it, our liberals may admit as indisputable the
> second half of the doctrine too: that Christianity, also, is untenable.[33]

It was to avert this danger that *Literature and Dogma* was written;
it was specifically to offset the negations of the Tübingen school
that *God and the Bible* followed. In the latter work appears a
sentence which might serve as a motto for the whole of Arnold's
religious criticism: 'I write to convince the lover of religion
that by following habits of intellectual seriousness he need not,
so far as religion is concerned, lose anything.'

Starting with Arnold's assumption that a broad culture and
literary insight are indispensable for 'restoring the intuition',
for basing the permanent truth of the Bible on psychological
experience rather than on dogmatic authority or systematic theoriz-
ing, we may notice here a few instances of the critical 'tact' at
work. With demonstration impossible, and plausibility sterile,
probability remains, and for a safe treatment of this idea culture
and common sense are the best guides. Are miracles in question?

Human nature, says Arnold, is prone to miracles: 'Under certain circumstances, wherever men are found, there is, as Shakespeare says,

> No natural exhalation in the sky,
> No scape of nature, no distemper'd day,
> No common wind, no customed event,
> But they will pluck away his natural cause,
> And call them meteors, prodigies, and signs,
> Abortives, presages, and tongues of heaven.

Imposture is so far from being the general rule in these cases, that it is the rare exception.' [34] Did the prophets foretell the coming of Christ? They merely made general promises of a successor to David and created a 'futurist' state of mind, partly as compensation for current misery, partly in impressive testimony to the continuing power of Israel's great experience, by dwelling on the ultimate triumph of the 'Eternal which makes for righteousness'. Is Jesus credited with statements concerning a future life, a resurrection, the kingdom of God? Then we must conclude that his reporters erred, naturally, in representing these as external and physical phenomena. For the mark of Jesus is the inwardness of his teaching—'The kingdom of God is within you', 'Cleanse thou the inside of the cup'—and his appearance after death is to be construed as an inward influence on those capable of receiving it. Similarly, the resurrection is the rising to a higher spiritual life by following righteousness, and immortality is merely the resulting sense of life so strongly developed that it suggests continuance to the spiritually enlightened. In fact, Arnold's positive and cultural method is the rather paradoxical one of preserving the authority of the Bible by showing the fallibility of the reporters. Morally, the disciples of Christ were far above the average; intellectually, they shared the mental outlook of the average Jew who caught at the letter in Old Testament exegesis and prophecy.

We have seen how Paul, to Arnold, rises above his inevitable orientalizing and judaizing by virtue of his hold on the practical matter of righteousness, and his spiritualizing of such concepts as that of the Messiah and the resurrection. Having satisfied himself of the Pauline genius for true religion, Arnold denies that the Epistle to the Hebrews could be Paul's. It is 'full of beautiful things' and it is 'clear in exterior argument', but it has not a religious idea at the centre. The work is 'notional', not experimental. Here and there 'one is tempted' to see the 'line' of Jesus, but Jesus never theosophized, nor did Paul after him. Hence this epistle must not be placed among the Pauline writings. Reversing this procedure, Arnold denies Baur's whole theory of the crucial Fourth Gospel as a work of the imaginative intellect composed by an artistic Greek with an anti-Semitic bias. No, says Arnold: 'It has the character of a work proceeding from the soul. It is solemnly and profoundly religious. . . . He is too much subjugated by Jesus to deal freely with him in this fashion, as a mouthpiece for his own purposes and his own ideas.'[35] There is no Gnosticism, as the Tübingen professors would have us believe in their zest for *Tendenzschriften*. Yet there is 'a philosophical turn of mind', and the unknown Greek editor of the Evangelist achieves in his redaction, under the exaltation of the *logia* and gnomic sayings reported of Jesus, the connection of these sayings into an articulated and smoothly flowing discourse. These examples of 'tact' at work in the field of the Higher Criticism, serenely settling questions of Pauline and Johannine authorship, show us the sort of thing which fascinated some readers of Arnold, and infuriated others.

In his treatment of the 'barren and retarding question of Church and Dissent', several of Arnold's ideas come into play: the cultural totality of man, the nature of religious development, the need in man for beauty. Just as being a Christian at any time during 'the last eighteen hundred years' meant being in the main stream of human life, so, for an Englishman, being a member of the Established Church meant having the chance to share in the total cultural life of the nation. So important are unity and continuity in religious life that separation can be justified only on moral grounds. The separation of the English Church from Rome at the Reformation can be so justified, but the separatism of the Puritan Dissenting sects, which is based on opinion, cannot be justified. Misinterpreting Paul in the first place, holding fiercely to doctrinal points of difference and mechanically to the literal interpretation of certain texts, the Puritans developed an aggressive self-righteousness, a righteousness which consisted mainly in 'smiting the Lord's enemies and their own under the fifth rib'. In the nineteenth century, with 'election' and 'justification' less firmly believed in than formerly, the reasons for separation come to be increasingly sought in matters of Church government and discipline. In other words the Puritan (read Philistine) is resting his case increasingly on machinery and externals, doing battle for non-essentials and thwarting his own total development. For this he is to blame. Remember, said Arnold to the Puritan, 'the Church cannot help existing—you can!' In spite of the historians, who favoured the Puritans as the party of civil liberties, Arnold maintained that the greater degree of tolerance and open-mindedness had been on the side of the Church. Nonconformity had resulted as much from the Church's refusal to be strictly Calvinist, as from her insistence on her own formularies. It was the Puritans who had dogmatically and fiercely held to rigid interpretations and had refused all conciliatory measures.

The type of Church government is not important, says Arnold. Let us have both Episcopalian and Presbyterian order within the Establishment, as there once was, and so reconcile the largest body of sectarians. Let us have union now, on the basis of the proposals of Tillotson and Stillingfleet, not on the basis of 'scriptural Protestantism'. But let the Dissenters make concessions too, chiefly the concession that the antiquity of the Church must be allowed to count for something. Then the Church will gain by the incorporation of so much new blood, energy, honesty, and multiplicity of views; the Dissenters will gain by becoming part of the main current of national life, by having their fine energies free for something other than 'the Dissidence of Dissent and the Protestantism of the Protestant religion'. Many times Arnold protests his friendship for the Dissenters, in terms which he echoes at the close of his last religious essay: 'Whether the Dissenters will believe it or not, my wish to reconcile them with the Church is from no desire to give their adversaries a victory and them a defeat, but from a conviction that they are on a false line; from sorrow at seeing their fine qualities and energies thrown away, from hope of signal good to this whole nation if they can be turned to better account.'

The Church Arnold finds to be a reasonable Establishment, a 'great national society for the promotion of goodness'. She has been accused of an alliance with property, but this is not her authentic tradition, not the 'line' of her great men. True, at times she has her faults—inertia, intolerance, reaction. But her reasonableness, comprehensiveness, and continuity, the integrity of her great men, and their largeness of mind as compared with the leaders of Dissent, have made for the full operation within her borders of the principles of development and growth.

(Trilling points out that for Arnold development proceeds in an undulant line, not in a straight line as for Newman. This is naturally so, since it is a gradual discovery by the 'imaginative reason', under conditions fixed by the *Zeitgeist* at different times, of the truth in the historically recorded psychological experience of a 'divine' law, and not the steady movement of human intelligence towards the fuller comprehension of an original divine revelation.)

Finally, there is the question of beauty, of the poetry of the service and the advantages of collective worship. The hideous red-brick-chapel Nonconformity of the Puritan meeting-places is no more depressing than their hymns and services, surely 'the most dismal performance ever invented by man'. The power for beauty which Arnold posits as one of the four powers in man is not to be satisfied by this. In the Church are grace and peace, dignity and permanence, the poetry (not the science) of the Creeds and Prayer Book, the rich symbolism of traditional ceremony and ritual. Here lies its strength, justifying a prophecy as to its future, a future dependent, of course, on the extent to which 'sweetness and light' distinguish its ministers:

> Force the Church of England has certainly some; perhaps a good deal. But its true strength is in relying, not on its powers of force, but on its powers of attractiveness. And by opening itself to the glow of the old and true ideal of the Christian Gospel, by fidelity to reason, by placing the stress of its religion on goodness, by cultivating grace and peace, it will inspire attachment, to which the attachment which it inspires now, deep though that is, will be as nothing; it will last, be sure, as long as this nation.[36]

On the Church question Arnold admits that he is not likely to make much of an impression, but he feels he has to speak, for the sake both of the Church of England and of Dissent. Dissent is driving people into the Church of Rome, noticeably in the United States, and prolonging by this accession of numbers the old untransformed Catholicism, not ushering in the Catholicism of the future. What this might be he describes in a summary of his religious aims and aspirations: 'Unity and continuity in public worship are a need of human nature, an eternal aspiration of Christendom; but unity and continuity in religious worship joined with perfect mental sanity and freedom. A Catholic Church transformed is, I believe, the Church of the future.'[37]

The word 'nature' here recalls the list of words offering a key to Arnold's thought. Arnold is always praising the 'natural truth' of Christianity. He finds it a *fact*, unlike the theorizings of orthodoxy. The *logia* of Christ are full of natural truth. John Smith and his fellow Cambridge Platonists are praised for making clear the natural truth of Christianity. The future of Christianity depends on its natural truth. This is not, however, the old 'natural religion'. Arnold speaks of 'the poor old dead horses of so-called natural theology, with their galvanic movements', brought in by the author of *Supernatural Religion*. And against the Dissenters, mixing religion with politics at the level of their ordinary busybody selves, Arnold can say 'Christianity is not natural', that is, not in conformity with our ordinary self or lower nature. The explanation is that only by our higher nature can Christ and Christianity be apprehended even dimly, as the (moral) cures wrought by Christ were made possible only at a level above ordinary animal nature. The true antithesis to 'revealed' is to Arnold not 'natural' but 'artificial'. Revealed religion is simply natural religion operating exclusively at the level of the higher self to which we are enabled to rise by virtue of Christ's example and our love for Him. Christ represented perfect harmony with 'the Eternal not ourselves that makes for righteousness', the 'divine' moral law which is natural in its operation and visible to men like Paul in those supreme moments of enlightenment when the lower self is submerged and the spiritual resurrection is complete.

This doctrine of the two selves in man is central to Arnold's ethico-religious criticism, as we saw in his reinterpreting of the Pauline message. It colours his usage of terms and, carried on from *Culture and Anarchy* as it is, unifies his critical thinking in general on a moral basis. The clearest statement of this central doctrine is made in the preface to the *Last Essays on Church and Religion*:

It will generally be admitted that all experience as to conduct brings us at last to the fact of two selves, or instincts, or forces,—name them how we will, and however we may suppose them to have arisen, —contending for the mastery in man: one, a movement of first impulse and more involuntary, leading us to gratify any inclination that may solicit us, and called generally a movement of man's ordinary or passing self, of sense, appetite, desire; the other, a movement of reflection and more voluntary, leading us to submit inclination to some rule, and

E

called generally a movement of man's higher or enduring self, of reason, spirit, will. The thing is described in different words by different nations and men relating their experience of it, but as to the thing itself they all, or all the most serious and important among them, agree. This, I think, will be admitted. Nor will it be denied that they all come to the conclusion that for a man to obey the higher self, or reason, or whatever it is to be called, is happiness and life for him; to obey the lower is death and misery.

Two paragraphs further on, the resulting 'naturalistic' presentation of the essentials of the religious life is given, in a passage which offers an even more compact summary than the 'Arnoldian catechism' quoted earlier:

Eternal life? Yes, the life in the higher and undying self of man. Judgment? Yes, the trying, in conscience, of the claims and instigations of the two lives, and the decision between them. Resurrection? Yes, the rising from bondage and transience with the lower life to victory and permanence with the higher. The kingdom of God? Yes, the reign amongst mankind of the higher life. The Christ the son of God? Yes, the bringer-in and founder of this reign of the higher life, this true kingdom of God.[38]

CHAPTER III

Major Formative Influences

Moral culture [is] so intimately allied to, nay incorporated
with æsthetic culture, . . . that to their mutual perfection the
one cannot be conceived without the other.

GOETHE, in Truth and Poetry

Nous irons vers l'avenir pleins du passé et remplissant nos jours
présents par l'étude, la méditation, et un continuel effort vers la
perfection.

GEORGE SAND, quoted in Note-books

THE eclectic nature of Matthew Arnold's reading, of the
sources that furnished and the influences that shaped many
of his ideas, was to some extent evident in the early selection from
his note-books, that intellectual and spiritual record described as
'the breviary of a humanist', and as 'one of the great devotional
books of the world'. Now that the complete note-books have been
published the image of the treasure-house replaces that of the
breviary, as one contemplates the richness and diversity of the
materials gathered from half a dozen languages and literatures.
Fullness of quotation and frequency of repetition go far to confirm
the impressions gathered from essays and letters as to the major
formative influences upon Arnold and warn against the seductions
of mere parallel hunting or source discoveries, to both of which
sometimes rather disparaging forms of attention Arnold has had
his full share of exposure.

The attempt to assess Arnold's religious thought in terms of
obligations and affinities, to indicate the 'streams of tendency' in
which that thought moves, is aided by occasional direct acknow-
ledgements. One such occurs in the course of his correspondence
with Cardinal Newman in 1872: 'There are four people in
especial, from whom I am conscious of having learnt—a very
different thing from merely receiving a strong impression—learnt
habits, methods, ruling ideas, which are constantly with me; and
the four are—Goethe, Wordsworth, Sainte-Beuve, and yourself.' [1]
This explicit acknowledgement seems very much to the purpose,
particularly in a letter addressed to the most prominent religious
figure in nineteenth-century England. Yet caution is necessary,
before we attribute to any of the four here mentioned a formative

influence in the shaping of Arnold's specifically religious ideas. With regard to Newman, the question is settled for us in an earlier letter, when Arnold declared, 'Nothing can ever do away with the effect you have produced upon me, for it consists in *a general disposition of mind rather than in a particular set of ideas.* In all the conflicts I have with modern Liberalism and Dissent, and with their pretensions and shortcomings, I recognize your work.' [2] In other words, Newman was a spiritual ally in Arnold's prolonged campaign against hard, unlovely Puritanism and crassly utilitarian Philistinism, one of the spiritual fathers of *Culture and Anarchy* rather than of the later and distinctively religious works. Newman recognized this important distinction himself when he replied, 'I am so sensitively alive to the very great differences of opinion which separate us. I wish with all my heart I could make them less.' Arnold's considered estimate of Newman emerges rather in the essay on Emerson, which opens with the lyrically eloquent eulogy to 'the charm of that spiritual apparition', and the 'religious music' of his voice. 'The name of Cardinal Newman is a great name to the imagination still'; but 'he has adopted, for the doubts and difficulties which beset men's minds today, a solution which, to speak frankly, is impossible'.

Two of the remaining acknowledgements must also submit to qualification. Sainte-Beuve's influence was mainly in the field of literary criticism, a matter of 'method', to use Arnold's own word. His tact, his humanistic standard, the objectivity and *curiosité* which made of him a 'naturalist' in literary and other criticism, above all, the balance struck with unerring precision—these were what Arnold admired and tried to emulate. 'He did but follow his instinct', runs Arnold's final tribute, with reference to a 'Liberal' speech of Sainte-Beuve in the French Senate, 'of opposing, in whatever medium he was, the current of that medium when it seemed excessive and tyrannous.' [3] Here, certainly, we find a 'ruling idea' which extended throughout Arnold's critical writing and thought, perhaps *the* ruling idea, which will come in for fuller treatment in a summarizing chapter. Arnold could not follow the 'naturalist' when he applied his naturalism to the Bible: 'M. Sainte-Beuve, the finest critical spirit of our times, conceived of the Bible so falsely, simply from not knowing it, that he could cheerfully and confidently repeat the Liberal formula: "Unless we mean to prefer Byzantinism to progress we must say goodbye *aux vieilles Bibles*." ' [4] But he could take the critical principle of Sainte-Beuve and, knowing his Bible, use it to preserve moral at the expense of literal inspiration.

The inclusion of Wordsworth does not mean, of course, that Arnold was a worshipper of Nature. What he found early in Wordsworth was what he was later to affirm as the hallmark both of great poetry and of religion stripped of pseudo-science, namely, moral profundity and joy. In the well-known passage which begins the essay on *The Study of Poetry*, the prophecy is made that mankind will more and more find its stay in poetry as religious creeds become fluid or dissolve under the heat of science. Indeed, 'the strongest part of our religion today is its unconscious poetry'. And the superiority of the poet consists in his capacity to make a powerful application of moral ideas to life, to deal with life, to make us feel 'the joy offered to us in nature, the joy offered to us in the simple primary affections and duties'. That Arnold used the word 'moral' here in the widest possible sense hardly needs affirming, though Professor Lowry did well to remind us that people who attack the famous definition, 'Poetry is a criticism of life', too often forget that Arnold added 'under the conditions fixed for such a criticism by the laws of poetic truth and poetic beauty'. Among the quotations from Goethe in his *Note-books* are the words 'A good work of art may and will have moral results; but to require of the artist a moral aim is to spoil his work.' Of course Arnold shared in the Victorian moral earnestness that Wordsworth himself helped to foster. Even Swinburne believed that 'good art produced a moral effect', and the care needed in assessing the whole intricate question is shown by a letter of Baudelaire. Having said that he hates all 'objective morality in a poem', he tells Swinburne, 'I merely believe, as you doubtless do yourself, that any poem, any work of art which is well done, naturally and inevitably implies a moral.' [5]

We have so far 'a general disposition of mind', a 'ruling idea', and a moral emphasis heightened by joy which suggests Arnold's definition of religion as 'morality, touched by emotion'. In Goethe, the fourth influence mentioned by Arnold in the letter to Newman, these factors may be said to coalesce; the 'physician of the iron age' is present in Arnold's pronouncements on matters pertaining to the imagination, the intellect, and conduct. The 'profound naturalism' of Goethe is throughout *Literature and Dogma* brought to bear upon man's anthropomorphism and the tendency to see in religious *Aberglaube* the science rather than the poetry of life.

The moral insight of 'the most naturalistic, the freest, the calmest of observers of these matters' supplies evidence that marriage as against free love represents a 'culture-conquest'. Most of all, it is as the representative of the 'modern spirit' at its best that Goethe is worthy of reverence. He is the liberator of 'the modern European from the old routine'; he puts the standard 'once for all, inside every man instead of outside him'; he opposes authority and custom with the critical question: 'But is it so? is it so to *me*? Nothing could be more really subversive of the foundations on which the old European order rested; and it may be remarked that no persons are so radically detached from this order, no persons so thoroughly modern, as those who have felt Goethe's influence most deeply.' [6] Steeped in and disciplined by the past yet no traditionalist, loftily surveying the possibilities of a world culture and condemning provincialism, devoted to natural science as the guide to truth yet always from the large point of view and aiming at an imaginative synthesis, Goethe was for Arnold *the* great figure of modern times.

Dr Arnold may be said to have exercised in general an influence combining that of Carlyle and Coleridge, without their respective brands of philosophical or transcendent idealism. With a moral seriousness as great as Carlyle's, though definitely Christian in tone and teaching, he applied a spirit of free historical inquiry, with important reservations, to the Bible. Tulloch and Pfleiderer agree that his main service to English religious thought was in advancing freer scriptural interpretation, and they expand this into the larger claim that, like Coleridge, he was a vitalizing force. Certainly he had not allowed his duties as headmaster of Rugby to keep him from scholarly work, strenuous though these were: 'My business as schoolmaster is a constant exercise in the interpretation of language, . . . and this habit of interpretation has been constantly applied to the Scriptures for more than twenty years; for I began the careful study of the Scriptures long before I left Oxford, and have never intermitted it.' [7] His most urgent and reiterated plea was for a liberal breadth of interpretation, that we should accept, for example, justification both by faith and by works, 'not to make one another offenders for a word'. And although Matthew pushed his father's liberal critical principles to lengths which would have appalled Dr Arnold, it was on this line that he rightly saw himself as continuing his father's work.

The arresting tributes to Butler, Coleridge, and the Cambridge

Platonists are made for the one reason, namely, that all stress the natural truth of Christianity. Nowhere is the need for careful consideration of Arnold's balanced statements and qualified judgments better shown. The essay on *Bishop Butler and the Zeit-Geist* leaves us with the impression that Butler, while an admirable man, a staunch defender of reason, and a great exponent of 'practical religion', has been discarded intellectually because of an unsound psychology and a logic based on faulty assumptions. Yet we find that this is only his 'embarrassment', that his true greatness remains: 'From Butler, and from his treatment of *nature* in religion, the idea of following out that treatment frankly and fully, which is the design of *Literature and Dogma*, first, as we are proud to acknowledge, came to us; and, indeed, our obligations of all kinds to this deep and strenuous spirit are very great.' [8] This is indeed unequivocal, and the number of references scattered throughout Arnold's writings show that the days when 'we at Oxford used to read our Aristotle or our Butler with the same absolute faith in the classicality of their matter as in the classicality of Homer's form' had left a deep impression.

The metaphysical speculations of Coleridge, on which J. H. Green was later to found his *Spiritual Philosophy*, had no attraction for Arnold, but he acknowledged Coleridge's importance as an influence in the direction of critical inquiry. With all his reverence for the Church and his spiritual idealism, Coleridge was insistent that the Bible as history be approached from a rational and scholarly point of view. Guarded and guided in reading the Bible, like Dr Arnold, by 'a strong and awful prepossession in its favour', he attacked the 'extravagant notion of the absolute truth and divinity of every syllable of the texts of the books of the Old and New Testaments'.[9] Those who believed in 'plenary inspiration' and tried to harmonize all discrepancies were the ones who degraded Scripture, said Coleridge, by making all equal. He read with reverence, but not with superstitious reverence; 'whatever finds me [in the Bible] bears witness for itself that it has proceeded from the Holy Spirit'. In a further plea for free inquiry, he reduced the bias or 'persuasion' to a minimum: 'I demand for the Bible only the justice which you would grant to other books of grave authority and to other proved and acknowledged benefactors of mankind.' [10]

The paucity of references to Coleridge in Arnold's writing is at first surprising, but the tone and point of the references themselves indicate both the extent of Arnold's knowledge and the focal point of the critical relationship:

> Coleridge had less delicacy and penetration than Joubert, but more richness and power. . . . Yet in all his production how much is there to dissatisfy us! How many reserves must be made in praising either his poetry, or his criticism, or his philosophy! . . . But that which will stand of Coleridge is this: the stimulus of his continual effort,—not a moral effort, for he had no morals,—but his continual instinctive effort, crowned often with rich success, to get at and lay bare the real truth of the matter in hand, whether that matter was literary, or philosophical, or religious.[11]

The 'moral' reservation is abrupt, but Arnold seems familiar enough with 'all his production' to speak with confidence of Coleridge's power to get at 'the real truth', the truth which to Arnold is 'scientific' and 'verifiable'. Similarly he speaks, in two essays, twenty-three years apart, of Coleridge's 'fine expression' with respect to Christian truth, as 'that which finds us'. In the latter essay, where he quotes with approval a number of tributes to Coleridge, and characteristically deprecates the attempts of Coleridge's disciples to systematize the master's ideas, Arnold shows us wherein he considers Coleridge's true greatness for Christian thought to consist:

> The 'great Coleridgean position', that apart from all question of the evidence for miracles and of the historical quality of the Gospel narratives, *the essential matters of Christianity are necessary and eternal facts of nature or truths of reason,* is henceforth the key to the whole defence of Christianity. When a Christian virtue is presented to us as obligatory, the first thing, therefore, to be asked, is whether our need of it is a fact of nature.[12]

Arnold may well have been introduced to the Cambridge Platonists by Coleridge, who speaks with enthusiasm of the 'Cambridge divines', and particularly of John Smith. Hales of Eton and the Cambridge men 'have in their conception of religion a boon for the religious wants of our own time', most fully revealed, according to Arnold, in Smith's *Select Discourses.* Of these sermons he says, 'Their grand merit is that they insist on the profound *natural truth* of Christianity, and thus base it upon a ground which will not crumble under our feet.'[13] Here, as in the tributes paid to Butler and Coleridge, is apparent the main idea in

Arnold's religious thought, the strategy he would substitute for the Maginot line of theological orthodoxy, and oppose to the dangerous combination of frontal attack and infiltration marking the advance of sceptical rationalism. By emphasizing in a naturalistic age the correspondence of Christ's teaching with the highest aspirations and needs of evolving human nature, Arnold was convinced that Christianity would go forward to a still greater future, in a form that humanity would find satisfactory to the reason, inspiring to the imagination, and fundamental to the moral sense.

The impact of Emerson and the Stoics upon Arnold was rather in terms of moral and spiritual guidance than in terms of ideas. We may couple them because Arnold himself, after denying to a Boston audience that Emerson was a great poet, writer, or philosopher, concluded that 'his relation to us is more like that of the Roman Emperor Marcus Aurelius'. This meant, as Arnold went on to add in a typically balanced and judicious estimate, one full of rich meaning, that 'he is the friend and aider of those who would live in the spirit'. This it was that made Emerson greater than Carlyle, who had a 'perverse attitude towards happiness'. In his desire to base religion in human psychological needs, Arnold came to believe that nothing was more essential than to see true happiness as attached to the life of the spirit, to right conduct. 'Epictetus and Augustine', he said, 'can be severe moralists enough; but both of them know and frankly say that the desire for happiness is the root and ground of man's being.' Such was Emerson's gospel—'Happiness in labour, righteousness, and veracity.' For Arnold the influence of Emerson went back to Oxford days, to 'a clear and pure voice, which for my ear, at any rate, brought a strain as new, and moving, and unforgettable, as the strain of Newman, or Carlyle, or Goethe'.

When we come to consider Renan, a careful balancing of positive and negative comment shows a surplus on the credit side. Renan is wrong on St Paul; he lacks Sainte-Beuve's genius in opposing excess; he is not critically 'sound, . . . in proportion to his brilliancy'. Yet, Arnold tells us,

M. Renan's attempt is, for criticism, of the most real importance and interest, since, with all its difficulty, a fresh synthesis of the New Testament *data*,—not a making war on them, in Voltaire's fashion, not a leaving them out of mind, in the world's fashion, but the putting a new construction upon them, the taking them from under the old traditional conventional point of view and placing them under a new one,—is the very essence of there ligious problem, as now presented; and only by efforts in this direction can it receive a solution.[14]

Writing to his sister Jane in 1859, Arnold had remarked on a 'considerable resemblance' between Renan's 'line of endeavour' and his own, and had also noted the difference:

The difference is, perhaps, that he tends to inculcate *morality*, in a high sense of the word, upon the French nation as what they most want, while I tend to inculcate *intelligence*, also in a high sense of the word, upon the English nation as what they most want; but with respect both to morality and intelligence, I think we are singularly at one in our ideas, and also both with respect to the progress and the established religion of the present day. The best book of his for you to read, in all ways, is his *Essais de Morale et de Critique*, lately published.[15]

One would hardly claim for George Sand a shaping influence upon Arnold's religious ideas. Rather she was a liberalizing force. Her inspiration may be traced in *Culture and Anarchy* where Arnold declares that equality is the social idea, that 'the men of culture are the true apostles of equality'. The shared excitement and flavour of forbidden fruit among the young men at Oxford reading her novels, the romantic touch in Arnold's pilgrimage to Berry and meeting with the famous author, the passion of youthful longing to set things right—no doubt all this increased the glamour of this rebellious genius. But even when Arnold had taken to lecturing the French for their inattention to conduct he was ready to make excuses for George Sand. A hint of the censorious crept into a letter at the time of her death: 'She was the greatest spirit in our European world from the time that Goethe departed. With all her faults and Frenchism, she was this.' In the essay he wrote on her a year later the censorious hint has gone. He recalls her large and generous utterance, her faith in the French peasant, her love of Nature. But what he stresses, and repeats, is 'the ruling thought of George Sand', her belief in 'the sentiment of the ideal life, which is none other than man's normal life as we shall one day know it'.[16] This was the woman who wrote to the self-analytical and tortured Flaubert, seeking her wisdom and rejecting it, 'I do not need to be sure of the safety of the planet and its inhabitants to believe in the necessity of the good and the beautiful.' [17] And again: 'Humanity is not a vain word. Our life is composed of love, and not to love is to cease to live.' We can say that George Sand, as a liberalizing and humanizing influence upon the young Arnold, contributed to the element of social sympathy in his ethical idealism.

In any further consideration of writers and moralists who influenced Arnold's ethical and religious thinking, there is a danger of moving out to a periphery. There is, for example, the French teacher and theologian, Alexander Vinet, 'who', Arnold said in a letter of May 1, 1865, 'has been occupying me a good deal lately'. A firm believer in a doctrinal and dogmatic Christianity, he was yet so liberal in his interpretations and withal so firm a moulder of character that he was compared with Arnold of Rugby. His view of Christianity as reasonable and natural, as 'conscience raised to its highest exercise', fitted well with Matthew Arnold's ideas. But there are many who received respectful reference and a niche in the *Note-books* without having a shaping or formative influence in the realm of ideas. Of those who had such an influence one, intellectually the most impressive figure, remains to be considered.

I have deliberately left to the last the purely philosophic influence, both because Spinoza furnishes the best transition from a preliminary glance at sources to a fuller treatment of ideas, and because he may serve to offset the negative impressions of Arnold as a thinker which have persisted since the severe attacks in the last century by F. H. Bradley and J. M. Robertson. The frequency with which Arnold confessed the lack of a 'philosophy with coherent, interdependent, subordinate, and derivative principles', and asserted that his was a plain man's approach to problems left 'pinnacled dim in the intense inane' by metaphysicians and theologians, has perhaps misled the majority of his critics and biographers, who have shown a curious eagerness to accept this mock humility at its face value. When the brilliant logician Bradley had, as Trilling maintains, exposed Arnold's 'terminological juggling with irresistible ferocity', and so prominent a biblical scholar as T. K. Cheyne had described Arnold's Hebrew scholarship as 'a smoking flax', there seemed little for succeeding students of Arnold to do but dismiss his religious writings, like Russell with a sigh, or like Saintsbury with a sneer. Herbert Paul deprecated this double dismissal, but was not convinced that this side of Arnold's work deserved serious study. Stuart Sherman, in fact, was the only one of the earlier critics to offer a reasonably serious and sensitive analysis of Arnold's religious thought, but in the rather general way appropriate to a volume written for a popular series.

It has remained for later scholars, notably Lowry and Trilling, to suggest the possible extent of Arnold's philosophical and theological reading, and to indicate the importance of this eclectic indebtedness in any adequate estimate of Arnold's thought as a whole. Professor Lowry observed in 1932 that the note-books in manuscript gave an impression of wide and deep theological reading, and added that half the religious thought of Arnold is mastered when one masters Spinoza's teaching that the image and knowledge of God are recorded in the enduring substance of the human heart.[18] Professor Trilling has examined the relation to Spinoza, laying great stress on Spinoza and Coleridge as the parents of Arnold's religious thought. The important thing is that the presence of thought, with antecedents and ramifications, is admitted, and Arnold is not dismissed on the score of inadequate logical definitions and exegetical minutiæ, which after all are peripheral to his purpose. It should be rewarding to examine in some detail the Spinozist elements in Arnold's thinking.

A striking fact is that Spinoza is the only philosopher of whom Arnold makes more than incidental mention. His article on 'The Bishop and the Philosopher', in 1863, later altered to 'Spinoza and the Bible' and published in *Essays in Criticism, First Series*, is as wholehearted a tribute as Arnold paid to any writer. We have already seen how Colenso's 'negative' aim suffers by contrast with Spinoza's 'positive' one, and his 'weak trifling' by contrast with the 'strong thought' of Spinoza. It is the latter's highest praise that he succeeds uniquely in 'edifying the well-instructed', men like Goethe and Lessing. Nor was this a late discovery, advanced a few years before Arnold was to make his own critical contribution to religious thought and biblical studies. As early as 1850, Arnold told Clough what human agencies were furnishing him with a corrective to the *mal du siècle* colouring so much of his verse: 'I go to read Locke on the Conduct of the Understanding: my respect for the reason as the rock of refuge to this poor exaggerated surexcited humanity increases and increases. Locke is a man who has cleared his mind of vain repetitions, though without the positive and vivifying atmosphere of Spinoza about him. This last, smile as you will, I have been studying lately with profit.' [19]

This statement is important as an early glimpse of the synthesis Arnold was seeking. The reason, yes; but as well the *positive* aim (conduct, edification) and the *vivifying* atmosphere (poetry and the imagination). We are prepared for the later formulation of the 'imaginative reason' as the critical faculty *par excellence* for the establishment of a modern and adequate culture and religion. We are prepared, too, I think, to find in Spinoza one of the major formative influences in Arnold's thinking during the central fifteen years when his critical principles and dominant ideas were maturing to the point of repetitive expression. What Arnold was searching for, what presumably Spinoza helped supply him with, he described in 1848 as 'an Idea of the world in order not to be prevailed over by the world's multitudinousness'. This the reason could supply. But there was another side, particularly important with regard to religion, and here thinkers like Locke were of no avail:

If one loved what was beautiful and interesting in itself *passionately* enough, one would produce what was excellent without troubling one-self with religious dogmas at all. As it is, we are *warm* only when dealing with these last—and what is frigid is always bad. I would have others—most others stick to the old religious dogmas because I sincerely feel that this *warmth* is the great blessing, and this frigidity the great curse—and on the old religious road they have still the best chance of getting the one and avoiding the other.[20]

Here Arnold sketches the *desiderata* of the higher life in terms of the rational, the moral, and the religious. The transitions he makes from poetry to literary criticism to social criticism to religious criticism are seen as not only natural, but inevitable. At this stage the affirmations rewarding the search for 'joy whose grounds are true' are yet to come, but of the object of the search there is from the beginning no uncertainty.

The article in which Spinoza is used as a touchstone to show up the inadequacy of theologians like Colenso, whether as textual critics or as religious philosophers, is written in a manner which suggests long acquaintance and undiminished respect. Arnold limits his discussion almost entirely to the *Tractatus Theologico-Politicus*, though he is familiar with the *Ethics* and the *Correspondence*. In the latter part of the essay he speaks more fully of 'certain governing ideas of Spinoza, which receive their systematic expression in the Ethics . . . but which are yet never absent from

Spinoza's mind in the composition of any work'. But until there is a translation of the *Ethics*, its criticism is 'far too serious a task to be undertaken incidentally'. Meanwhile, Arnold is quite clear on the 'governing ideas'. They are the denial of final causes, the belief in an active stoicism, and the distinction (which became 'a current notion for educated Europe') between adequate and inadequate ideas. All these ideas inform Arnold's own writing and thinking, and the third, indeed, is omnipresent in his social and religious criticism.

Though Arnold could claim adequate first-hand knowledge of Spinoza, it is safe to say that his reading of Goethe antedated his reading of Spinoza, and perhaps coloured it. The theory of final causes is given the death-blow by the dual authority:

For a mind like Goethe's,—a mind profoundly impartial and passionately aspiring after the science, not of men only, but of universal nature,—the popular philosophy which explains all things by reference to man, and regards universal nature as existing for the sake of man, and even of certain classes of men, was utterly repulsive. Unchecked, this philosophy would gladly maintain that the donkey exists in order that the invalid Christian may have donkey's milk for breakfast; and such views of nature as this were exactly what Goethe's whole soul abhorred. Creation, he thought, should be made of sterner stuff; he desired to rest the donkey's existence on larger grounds. More than any philosopher who has ever lived, Spinoza satisfied him here.[21]

The other aspect of Spinoza's thought which satisfied Goethe, according to Arnold, was the active, rather than passive, stoicism. Certainly, in *Truth and Poetry* Goethe stressed the influence of Spinoza upon him, in calming him and in freeing him to think when he was most restless, especially by virtue of the principle of 'disinterestedness'. He owed to Spinoza chiefly the conviction that 'Nature works after such eternal, necessary, divine laws, that the Deity himself would alter nothing in them.'[22] That they were opposites in temperament he recognized. No man could fully understand another, especially one at 'the highest reach of thought', one 'whose name even to this day seems to mark the limit of all speculative efforts'.

What most impresses Arnold in Spinoza is the combination of critical honesty and acumen with a moral earnestness which insists that so sturdy a support for frail humanity as the Christian religion should be preserved, even if it means placing ethical values above intellectual rigour. This involves leaving the pure air of the *Ethics* for the slightly hazier (but 'warmer') atmosphere of the *Tractatus*, where the weaker understanding of the many can be reached and where the humanist and moralist can gently return with the left hand what the logician and philosopher took away with the right. Spinoza rejects anthropomorphic deity, literal inspiration, and the whole metaphysical basis of traditional theology. Miracles do not happen, since they would transgress the eternal and immutable laws of nature, which are laws of God, are in fact of His essence. The prophets were men of vivid imagination, speaking Hebrew poetry, of extraordinary piety but of ordinary minds.

This negative criticism is, however, accompanied by equally positive inferences. We do not infer that the message is no longer valid—only that it needs clarifying and reinterpreting. Are some things in scripture not clear to the reason? It 'narrates them in the order and style which has most power to move men, and especially uneducated men, to devotion; and therefore it speaks inaccurately of God and of events, seeing that its object is not to convince the reason, but to attract and lay hold of the imagination'.[23] Since the power of clear reasoning is limited, scripture addresses the understanding and experience of men. But the condition of blessedness lies in the result (i.e., conduct). Here the Spinoza of the Tractate makes the pragmatic emphasis which must have attracted Arnold: 'If a man abounds in the fruits of the Spirit . . . whether he be taught by reason only or by Scripture only, [he] has been in very truth taught by God, and is altogether blessed.'[24] The basis on which Spinoza operates as a moralist is made clear when he tells us that the whole aim of his treatise is to separate faith from philosophy, and to indicate their proper spheres: 'The sphere of reason is . . . truth and wisdom; the sphere of theology is piety and obedience.' In the latter sphere, where reason cannot prove or disprove the truth of revelation, it accepts, only demanding a moral certainty. Nor is this difficult. We accept the teachings of the prophets, because 'the morality they teach is in evident agreement with reason, for it is no accidental coincidence that the Word of God which we find in the prophets coincided with the Word of God written in our hearts'.[25]

The appeal to experience and the judgment by results call for a level of accommodation in scripture to the needs of the many.

In words which suggest a direct inspiration for Arnold's approach to the Bible, Spinoza says:

> Scriptural doctrine contains no lofty speculation or philosophic reasoning, but only very simple matters, such as could be understood by the slowest intelligence. I am consequently lost in wonder at the ingenuity of those . . . who detect in the Bible mysteries so profound that they cannot be explained in human language, and who have introduced so many philosophic speculations into religion, that the Church seems like an academy, and religion like a science, or rather a dispute.[26]

In fact, Spinoza continues, 'Scripture does not aim at imparting scientific knowledge; . . . it demands from men nothing but obedience, and censures obstinacy, but not ignorance.' Revelation (which is clearly to Spinoza the heightened experience, the intuition, of a natural moral truth) operates quite naturally in this sphere and is needed, since 'all are able to obey . . . but very few . . . can acquire the habit of virtue under the unaided guidance of reason'.[27]

This careful division of the two spheres provides, as Sir Frederick Pollock drily remarks, a euthanasia for theology; more pertinent here is the fact that the virtual equation of religion and ethics which underlies it is strongly suggestive of Arnold's position. The position is even more clearly shown when Spinoza considers the Apostles, universal in their mission, writing by the light of natural reason, as against the Prophets, temporary and particularist, communicating truths by 'revelation': 'Although religion, as preached by the Apostles, does not come within the sphere of reason, in so far as it consists in the narration of the life of Christ, yet its essence, *which is chiefly moral, like the whole of Christ's doctrine*, can readily be apprehended by the natural faculties of all.'[28] Putting this more largely, the aim of scripture is simply to bring out the truth of human nature, and to assert that the essence of the divine law is love for God (or perfection) and for one's neighbour (an extension of oneself). Who follows this out is blessed, is moral, is religious. And 'for this end, it is not even essential to have true opinions about the course of nature, or God's relation to nature, or about God's nature from a speculative point of view'.[29]

The main critical ideas common to Arnold and Spinoza we may summarize as follows: the dismissal of anthropomorphic deity, miracles, plenary inspiration, and general Bibliolatry; the treatment of the resurrection in a spiritual sense; the stress on the Bible as addressing the experience and imaginations of men, not the reasoning powers of metaphysicians and theologians; the pragmatic test for faith and good conduct as resulting in blessedness; the treatment of revelation as intuition, the heightened experience of a natural truth; the virtual equation of morality and religion. Not only these critical ideas, however, but the foundations of Arnold's psychology are from Spinoza. To Spinoza, there is neither morality nor reason in the 'natural' state, but just power and desire. But in man, by the necessity of his nature, the potentialities are there, enabling him to escape from the miseries of this state of nature, of unlicensed freedom, to a civil and religious state. To work towards that life is to fulfil the 'deepest law of his being', to obey a divinely implanted impulse, to realize his moral, social, and religious happiness in terms of the laws peculiar to his own nature.

This approach Arnold uses, if we may return briefly to Bishop Butler, in disposing of 'psycho-physiology'. Butler is quite right, he says, in positing a need in human nature for religion, and in appealing to right and wrong, reason and conscience, as facts of human experience. But his attempt to show human nature as a neatly equated array of instincts and principles presided over by a conscience, the voice of God, is an arbitrary, not a 'Newtonian', psychology, a fanciful hypothesis. To say that we have an instinct of hunger for our self-good, of compassion for the public good, of deliberate anger to further the ends of justice as against sudden anger for self-defence, is to offer an artificial and unverifiable teleology. The stress is on the negative mitigating of misery, not on the positive desire for happiness. One must appeal instead, says Arnold, to the genesis of these emotions in a single primary instinct, the instinct to live. This becomes the search for happiness; we find that our achieving this depends upon our being 'solidary' with mankind, that 'our nature is violated' if this instinct is thwarted, and that 'this sense finds in us a pre-adaptation to it'.[30] The whole process, in other words, is one of immanent necessity. It is typical of Arnold that he goes on to find the proof in 'the real experience of the race', but the weapons of attack are from Spinoza's armoury.

Yet a great deal is left of Butler to aid the seeker for a truer faith; his stress on the *natural* in religion, which, by Arnold's own statement, was the source for the main idea in *Literature and*

F

Dogma; his practical sense of religion; his moral scrupulousness; his emphasis on the inner law and the word of God written in our hearts. In these things, as in the grandeur of his personal rectitude as an inspiring example, his influence is akin to that of Spinoza, only more distinctively religious. Arnold pays final and decisive tribute to Butler's 'profound sense, that inattention to religion implies "a dissolute immoral temper of mind" '; to his 'fidelity to that sacred light to which religion makes too many people false— reason'; to 'his conviction, that religion and Christianity do some- how "in themselves entirely fall in with our natural sense of things", that they are true, and that their truth, moreover, is somehow to be established and justified on plain grounds of reason'.

The words *natural sense, truth,* and *reason,* remind us of what Arnold was seeking in great writers and thinkers, in the philoso- pher Spinoza and in the theologian Butler, namely, a psycho- logical and historical witness to moral and religious truth. It is his use of such words that we must consider in the following chapter, as we examine his attempt to make the best of both worlds, the world of science and the world of religion.

2. THE MAIN THEMES

CHAPTER IV

Experience and Dogma

I write to convince the lover of religion that by following habits
of intellectual seriousness he need not, so far as religion is con-
cerned, lose anything.

Introduction to God and the Bible

Le rationalisme populaire, conséquence inévitable des progrès
de l'instruction publique et des institutions démocratiques, rend
les temples déserts.

RENAN, quoted in *Note-books*

IT is a commonplace that the reconciler, the peacemaker who
sets out to build a middle way broad enough for opposing
forces, is liable to find himself running the gauntlet. So Arnold
found, and tried to meet the attacks on *Literature and Dogma: An
Essay towards a Better Apprehension of the Bible* by writing his *God and
the Bible: A Review of Objections to Literature and Dogma*. In this
work he restated the two main principles of his biblical criticism:
'To people disposed to throw the Bible aside *Literature and Dogma*
sought to restore the use of it by two considerations: one, that
the Bible requires for its basis nothing but what they can verify;
the other, that the language of the Bible is not scientific, but
literary.' [1] The seeming contradiction here is easily resolved, when
we remember that the verification refers to an assumed universal
experience of the supreme importance of conduct, which, how-
ever, has achieved and can achieve its supreme expression only in
the language of imaginative power. Elsewhere Arnold leaves no
doubt as to what he considers the main avenue to significant
human truth, when he exalts poetry over art (because it thinks)
and over science (because it thinks emotionally): 'Poetry gives the
idea, and it gives it touched with beauty, heightened by emotion.' [2]

It was not the physical scientist who was outraged by Arnold's
views. Huxley, as we shall see, was sympathetic to Arnold's pur-
pose. It was rather on the one hand the conservative theologian,
who was blandly informed that the whole of dogmatic theology
was a mistaken effort to pronounce with scientific exactness on
unverifiable matters, and on the other hand the radical scholar and
critic who was warned that his scientific aims in historical and
textual research resulted in theories which served merely to

73

obscure the true value of the documents and institutions being studied. On the one hand was 'a want of intellectual seriousness' in tying ideas of God and morality to miracles and meta-physics, on the other 'the imperturbable resolution of a German professor in making all the facts suit a theory which he has once adopted'.

These strictures were especially irritating coming from a critic who seemed to be continually shifting his ground, at one time claiming that his own definitions and interpretations were verifiable in a scientific sense, at another describing them as the fruit of superior insight by a man of broad literary culture. For Arnold, however, these were not mutually exclusive points of vantage. If he denied to the professional theologian the sole authority to pronounce on questions of religion and morality, he did not concede to the man of physical science the exclusive right to the word 'scientific'. His object in writing was not to dazzle the reader with intellectual gymnastics, but to be of practical aid in helping him 'to enjoy the Bible and to turn it to his benefit'. To this end the reader must come to the inquiry, like Arnold, 'absolutely disinterested, with no foregone conclusion at the bottom of [his] mind to start with, no secondary purpose of any kind to serve; but with the simple desire to see the thing, so far as this may be possible, as it really is'.[3] The phrase 'so far as this may be possible' never acted as a deterrent upon Arnold in his claim to be scientific as well as practical.

Arnold's whole approach was consistent in motivation and conservative in aim, being the idealizing of man's moral nature and moral experience as witnessed in literature and in history. To reject intellectual development, specifically the growth of the modern scientific outlook, was to risk antagonizing the educated world and losing for the masses the as yet indispensable religious sanctions for morality. Hence his radical attempts to eliminate the obsolete and to place questions both of religion and of morality upon foundations acceptable to a scientific age. The rash application of 'scientific' methods to traditional materials, how-ever, could result in the same loss, and was a greater danger because of the attractions of novelty. Hence his attack upon Colenso, his mockery of the 'vigour and rigour' of theorizing German critics, his description of even *Essays and Reviews* as not 'a free handling, in *a becoming spirit*, of religious matters'. Though gratified by a German tribute to his originality, to his 'much-doubted *Radicalismus*', he was more gratified that *Literature and Dogma* came increasingly to be seen as an 'entirely religious' work, especially in the United States, and earnestly defended himself to his sister Fan against a charge of levity in treating of sacred subjects: 'The two concluding parts of my "Review of Objections" will be in general conservative, and directed against negative criticism of the Bible, both German and of home production, although, of course, I do not mean to say that the subject will be treated from the point of view of the ordinary defenders of the Bible against innovators.' [4] The defence concludes with a classic example of understatement; what we may more profitably notice is that the privacy of a letter bears witness to the sincerity of Arnold's public avowal, bland or patronizing as this may have seemed, that he was the friend and champion of renovated religion. Among the tributes to Arnold after his death one of the shrewdest was the epigrammatic remark of F. W. H. Myers: 'He has been treated as a flippant and illusory Christian, instead of as a specially devout and conservative agnostic.' [5]

In this balance of radical mind and conservative temper, Arnold is in a humanist tradition of which the most distinguished representative is Erasmus. Driven by a passion for the pure truth of scholarship and fighting the battle of biblical criticism, Erasmus did not realize how his 'philosophical-critical methods must shake the foundations of the Church', or how radical was his simple statement: 'We have defined so much that without danger to our salvation might have remained unknown or undecided. . . . The essentials of our religion are peace and unanimity.' [6] Calling for change, he was yet in a crisis conservative, as his letters to and about Luther show. He told Martin Bucer in 1527 that leaders like Luther should not 'have heedlessly wrecked anything without having something better ready to put in its place', but he had himself written a gentle letter to Luther in 1519, in which the peaceful tone did not disguise the revolutionary principle: 'As for me, I keep myself as far as possible neutral, the better to assist the new flowering of good learning; and it seems to me that more can be done by unassuming courteousness than by violence. It was thus that Christ brought the world under His sway, and thus that Paul made away with the Jewish Law, by interpreting all things allegorically.' [7]

There is another humanist tradition in which Arnold has his place, that of the intelligent amateur occupying himself with religious questions. Of that tradition we have a later representative in Edmund Wilson. Learning Hebrew in order to read Genesis for the first time as 'neither a Jew nor a Christian', and disregarding 'the tons of theological controversy', Wilson finds in 'these fragmentary legends . . . that specialty of the Jewish genius —the development of the moral consciousness of man's relations with God'. There is much in Mr Wilson's interesting essay that reflects later knowledge and modern thinking. There is a more analytical treatment of language, especially of the force of Hebrew verbs in revealing a concept of time different from the Western; there is a suggestive comparison of this primitive time sense, and its relation to the prophetic mode of utterance, with the Russian; there is a comprehensive view of four world religions of which Marxism is the latest. Yet here as in Arnold is the literary critic of wide culture and sensitive insight examining the biblical material afresh. The judgments made on 'these fumbling and awkward old stories' lack the ingrained reverence of the Victorian Arnold, but the similarity of tribute is all the more striking when we read that even the most savage biblical stories show 'the emergence of the moral sense', that in them 'we can see man becoming aware of the conscience that begins to dignify him, that seems to tower above him'. One such (purely literary) judgment expresses in a more telling sentence a good deal of what Arnold was saying:

These strokes of human feeling, of insight, are so trenchant and so authentic, and they so surely awake a response in all kinds and conditions of people, that there are moments when the gods and the heroes of the so much more expertly handled, the so much more sophisticated Homeric poems seem less real than the nomads of Genesis when the finger of the unknown scribe, tracing the ancient story, flashes across the page the verses that make them live.[8]

Criticism of this sort and at this level is an art, even if it is based on an approach that may, in the sense of disinterested or objective, be called scientific. The element of puzzle in the irritation at Arnold arose in part from this approximate use, in an age when the word 'scientific' was increasingly being restricted to a methodology and a technique and to a logic operating from the basis of facts arrived at by experiment and observation. Arnold knew the approved use. 'Science makes her progress,' he told his readers, 'not merely by close reasoning and deduction, but also, and much more, by the close scrutiny and correction of the present commonly-received data.' [9] As a science, theology went upon 'the uncorrected data of a time of imperfect observation and boundless credulity', and so could not be taken seriously. But it was impossible to have a complete demonstrative case against miracles, a complete induction. What they had was a 'more complete induction' against miracles as untrustworthy, a high degree of probability, in view of growing naturalistic explanations, that they did not happen.

The crux of Arnold's case was that in the modern age, with a truly scientific spirit displacing pseudo-science, it was becoming impossible to base religious faith upon proofs incapable of demonstration, having at the best 'a low degree of probability'. What *could* be demonstrated, or verified, was the witness of life itself, of all the productions of man's spirit, to the operation of the moral law, of the power making for righteousness. To penetrate to this truth, however, and to present it as a rational object of man's faith required not a misused scientific apparatus, as in so much of biblical criticism, but the cultivated judgment of a critic practised in discriminating among the literary forms of man's emotional and imaginative utterance. This double anxiety, to keep in step with the march of the scientific mind yet to check illegitimate applications of scientific method, made Arnold vulnerable in a way that we must presently notice.

There was a special aim in Arnold's religious writing. We have seen his attack on Colenso for not edifying, his praise of Spinoza for edifying, the multitude. For Arnold, religious criticism must be rational, it must be imaginative, but it must above all be edifying. He was widely read in the products of biblical scholarship, he studied Hebrew in order to get at original meanings, and his revision of Isaiah received high praise in *The Times* and at least favourable notice in the *Academy*. Yet his aim here was pleasurable edification, not scholarly production. He would 'amend the authorized translation without destroying its effect', and 'meet the wants of the mass of mankind' by preserving the 'charm' and the 'general sense'. His conclusion is explicit: 'My paramount object is to get Isaiah enjoyed; and the right way to get a great author enjoyed is to raise not as much discussion as possible over his meaning, but as little as possible.' [10]

Here there is not even a gesture towards the 'scientific' mind; what is striking is the fusion of moral and æsthetic values, to

which mere accuracy of knowledge is subservient. To get at
these values, to lay bare significant truth in documents that
express the nature and needs of the total man, the equipment
called for is not that of scientific or theological training. It is
rather a practised intuition. We may see in Thomas Arnold's
'signs' or 'marks of divinity', in Coleridge's 'whatever *finds* me',
the attitude towards the question of proof that appears again in
Arnold's 'tact', his conviction that a special bent in Israel for
moral perceptions 'declares itself by the accent and power with
which its utterances are made'.[11] It is the literary critic, the man
of broad culture, who is responsive to these utterances and can
best assess their truth to experience. There was a good strategical
reason for Arnold's course. As he told M. Fontanès: 'En parlant
de St Paul, je n'ai pas parlé en théologien, mais en homme de
lettres mécontent de la très mauvaise critique littéraire qu'on
appliquait à un grand esprit; si j'avais parlé en théologien,
on ne m'eût pas écouté.'[12] But strategy apart, Arnold was
certain that in history as well as in poetry, the fusion of powers he
came to call the 'imaginative reason' was essential to the under-
standing of the records of human experience.

To claim scientific or verifiable certainty for these critical
judgments, this discovery by 'tact' and insight of eternal moral
truth in the flux of experience and the records thereof, made
Arnold vulnerable to the attacks of more consistent or logical
reasoners. How could one assert objective authority for what were
in effect subjective findings, or universal sanction for intuitions
that reflected the formative influence of a particular culture
selectively studied? 'We hear the word "verifiable" from Mr
Arnold pretty often', said F. H. Bradley scornfully. 'What is it
to verify? Has Mr Arnold put "such a tyro's question" to him-
self?' The object of true religion could not be verified in the
ordinary sense, he went on, since 'it can not be found as this or
that outward thing or quality'. As for Arnold's evidence: 'If what
is meant by this, that what is ordinarily called virtue does always
lead to and go with what is ordinarily called happiness, then so
far is this from being "verifiable" in every-day experience, that
its opposite is so.'[13] Even Mr Arnold must know that it was not
a 'fact' that 'happiness always comes from virtue'.

Now Arnold's position was not so intellectually naïve as
Bradley makes out, as I hope to show in a later chapter—but he
did not explicitly allow for, although he was fully aware of, the

limitation suggested by Bradley's 'ordinary sense' and 'ordinarily'. His desire to have the best of two worlds left him open to attacks. To assert that his elucidations of literature and history, his ethical evaluations of man's nature and destiny, were demonstrably true in any scientific sense, was to invite Bradley's flat denial and sarcasm. At the same time to reject metaphysics and its logic as dealing only with abstractions, and then to posit an Eternal absolute force making for righteousness as a valid inference from the interpretation of relative and historical experience, without admitting that such a force was both an abstraction *and* an object of faith—such audacious inconsistency inevitably drew fire from all sides, especially in view of the disturbing popularity of *Literature and Dogma*, and, perhaps, of a rankling suspicion that in the long run what Arnold was saying might have a value independent of logical precision, scientific demonstration, or biblical exegesis.

Arnold's attitude to the scientific or verifiable has exercised his critics from his day to our own, even those who have found high merit in his religious writings, especially in *St Paul and Protestantism*. J. E. Carpenter thought Arnold's stand on the question of the authorship of the Fourth Gospel worth mention, but added that Arnold thought it possible 'by pure literary judgments to isolate specific sayings as undoubtedly authentic, a method which severer critics do not sanction'.[14] To Trilling, Arnold's science is nothing but 'organized common sense', a description which recognizes that his interpretations to some degree reflected the audience he designedly wrote for, rather than his (ironically) confessed inaptness for logic or reasoning. A favourable view by Dickinson Miller in 1906 was that Arnold's criticism, though simple, was not shallow, and was at least 'an effort conceived in the spirit of science itself' by 'a philosopher of middle principles' who never pushed analysis to 'the bitter or insipid end'. He gave the 'sublimation of a rule of thumb, a distinction that can be verified without apparatus. . . . In the study of men, societies, sentiments and philosophies it forwards us.' [15]

This genial summary may well be recalled when we come to estimate Arnold's total achievement; meanwhile we must consider his use of such words as fact, truth, reason, nature, and experience. For Arnold's religious criticism may be regarded as a daring attempt to steer between the Scylla of logic and the Charybdis of semantics, as he sought the haven of a compromise between the forces of science and those of religion. The degree of skill or success conceded to the navigator depends upon the nature and position of the observer. Complete wreckage, a badly battered craft no longer seaworthy, a relatively unscathed passage, and the glad cry of 'Land ahead!'—the reports vary.

Professor Trilling observes that Arnold cannot bring himself to say that Christianity is true: 'That Christianity contains the highest moral law, that Christianity is natural, that Christianity is lovely, that Christianity *contains* the truth—anything but that *Christianity is true.*' [16] This is an instructive example of the care needed in estimating the value accorded certain words by Arnold. We have his praise of Butler for the latter's insistence that Christianity and religion are true, and that their truth may be established by reason. Turning to the passage on the Cambridge Platonist John Smith, we find Arnold saying emphatically, 'Christianity is true.' 'But', he continues, 'in general the whole plan for grounding and buttressing it chosen by our theological instructors is false, and, since it is false, it must fail us sooner or later.' [17] This 'natural truth' of Christianity is not that of either naturalistic science or metaphysical science; it is for Arnold a truth operative at the level of 'resurrected' human nature, to be apprehended by the imagination, that imagination whose emotional alliance with conduct brings us to religion. What the imagination seizes on as poetically true, what conduct accepts as morally true, has for him a practical and experiential truth superior to that of a logically verifiable proposition, which is to be contrasted to an emotionally verifiable experience. Nor is this experiential verification merely an emotional response akin to wishful thinking. Arnold believes that Christianity has, in Spinozist idiom, 'all the grandeur of a natural law'.

'What pitfalls are in that word nature', Arnold once remarked; certainly there is not uniform precision in his own use of this treacherous word. It is obvious that his 'nature' is not that of the scientist, nor that of the poet, though it shades into the one when he strikes out a formula for the intellect, and into the other when the hold of religion over the imagination is being emphasized. It is rather (as in the 'natural truth' on which religion, and particularly Christianity, is based) a term suggestive of the Christian-stoic-humanist moral psychology developed by Arnold on a Spinozist foundation: 'How much more safe is it, as well as more fruitful, to look for the main confirmation of a religion in its intrinsic correspondence with urgent wants of human nature, in its profound necessity.' [18] The right human nature is, then, human nature regenerate, risen above itself, as Arnold would have us see in his naturalistic interpretation of the sayings of both Jesus and Paul. Or again, in Spinozist idiom, it is human nature behaving according to its own necessary laws. Instead of a separation of two spheres, earthly and heavenly, everything moral and religious is spoken of in terms of two selves, the higher and the lower. This distinction occurs in the writing of Alexander Vinet, in words which present a natural state in the Arnoldian sense. Vinet sees the contrast of the earthly and heavenly spheres of orthodoxy as a false one:

It consists in taking the words of the apostle, 'the things above', in a too spiritual sense. The things above are not precisely those of another world, but those of another sphere than the habitual one of our thoughts. They are the things . . . above our natural sentiments. The things on high are here below, if we wish it; . . . the disposition of a heart renewed by the Spirit from above; . . . all those sentiments, motives, impulses, which belong to a regenerated soul. [19]

It is instructive to listen at this point to a theologian, without Vinet's 'rationalistic' turn, on the 'natural state' of man. Many things achieved by the natural man, says Newman, seem spiritually sufficient, for example, the impressive cultural and philosophical attainments of Greece. But 'you will find nothing of faith there, but mainly expedience as the measure of right and wrong, and temporal well-being as the end of action'. [20] The warning against the natural man in this sermon on 'Nature and Grace' is accompanied by a contempt for energy for its own sake, and for local and temporary ends, which suggests the influence of Newman upon Arnold as a critic of Philistinism. He speaks of 'the laborious, energetic, indefatigable world', which 'takes up objects enthusiastically, and vigorously carries them through. . . . And so pleasant is the excitement which those temporal objects create, that it is often its own reward.' Going further, Newman mentions the high and beautiful sentiments present in tales and poems, which cause us to think that 'he must be a man of deep religious feeling and high religious profession who could write so well'. But 'after all it is *but* poetry, not religion; it is a human nature exerting the powers of imagination and reason, which it has, till it seems also to have powers which it has not'.

It is at this point, where Newman is clearly about to introduce the theological doctrine of grace, that Arnold parts company with him, and walks instead with the naturalistic Goethe, who puts the standard 'inside every man'. The natural state described by Newman is *the* human nature, up to and including the powers of the reason and the imagination. To Arnold it is *a* human nature, subordinate to the higher nature at which level the 'imaginative reason' operates. Newman is contrasting the fallen state, where opinion and reason hold sway, with the restored state, to which humble faith and the power of grace may raise the natural sinner. To Arnold the state of grace is rather that regenerate moral insight and that practice (conduct) which bring man into harmony with the eternal moral law. Faith is simply a psychological process (most particularly the love men feel for Jesus, the great exemplar of moral goodness) which invests the otherwise rather barren stoicism of renunciation with an emotion of joy, and makes the higher life attractive as well as reasonable.

The mark of man operating at this higher level of nature, this distinctively human nature, is his use of the reason, and it is because they recognize in reason the only instrument whereby humanity may arrive at the truth that Arnold exalts theologians like Butler and Vinet. Defending revelation, says Vinet, the theologian 'applies himself to prove its necessity, as well as its harmony, with the nature of the human heart,—in a word, the perfect *reasonableness* of a system which *reason* has not discovered'. Reasonableness is exactly what Arnold finds in Christianity, and one has only to substitute 'religion' for 'revelation' to have a definition which might have been his on a Spinozist basis of necessity and harmony with nature. This is clearer in Vinet's extended definition:

Reason, that is to say, the nature of things, . . . will always be to us the criterion of truth and the basis of faith. The truth without us must always be measured and compared with the truth within us; with that intellectual conscience, which, as well as the moral conscience, is invested with sovereignty, gives judgments, knows remorse; with those irresistible axioms which we carry within us, which form a part of our nature, and are the support and groundwork of all our thoughts;—in a word, with *reason*.[21]

The stress on reason as a part of our higher nature suggests the point of view of the Cambridge Platonists and Coleridge, to both of whom the essentials of Christianity are facts of nature or truths of reason. We are in the region where reason has lost entirely its mere logical or discursive aspect, and wears instead that of intuition, of moral or spiritual insight. It is a region where mysticism is likely, though not inevitable. Arnold had no sympathy with a disguised subordination of reason to a belief in mysteries, even when so eloquently phrased as 'Reason, of which spiritual Faith is even the blossoming and fructifying process',[22] but he does invest reason with imaginative insight at the higher level of human nature, in complete harmony with Butler's declaration that 'Reason, almost intuitively, bears witness to the truth of this moral system of nature.'[23]

Arnold's 'reason' seems to be compounded of common sense, cultured understanding, imaginative insight and organized experience, in the tradition of Hooker, the Cambridge men, and Butler, rather than directly in that of either Plato or Locke. 'Hooker's greatness is that he gives the real method of criticism for Church-dogma, the *historic* method; . . . he assigns the one right criterion for determining whether a dogma is justly deduced, and what Scripture means, and what is its true character: the criterion of *reason*.'[24] To the same effect, 'Butler says of reason, that "it is indeed the only faculty we have wherewith to judge concerning *anything*, even revelation itself".' To this historical and common-sense reason Arnold adds experience and observation, and sums up his own religious criticism as proceeding 'from experience of the human spirit and its productions, from observing as widely as we can the manner in which men have thought, their way of using words and what they mean by them, and from reasoning upon this observation and experience'. This, again, is what Arnold means by his claim to deal in the scientific and verifiable.

There is a continual equation in the Cambridge men of the facts and truths of religion to those of nature and reason. The reason approves moral goodness: 'A good man, one that is attracted by religion, lives in concourse with his own reason; he lives at the height of his own being.'[25] He is enabled to do so only by recognizing the sovereignty of reason. Man's natural bent, by virtue of the Divine spark in his nature, is toward religion and goodness: 'A man's religion is himself, the sum of his powers, his nature in its ideal perfection. To be religious, a man must realize himself.' And 'he who best realizes himself also best realizes human nature'.[26] (One might here be reading Spinoza!) The inwardness of all this as a 'vital principle', the pursuit of perfection under the guidance of reason, the tendency wherever possible to emphasize human nature and human experience, are carried by Smith and Whichcote through to religious ultimates. Yet even where the theological or metaphysical or mystical turn is apparent, the guide is conduct, and the basis is the solid one of experience:

> If we see things as they are, we shall live as we ought, and if we live as we ought, we shall see things as they are. This is not a vicious circle, but the interplay of contemplation and action, of θεωρία and πράξις, in which wisdom consists. Action is the ritual of contemplation, as the dialectic is its creed. The conduct of life rests on an act of faith which begins as an experiment and ends as an experience.[27]

One can see why Arnold found this Cambridge Platonist so congenial; one can also see in the phrase 'an act of faith', at the centre of the beautifully compact final sentence, that element in the reasoning of the ethical idealist that Arnold overlooked in his anxiety to claim 'scientific' verification for the power that makes for righteousness.

Coleridge vigorously states the moral foundations of religion, the criterion of experience, the conformity of religious truth to man's reason, the separation of that reason (Platonic or Kantian) from the mere logical faculty:

> Too soon did the Doctors of the Church forget that that *Heart*, the *Moral* Nature, was the beginning and the end. . . . This was the true and first apostasy—when in Council and Synod the Divine Humanities of the Gospel gave way to speculative Systems, and Religion became a science of Shadows. . . . The Christian world was for centuries divided into the Many, that did not think at all, and the Few who did nothing but think.[28]

Saved from the 'sandy deserts of utter unbelief' by the mystics, saved from the arid systematizing of rationalist theologians and metaphysicians by a 'certain guiding light', Coleridge gives more and more weight to this higher faculty, the *real reason*, which runs the gamut from emotion through intuition to faith. 'The best way to bring a clever young man, who has become sceptical and unsettled, to reason', he tells us, 'is to make him *feel* something in any way.'[29] He follows Kant in denying that the intellect can grasp the supersensuous, but goes beyond him in asserting that the supersensuous can be given in experience. And under the influence of his rapidly solidifying orthodoxy in later years, Coleridge

cries, 'I am born a child of wrath. This fearful mystery I pretend
not to understand . . . but I know that it is so.'

We see here the limit of Coleridge's influence on Arnold.
When he writes, 'Christianity is not a Theory, or a Speculation,
but a Life. Not a *Philosophy* of Life, but a Life and a Living
Process. . . . Try it. It has been eighteen hundred years in exist-
ence'—when he makes this appeal to cumulative human experi-
ence, Coleridge is writing words which Arnold in later years is
virtually to duplicate. But the orthodox theologian is too strong in
Coleridge to let him stay in this position. He trembles at the
naturalness of sin, and for him 'the moment we rise above Nature,
we are compelled to assume a *Supernatural* Power'. He retains all
the apparatus of orthodox theology which Matthew Arnold is
later to discard, and philosophizes endlessly over it. In Muir-
head's words, 'he was too deeply involved in the "metaphysical
prolegomena" and the Laocoön-like coils of Trinitarian theology to
be content with the experiential fruits of Christianity'.[30] Where
Coleridge made his real contribution, Muirhead maintains (and
Arnold too saw it in this light), was in the psychology of religion:
'Beyond the beasts, yea, and above the nature of which they are in-
mates, man possesses love and faith and a sense of the permanent.'[31]

In Arnold's one essay on the mystics, we find him attracted
by two things: the inwardness, and the doctrine of the two selves.
'Dearly beloved and elect,' says Tauler, 'listen to the Voice of God
in your hearts . . . that ye be not led astray and blinded by tran-
sitory things and your own natural tendencies.'[32] Arnold finds
that Tauler's superiority over Luther, whose 'moral mythology'
succeeded with the masses and was bound to succeed at the time,
lies in the appeal to 'the Voice of God in your hearts' rather than
to justification—in other words, to our higher sin-abhorring
natures rather than to dogma: 'The mystics have the merit of
keeping always before their minds, and endeavouring earnestly
to make operative on their lives, just that in Christianity which is
not perishable but abiding.'[33] The sympathy stops short, how-
ever, at the mystic's plea to drop all external ties and obligations,
to 'ponder on the short transitory nature of this miserable life, and
the delusions of this faithless, treacherous and deceitful world'.
The intuitive insight of the mystic is to Arnold vain without
practical activity, just as the rational handling of the religious
problem by the intellect is barren without imaginative sympathy.
The happy blend of these two powers, representing for Arnold the

G

supreme example of the 'imaginative reason' at work in religion, is manifested by the 'piercing practical religious sense' of Paul:

It is at once mystical and rational; and it enlists in its service the best forces of both worlds,—the world of reason and morals, and the world of sympathy and emotion. The world of reason and duty has an excellent clue to action, but wants motive-power; the world of sympathy and influence has an irresistible force of motive-power, but wants a clue for directing its exertion. The danger of the one world is weariness in well-doing; the danger of the other is sterile raptures and immoral fanaticism. Paul takes from both worlds what can help him, and leaves what cannot.[34]

The pragmatic nature of the appeal to experience as against dogma is clear in Arnold's reiterated statement that we can judge only by results, that we cannot know the nature of a thing—only its operation: 'We no more pretend to know the origin and composition of the power that makes for righteousness than of the power that makes for gravitation. All we profess to have ascertained about it is, that it has effect on us, that it operates.' Here is the fact of experience Arnold offers, the 'scientific' certainty which arises from the correspondence of eternal moral law with 'irresistible axioms' in ourselves: 'As far as man's experience reaches, it comes out . . . ever more clearly, both by the operation of the law itself and by man's inward sense of affinity and response to it, that our welfare, which we cannot but pursue, is inextricably and unalterably, and by no procuring of ours but whether we will or no, dependent on conduct.'[35] As with conduct, so with Christianity and its 'experiential fruits'. Vinet puts the case most clearly, basing Christianity's claim to continuing authority in matters moral and spiritual on the pragmatic appeal to experience:

The true point at issue in reference to religion is this:—Does the religion which is proposed to us, change the heart, unite to God, prepare us for heaven? If Christianity produces these effects, we will leave the enemies of the cross free to revolt against its mysteries, and tax them with absurdity. . . . But behold what a new species of absurdity that certainly is, which attaches man to all his duties, regulates human life better than the doctrines of sages, plants in his bosom harmony, order and peace, causes him joyfully to fulfil all the offices of civil life . . . and which, were it generally received, would be the support and safeguard of society. . . . If that 'foolishness' we preach produces effects like these, is it not natural to conclude that it is truth itself?[36]

True, Vinet pleads here for an acceptance of the 'mysteries' as a part of this beneficent Christianity, but the stress is on the effects. Try it, and see for yourself! This is the message of Vinet, of Coleridge, of Arnold. And, in more philosophical terms, it is the position of William James. (As Trilling says, had James not read Arnold, we might suspect that Arnold had read James.) The ethical philosopher must everywhere wait on the facts. No system is now possible: 'Moral scepticism can no more be refuted or proved by logic than intellectual scepticism can.' The heart, the whole nature is involved, and faith, that is, faith in oneself and one's experience, must achieve its own verification. James goes even further in his pragmatic individualism, and tends to make the world of eternal verities, seen by Arnold as corresponding to affirmations in ourselves, to some extent dependent upon the element of personal experience which we contribute. In considering what may lie behind phenomena, James says that *'maybes* are the essence of the situation. I confess I do not see why the very existence of an invisible world may not in part depend on the personal response which any one of us may make to the religious appeal—God himself, in short, may draw vital strength and increase of very being from our fidelity.' [37] This may be a legitimate extension of such an experiential emphasis as Arnold's, but it was not one which he, with his (illogical) need for an external and eternal moral law, was prepared to make.

It is probable that had James been a contemporary, Arnold would have recognized and surrendered this persistent transcendental element in his own equation, and found in pragmatism the philosophical statement of his position. When James defines religion as 'the belief that there is an unseen order, and that our supreme good lies in harmoniously adjusting ourselves thereto'; [38] when he agrees that the 'ultimate test of religious values is nothing psychological . . . how it happens, but something ethical, . . . what is attained'; when he coolly remarks that all the metaphysical attributes of God have no bearing on our conduct, but that 'God is the natural appellation, for us Christians at least, for the supreme reality'—in all this, he is virtually repeating Arnold. What James would have shown him (what Arnold might have learned from John Smith) is that an act of faith *is* involved, 'faith in oneself and one's experience', and that this must achieve its own verification. Arnold would not have been enough of the detached psychologist to limit himself to personal as against institutional religion, but he would have followed James in finding that for the criticism of the *facts* of religious experience, 'philosophical reasonableness and moral helpfulness are the only available criteria'. And having cordially agreed that personal experience, or *feeling*, is deeper than philosophy or theology and precedes them in religion, he could easily have accepted James's quiet reminder that philosophy has its place, to remove and refine from the private and mysterious areas of feeling the 'truth objectively valid for all thinking men'.

The conflict implicit in the title of this chapter has been stated in terms of reason and experience against mystery and dogma, rather than in terms of science against religion. This is deliberate, since an over-simplified statement of the major nineteenth-century dilemma is too suggestive of St George and the Dragon, with the principals alternating in the two roles. Arnold did not attack religion; he attacked what he considered to be the accretions and non-essentials of religion, and the intellectual systematizing by metaphysical theologians who erected a shadowy superstructure on the moral and imaginative utterances of Jesus. He did not attack science; he attacked the stubborn dogmatism which refused to accept any but empirical evidence of a classificatory kind.[39] Eager to be a 'healing and reconciling influence' as well as a 'dissolvent', he tried to get theology to relinquish intellectually indefensible positions, and science to admit that poetic or imaginative insight was one way of arriving at the truth. A true religion, based upon facts of human experience, facts whose solidity and authority would be admitted by both theology and science, would then emerge. What it lost in intellectual 'vigour and rigour' it would gain in broadly human comprehensiveness. It would still be a philosophy, at least at the level at which, as Joubert remarks, 'Religion is the only philosophy which the common mind is able to understand and adopt.'[40]

We may see the application of the strictly scientific spirit in the work of Renan, of whose criticism Arnold approved, with important reservations. Renan begins with a flat denial of miracles and literal inspiration: 'Ce n'est pas au nom de telle ou telle philosophie, c'est au nom d'une constante, expérience, que nous bannissons le miracle de l'histoire.' Studies in Christianity must be conducted in the manner of scholars engaged in secular studies, 'qui ne songe ni à édifier ni à scandaliser, ni à défendre les dogmes ni à les renverser'. Only science is pure, bound to prove, not to persuade or convert. There is no praise or blame in the naturalist. This, however, is not to take the attitude of the materializing rationalist, and Renan utters a warning to the rational intellect:

> *Est Deus in nobis.* Fausses quand elles essayent de prouver l'infini, de le déterminer, de l'incarner, si j'ose le dire, les religions sont vraies quand elles l'affirment. Les plus graves erreurs qu'elles mêlent à cette affirmation ne sont rien comparées au prix de la vérité qu'elles proclament. Le dernier des simples, pourvu qu'il pratique le culte du cœur, est plus éclairé sur la réalité des choses que le matérialiste qui croit tout expliquer par le hasard et le fini.[41]

Many of Renan's views are those of Arnold: 'C'est la race sémitique qui a la gloire d'avoir fait la religion de l'humanité.' But this was not a matter of dogma, creed and speculation: 'Le juif de cette époque était aussi peu théologien que possible.' Jesus followed the current taste in allegory; the prophets were his masters. But 'la vraie poésie de la Bible, qui échappait aux puérils exégètes de Jérusalem, se révélait pleinement à son beau génie . . . la poésie religieuse des Psaumes se trouva dans un merveilleux accord avec son âme lyrique'. For Jesus 'Le merveilleux n'était pas . . . l'exceptionnel; c'était l'état normal.' Finally, in terms which approximate Arnold's, Renan insists on the validity of the inner experience in religion to the great figures of Christianity:

> Les preuves physiques et métaphysiques de l'existence de Dieu eussent laissé ces grands hommes [Paul, Francis of Assisi, Augustine] forts indifférents. Ils sentaient le divin en eux-mêmes. Au premier rang de cette grande famille des vrais fils de Dieu, il faut placer Jésus. Jésus n'a pas de visions; Dieu lui parle pas comme à quelqu'un hors de lui; Dieu est en lui; il se sent avec Dieu, et il tire de son cœur ce qu'il dit de son Père.[42]

The parallel between the conclusions of Arnold and Renan, or, conceding influence, the extent to which Arnold follows Renan, is reasonably obvious. So are the differences. Renan says that there is 'no science of the individual soul', which is tantamount in his case to denying authority to inner psychological truth, at least authority acceptable to the scientific historian. As Babbit points out, the exclusive emphasis on historical science ignores

the fact that theories drawn from historical study are contradic-
tory, and the moral sense is left suspended in a void. Arnold
escapes this by denying the relativity of Christian truth, by
regarding 'the really essential ideas of Christianity' as having a
'truth, depth, necessity and scope' making for permanence. Jesus
is their embodiment: 'Being so evidently great and yet so un-
comprehended, and being now inevitably to remain so for ever,
he thus comes to stand before us as what the philosophers call an
absolute.'[43] Renan's romanticizing, his tendency to treat Jesus as 'a
delicate and amiable moralist', is what Arnold has in mind when
he finds something 'insubstantial' about Renan's work, something
'in the air'. But of Renan's skill and scholarship there is no
question; nor can there have been, for Arnold, of his general aim.
As expressed in full in the *Essais de Morale et de Critique*, Renan's
credo may well have suggested the main lines of his religious
criticism to Arnold in 1859.[44]

How far was Arnold justified in thinking himself to be in line
with the true scientific spirit? Here the problem emerges in its
true form. Are his 'facts of experience' and 'facts of (human)
nature' valid as witnesses to permanent religious truths? Or are
logically intact propositions, verified by quantitative research and
by 'controlled' experiments and situations, the only bases upon
which 'truths' may be established? The systematic Spencer has
no doubts about the answer. He concedes, however, that religious
beliefs must have a basis in some ultimate fact. They have
vitality, omnipresence, permanence. 'If not supernaturally
derived as the majority contend, they must be derived out of
human experience, slowly accumulated and organized.'[45] On
either hypothesis, the religious experience is normal and conducive
to human welfare. Also, there is always a sphere for the operation
of the religious feeling, in that nescience which is continually
encroached upon by science, but never eliminated. Spencer
visualizes a permanent peace between religion and science, on a
basis of 'that ultimate truth which both will avow with absolute
sincerity'. This basis must be in the most abstract conception
common to both, since the dogmas of the one and the particular
findings of the other are equally certain of a hostile reception.

Here the Unknowable raises its invisible head, but the dis-
cussion of this particular concept must be postponed to the fol-
lowing chapter. What is evident here is that Spencer, logically
consistent, has offered in his 'abstract conception' just that kind

of exclusively intellectual 'fact' which to Arnold would be not only
fruitless, but fundamentally untrue to man's moral and religious
experience. There is nothing here of the 'warm' and the 'vivi-
fying' which Arnold wanted, and which he claimed to find in
Spinoza; there is rather, for the spirit, a particularly chilly death.
The reality of the religious experience is recognized, but this in
turn is nullified by the anæsthetizing of that experience in the
indefinable area of nescience. Mill seems almost 'warm' by
contrast, when he remarks that 'it is perfectly conceivable that
religion may be morally useful without being intellectually
sustainable'.[46]

Turning to Huxley as the eloquent champion of physical
science, we find more sympathy with and understanding of the
sort of thing Arnold is trying to do. His appreciation of Arnold's
effort is best given in his own words:

> One of the best [points made in *St Paul and Protestantism*] is what you
> say near the end about science gradually conquering the materialism
> of popular religion. It will startle the Puritans who always coolly put
> the matter the other way; but it is profoundly true. These people are
> for the most part mere idolaters with a Bible-fetish, who urgently stand
> in need of conversion by extra-Christian missionaries. . . . It takes all
> one's practical experience of the importance of Puritan ways of think-
> ing to overcome one's feeling of the unreality of their beliefs. . . . If you
> can persuade them that Paul is fairly interpretable in your sense, it
> may be the beginning of better things, but I have my doubts if Paul
> would own you, if he could return to expound his own epistles. . . .
> My business with my scientific friends is something like yours with the
> Puritans, nature being *our* Paul.[47]

It may surprise us to find this cordial agreement, in aim and in
critical principle, on the part of a man forced into the role of con-
troversialist, as Huxley was by the exigencies of his position,
though the strangeness disappears in the degree of mutual affection
and respect, genuine if infrequently expressed, revealed in their
correspondence. Not that Huxley ever compromises on the intel-
lectual rigorousness demanded by a mistress as jealous as Science.
He defines his agnosticism. It is no creed, except 'as it expresses
absolute faith in the validity of a principle, which is as much
ethical as intellectual'; that is, that 'it is wrong for a man to say
that he is certain of the objective truth of any proposition unless
he can produce evidence which logically justifies that certainty.'[48]
He is an unrelenting enemy of ecclesiasticism, as represented by

men like Newman. He can utter an Arnoldian definition, with the substitution of the significant (and more Spinozist) word 'knowledge' for Arnold's 'experience': 'The faith which is born of knowledge finds its object in an eternal order.'[49]

But Huxley, unlike Spencer, does more than recognize the existence of a religious feeling and experience. He agrees with Arnold that culture and science working hand in hand for a better religion and ethic must keep their feet solidly on the ground of human nature and experience. The 'Christianity of the Churches' will stand or fall by the results of critical investigations, but the Bible itself is the best 'antidote to the poison which has been mixed with Christianity'—'an undefiled spring'. It 'contains within itself the refutation of nine-tenths of the mixture of sophistical metaphysics and old-world superstition which has been piled around it by the so-called Christians of later times'.[50] This makes us curious as to the kind of religion which would satisfy Huxley, and he tells us in a letter of 1892, in a formula over which he and Arnold could have shaken hands: 'I have a great respect for the Nazarenism of Jesus—very little for later "Christianity". But the only religion that appeals to me is prophetic Judaism. Add to it something from the best Stoics and something from Spinoza and something from Goethe, and there is a religion for men.'[51]

Huxley's concessions to religion are not merely a recognition of human frailty and unintelligence—if so, they would be little to our purpose. In one of his richest claims on behalf of science, he shows at the same time that he fully understands the kind of verification which Arnold describes as a 'fact' of human experience, and fully agrees that it reveals a harmony between our higher selves and the 'Eternal not ourselves which makes for righteousness'. Even the superior certainty of a proof within the experience of all is admitted: 'Science seems to me to teach in the highest and strongest manner the great truth which is embodied in the Christian conception of entire surrender to the will of God.' But we must 'sit down before fact as a little child'. After dismissing desires for immortality, compensatory or otherwise, as irrational, Huxley goes on: 'The absolute justice of the system of things is as clear to me as any scientific fact. The gravitation of sin to sorrow is as certain as that of the earth to the sun, and more so—for experimental proof of the fact is within reach of us all—nay, is before us all in our own lives, if we had but the eyes to see it.'

It is perhaps a fitting conclusion to this chapter to have the great champion of nineteenth-century science agreeing with Arnold on the reality of the ethical ideal, with or without religious overtones, and declaring that the reality is substantiated in the experience of the race. In this blending of a moral truth and an emotional experience acceptable to both the scientist and the ethical humanist, the 'imaginative reason' does its work under the approving eye of the modern *Zeitgeist*. The demand for verification is met by the facts of human nature as they are revealed at this higher level of moral responsibility and imaginative insight. Nor is this a line of thought scorned by the religious philosopher, in an increasing emphasis on humanistic and naturalistic sanctions:

> Certainly in no sphere of our experience is the implication of objectivity . . . more insistent . . . than just in the moral and religious life. Reverence for the moral law, the self-humiliation caused by failure to fulfil its demands, the sense of sin, the attitude of worship and utter self-surrender, are possible only if the subject feels himself in presence of a Reality beside which all else pales into insignificance. And it is to the moral and religious man himself we must go, not to the philosopher weaving theories about him, if we are to understand his experience aright.

There are accretions on which criticism and research may work,

> but the fundamental pre-suppositions of any experience must be accepted from the experience itself. . . . On the evidence of the moral and religious life, therefore, we are bound to treat the ideals of that life not as devout imaginations . . . but as having their authentic basis in the nature of the world.[52]

Here is agreement on the source for evidence of religious experience. But is the source quite the same for evidence of the ultimate object of religious (and moral) experience? It may satisfy Arnold and Huxley, but for religion it is hardly the traditional approach, nor, as Trilling points out, the safest one. The question seems to hinge on the Reality of which Pringle-Pattison speaks, the nature of which for him seems clear enough in his suggestion that an 'attitude of worship and utter self-surrender' is part of the experience he posits. But what of a Reality, also seen as an object of experience, which is simply the combination of all the forces making for moral and spiritual perfection, 'the stream of tendency by which all things fulfil the law of their being'? What of a God whose religion is 'morality, touched with emotion', and whose lineaments are those of Spinoza, touched with the Gospel?

CHAPTER V

The Idea of God

Our contemplations of God should always be the most serene
and lovely; such as might ennoble our spirits and not debase
them. A right knowledge of God would beget a freedom and
liberty of soul within us.

JOHN SMITH, as quoted in *Note-books*

Im Innern ist ein Universum auch,
Daher der Völker löblicher Gebrauch,
Dass jeglicher das Beste was er kennt,
Er Gott, ja seinen Gott benennt.

GOETHE, 'Prooemion', in *Gott und Welt*

A RNOLD'S poetry has often been contrasted in mood and
theme with the assurance and serenity of his prose. Con-
sequently, the sustained presence in his poetry of two of his most
characteristic themes, the need for moral authority and for
personal integrity, has frequently been overlooked, leading to the
false conclusion that his work as a whole lacks unity. This faulty
emphasis has been corrected by later critics. Yet it remains true
that his spiritual conflict, and his negations and uncertainties,
appear in his poetry, and that a study of his mature religious
thought is incomplete without some attention to this imaginative
reflection of his wandering between two worlds. What strikes us
most is the variety of hypotheses and ideas presented, the number
of the ways of God to man considered critically, nostalgically,
or tentatively, and dismissed as inadequate or futile. This
exploratory tentativeness is, I think, what Arnold had in mind
when he wrote the following words to his sister Jane, of whose
critical opinion, to judge from the tone and frequency of his
letters to her, he thought very highly:

The true reason why parts suit you while others do not is that my
poems are fragments—i.e. that I am fragments, while you are a whole;
the whole effect of my poems is vague and indeterminate—this is their
weakness. . . . I shall do better some day I hope—meanwhile change
nothing, resign nothing that you have in deference to me or my
oracles; and do not plague yourself to find a consistent meaning for
these last, which in fact they do not possess through my weakness.[1]

94

Now this self-accusation obviously does not refer to a distinctively *poetical* weakness, and certainly any weakness in Arnold even at this time was not a moral weakness. We may call the 'weakness' philosophical, in the largest sense, and with reference to the lack of any unifying conception of man's place in the scheme of things and his relation to forces outside himself.

The so-called 'natural religion' of an optimistic deism was impossible for Arnold from the beginning; he was too much a child of Goethe and the scientific *Zeitgeist* ever to find in external Nature teleological evidence for the existence of a moral and beneficent Governor of the universe. Nor could he, like the early Wordsworth, find in Nature the soul of all his moral being, although he could derive consolation and 'healing power' from Wordsworth's poetry. In his sonnets he finds Nature strong, purposeful, and cool, and hence an object of envy to feverish and fretful man, but he also asserts, in harsh condemnation of a 'restless fool' who crooned of being in 'harmony with Nature', that 'cruel' and 'stubborn' Nature is no safe guide for man, 'who would be mild and with safe conscience blest'. It is man's nature which concerns Arnold, man who

> hath all that Nature hath, and more,
> And in that *more* lie all his hopes of good.

Not all the beauty of Nature, given us in sensitive and loving detail in his own descriptive passages, could change his conviction that man must 'pass her', or else 'rest her slave'. He must seek

> the foundations of that shadowy throne
> Where man's one nature, queen-like, sits alone,
> Centred in a majestic unity.

In these sonnets, whose prosy titles, and often prosy lines, suggest their use as vehicles for the expression of his intellectual restlessness, the consideration of nature and man and the cosmos brings in the problem of man's will. Sometimes the emphasis is on

> the high
> Uno'erleap'd Mountains of Necessity,
> Sparing us narrower margin than we deem.

Again he can say,

> Yet the will is free;
> Strong is the soul, and wise, and beautiful;

> The seeds of godlike power are in us still;
> Gods are we, bards, saints, heroes, if we will!

only to go on and complete the ringing assertion with,

> Dumb judges, answer, truth or mockery?

What emerges is a grimly limited freedom:

> man can control
> To pain, to death, the bent of his own days.
> Know thou the worst! So much, not more, he *can*.

What comes out clearly in the early poems as a whole is the fluid state of Arnold's opinions. Man is the victim of necessity; he is free. Nature is a fellow-sufferer with man; she stands aloof and serene. She is a source of strength and consolation; she is a hostile, or at best callously indifferent Force. The world is a dream-world; it is a brute creation painfully evolving. There is even a period, under the influence of the *Bhagavad-Gita*, as the letters to Clough show, when the All and the Infinite have their attraction, with the thought of absorption into an all-embracing Nothingness. That this idea, which may possibly have suggested the stream of the 'general life' in the poem 'Resignation', was never very real to Arnold, is apparent from his late essay on Amiel, where he refers to the latter's Buddhism and says, 'It is a prosaic mind which has never been in contact with ideas of this sort, has never felt their charm.' But 'except for use in passing, and with the power to dismiss them again, they are unprofitable'.

The doubts and denials and suspended judgments in Arnold's poetry stem from the desire for an ideal or vision which will give warmth to the bleak moral stoicism that is his from the beginning. It can be modest and unphilosophical, but it must be true, he tells Clough—true for him. One possible source of the warmth he craves gleams through in 'Dover Beach', where the appeal to human love, contrasting with the rest of the poem, momentarily lightens the sombre background of dead faiths and warring ideologies. It recalls the hymn to a larger love in the closing lines of the 'Church of Brou', where the entombed pair slumber on eternally, while they

> The passage of the Angels' wings will hear,
> And on the lichen-crusted leads above
> The rustle of the eternal rain of love.

In 'Empedocles on Etna', considered by T. Sturge Moore 'the most considerable poem of a comparable length by a Victorian', the philosopher Empedocles sees clearly the true nature of man, of the universe, of God, in all their austere simplicity. Man is born to a life of suffering, largely because he confuses his will with his rights, basing his expectations upon a teleological view of the universe. But 'Nature, with equal mind, sees all her sons at play', indifferent alike to the virtuous and the vicious. 'So, loath to suffer mute', man peoples the void with gods, kindly or hostile, to account for good or bad fortune. He explains the limitations on human knowledge by assuming an omniscient God; he consoles himself for his incapacity to reach ultimate and satisfying joy by imagining gods who do. All this is childish and foolish to Empedocles, who recognizes only a Power which is Life itself, a universal and immanent Force manifesting itself by necessity.

> All things the world which fill
> Of but one stuff are spun,
> That we who rail are still,
> With what we rail at, one;
> One with the o'er-labour'd Power that through the breadth and
>   length
>
> Of earth, and air, and sea,
> In men, and plants, and stones,
> Hath toil perpetually,
> And travails, pants, and moans;
> Fain would do all things well, but sometimes fails in strength.
>
> And patiently exact
> This universal God
> Alike to any act
> Proceeds at any nod,
> And quietly declaims the cursings of himself.

Empedocles then tells Pausanias, the well-meaning and anxious old disciple, that he need not despair. He must look within for the truth, moderate his desires, and manufacture no gods to explain what cannot be explained:

> I say: Fear not! Life still
> Leaves human effort scope.
> But, since life teems with ill,
> Nurse no extravagant hope;
> Because thou must not dream, thou need'st not then despair!

Pausanias retires, half-convinced and vaguely comforted. But this counsel is useless to the counsellor. Uplifted with an austere and tragic exaltation at his insight into the ultimate truth, yet unbearably lonely because of the intellectual isolation this entails, Empedocles retains some of the exaltation and avoids the dreary return to the enslaving fears and depressions which clutch at him by leaping into Etna and dissolving into the original elements, escaping the arid existence to which he has come as

> A living man no more, Empedocles!
> Nothing but a devouring flame of thought—
> But a naked, eternally restless mind!

Clearly the course for humanity is not to follow the scepticism of Empedocles to its logical conclusion, but to embrace the melioristic stoicism suggested to Pausanias, as Arnold does himself.

Speculation on the nature of God was irresistible, however, as we see in two of Arnold's later sonnets. In 'The Better Part' (of which the first title was 'Anti-Desperation') the speaker reacts violently to the loss of an anthropomorphic and beneficent Deity and a divine Christ, and, since the supports are withdrawn, cries out, 'Live we like brutes our life without a plan.' The poet replies in terms of a moral and stoical humanism which anticipates the prose catechism quoted in chapter II:

> So answerest thou; but why not rather say:
> 'Hath man no second life?—*Pitch this one high!*
> Sits there no judge in Heaven, our sin to see?—
>
> '*More strictly, then, the inward judge obey!*
> Was Christ a man like us? *Ah! let us try*
> *If we then, too, can be such men as he!*'

When we add to this psychological and ethical religion the definition of God which appears in 'The Divinity', we have, clearly stated, the ideas fundamental to the whole of Arnold's religious writing, on which he is to ring the changes through four books of controversial and didactic prose. He quotes St Bernard to the effect that

> 'Tis God himself becomes apparent, when
> God's wisdom and God's goodness are display'd,
> For God of these his attributes is made.

But the metaphysicians have seized on the attributes and specu-
lated, and the theologians have dogmatized, until now their
'insubstantial pageant' threatens to collapse like a house of cards.
The original intuition must be restored in all its freshness, and
stated in language which the experiences of humanity and the
Zeitgeist will agree upon as verifiable, as true in a way which is
true for all time because true to the experience of the highest
human nature.

> *God's wisdom and God's goodness!*—Ay, but fools
> Mis-define these till God knows them no more.
> *Wisdom and goodness, they are God!* what schools
>
> Have yet so much as heard this simpler lore?
> This no Saint preaches, and this no Church rules;
> 'Tis in the desert, now and heretofore.

With the *desiderata* of the religious life struck out in these two
sonnets in terms of a moral stoicism, a psychological dualism, and
a God equated to wisdom and goodness, we are prepared for a
mature formulation of the principal ideas in Arnold's religious
thought. The psychology and morality have been touched upon,
and will be dealt with more fully in the chapter following. What
of the idea of God? Here I think we may see the influence of
Spinoza even more than in the question of experience as against
dogma. The sonnets themselves were probably composed in
1863, the year of the essay on Spinoza, and appeared in the
collection of 1867. In 1867, too, the series of papers later entitled
Culture and Anarchy began to appear, and the use of Spinozist
idiom colours all Arnold's definitions. The use of culture is 'to
draw towards a knowledge of the universal order which seems to
be intended and aimed at in the world, and which it is a man's
happiness to go along with or his misery to go counter to,—to
learn, in short, the will of God'. The teachers of culture merely
reveal the realizing process of the divine nature: 'Docile echoes
of the eternal voice, pliant organs of the infinite will, such workers
are going along with the essential movement of the world; and
this is their strength, and their happy and divine fortune.'
Arnold did not misunderstand or misrepresent Spinoza (if we
assume that the definition in the sonnet of God as 'wisdom and
goodness' owes more to Spinoza than to St Bernard), and he was
careful to draw the distinction between Spinoza's love of God

(the *knowledge* of God) and what the Christian means by the love of God:

> Spinoza's ideal is the intellectual life; the Christian's ideal is the religious life. Between the two conditions there is all the difference which there is between the being in love, and the following, with delighted comprehension, a reasoning of Plato. For Spinoza, undoubtedly, the crown of the intellectual life is a transport, as for the saint the crown of the religious life is a transport; but the two transports are not the same.[2]

The idea of God, or of the nature of God, is by Spinoza carefully accommodated to the needs and understanding of men. We may examine it at three levels. At the purely philosophic level, God is the 'immanent principle of all existence', the 'Infinite Being fulfilling in the uniformity of natural law the perfection of his own Nature'. He is not causal in either the Platonic or Christian meanings of the term. He may be described as having an immanent causality, but the quality stressed is the immanence, the necessary existence: 'In reality God acts and directs all things simply by the necessity of His nature and perfection. . . . His decrees and volitions are eternal truths, and always involve necessity.'[3] Below this is the level where accommodation begins. Recognizing that the power of God is identical with natural laws, we see that 'whatever human nature can furnish itself with by its own efforts to preserve its existence, may be fitly called the inward aid of God'. At this level one Arnoldian definition operates, that of 'the stream of tendency not ourselves by which all things fulfil the law of their being'.

From here we pass to the third level, where accommodation is complete, where attributes of justice, mercy, truth, and anger are seen as qualities of the divine mind. And here Spinoza insists on the same practical dichotomy. The only 'knowledge of God needful for all' is that

> God is supremely just, supremely merciful—in other words, the one perfect pattern of the true life. . . . We may draw the general conclusion that the intellectual knowledge of God . . . which cannot . . . be followed or imitated . . . has no bearing whatever on true rules of conduct, on faith, or on revealed religion. . . . God has required from man nothing but a knowledge of this Divine justice and charity, and that not as necessary to scientific accuracy, but to obedience.[4]

Now this puts into moral and religious terms what is a fact in

Spinoza's pantheistic scheme, namely, that man, a part of a system of necessary relations, is in very truth the slave or servant of God, who is Nature, the whole of existence, the sum total of cosmic forces. This of course raises an awkward question. Since man is only a minor self-determining unit in a larger self-determining Whole which embraces all things as determined possibles, must he not accept evil as having, too, a lawful and necessary and unavoidable existence? Spinoza concludes otherwise, on a pragmatic basis of relative values: 'The teachings of morality, whether or not they receive the form of a law from God himself, are yet divine and wholesome, and whether the good which necessarily follows from virtue and the love of God be received by us from God as a judge, or whether it issues from the necessity of the divine nature, it will not on that account be the more or less desirable.' [5]

It is obvious that Spinoza separates practical wisdom from theoretic knowledge and makes the former the means by which man may move towards that perfection which is a necessary part of his existence. In his *Correspondence*, he insists that to achieve salvation it is not necessary 'to know Christ according to the flesh: but with regard to the Eternal Son of God, that is the Eternal Wisdom of God, which has manifested itself in all things and especially in the human mind, and above all in Christ Jesus, the case is far otherwise'.[6] The thing to understand about the resurrection of Jesus, which Spinoza accepts in a spiritual sense, is that 'Christ to this extent raises his disciples from the dead, in so far as they follow the example of his own life and death'.

Yet the separation is more apparent than real. This practical wisdom, resulting in moral and religious living, results too in self-realization which is one form of thought, and hence is knowledge, however fragmentary, of God. Happiness comes through this, and only this, as a condition of human existence. But the end towards which man is carried by this wisdom, this knowledge of his own perfection, or of God, is a logical necessity of his existence, which true or adequate thinking makes clear to him. God has imposed on human nature the laws that determine '(1) the impulse of each individual nature to seek its own good, or happiness, so far as it knows it; (2) the constant dissatisfaction with anything short of complete knowledge of truth, and complete harmony and perfection of life.' [7] Here are two of the dominant notes in Arnold's gospel of culture: the desire in human

H

nature for perfection, and the dissatisfaction with anything that comes short of that perfection. What Arnold does is to substitute for the philosophical sanction of logical necessity the humanistic sanction of cumulative human experience.

To equate morality with religion, and God with perfected knowledge, was in the eyes even of Spinoza's faithful correspondents a subversive activity. This Spinoza strenuously denies. How can he be throwing off all religion, when he 'maintains that God must be acknowledged as the highest good, and must, as such, be loved with a free mind? or again, that the reward of virtue is virtue itself?. . . or lastly, that every man ought to love his neighbour, and to obey the commands of the supreme power?' [8] The fact remains that God is an intellectual absolute in Spinoza's scheme, the only absolute, while even the highest tests and sanctions for human behaviour are moral and pragmatic: 'The individual necessity in things destroys neither divine laws nor human. For moral principles, whether they have received from God the form of divine laws or not, are nevertheless divine and salutary.' And again: 'Whether I love God in freedom, or whether I love Him from the necessity of the divine decree, I shall nevertheless love God, and shall be in a state of salvation.' The use of the word 'love' as the equivalent of 'have knowledge of' is very significant. Indeed, it suggests as a parallel to Arnold's definition of religion as 'morality, touched with emotion', a Spinozist definition as 'knowledge, touched with emotion'. So Elwes, with an obvious reminiscence of Arnold, construes Spinoza's position: 'Emotion can only be conquered by another emotion stronger than itself, hence knowledge will only lift us above the sway of passions, in so far as it is itself "touched with emotion".' [9]

The intellectual God demonstrated in the *Ethics* was in Arnold's opinion hardly a substitute for the God of orthodoxy so far as the emotional and imaginative many were concerned (as Spinoza himself saw). Huxley, like Albert Einstein, could find the pantheistic abstraction satisfactory: 'When Spinoza says, "Per Deum intelligo ens absolute infinitum, hoc est substantiam constantem infinitis attributis", the God conceived is one that only a very great fool would deny, even in his heart.' [10]   But Arnold was not presuming to write for a self-sufficient scientist like Huxley, nor for a self-sufficient humanist like Jowett, who could turn back the reproaches of orthodoxy and define his own position. 'Newman, Manning and Gladstone', remarks Jowett blandly, 'would call me an infidel. Are they quite certain that they are not more infidel than I am, and more materialist? They believe in the Church only and an ecclesiastical organization. I try to believe in God and in the presence and possibility of God everywhere.' [11] Again, Arnold is not speaking to those satisfied people who, following the lead of the dogmatizing, metaphysical bishops, can speak of 'God as familiarly as if he were a man in the next street'. He has no desire, he says, to unsettle their faith; the *Zeitgeist* will attend to that.

The people for whom he wrote were those who had broken with the old faith, but could not approve in their religious instinct or psychological experience the rationalistic and utilitarian substitutes offered them. Liberal but devout, honest and anxious, they followed 'heterodox' clergymen like Maurice and Robertson of Brighton, who had no answer, but whose integrity and candour were reassuring, and whose perplexity, at a learned and theological level, reflected their own. For Robertson, whose *Life* and *Sermons* he had read, Arnold had sincere praise. In one of Robertson's letters to a troubled correspondent, the basis for sympathy is obvious: 'We are all anxious to know *all about* God, and meanwhile we never think of knowing *God*. God, instead of religion, and, much more, God, instead of theology, is what we need to believe in.' [12] He went on to admit that he read more of literature than of divinity, and said with desperate honesty, 'I try to trust in God and my own soul; there is nothing else to trust to.' Robertson spoke to those people for whom Arnold wrote; perhaps his representative quality in the 1850's is most clearly brought out in the following remark: 'The most satisfactory things that have ever been said on the future state are contained in the "*In Memoriam*".'

It was for these people, then, as well as for himself, that Arnold offered the 'strong thought of Spinoza' at the less austere level, where he felt sure that a God synonymous with the objectified values of wisdom and goodness would be found to correspond with that ideal of perfection towards which our experience moves, and of which we obtain glimpses in moments when the 'imaginative reason' is operating at the higher level of 'resurrected' human nature. That the objectification was a justifiable inference the analysis of the *Tractatus* has shown. Others besides Arnold have read Spinoza in this way. Pringle-Pattison points out that Spinoza's real attitude involved a restoration of values, after the extraction of all predicates from Being and the reduction of all human qualities to a dead level: 'Spinoza's reply to his critics is, in effect, the acknowledgement of an objective set of values, which reinstates the distinctions which he had apparently denied.'[13] And Strauss, in pointing to the failure of Schleiermacher to combine the historical with the ideal Christ, maintained that Spinoza had made the necessary distinction in setting up practical moral objectives for man: 'Spinoza made this distinction when maintaining, that to know the historical Christ is not necessary to felicity, but only to know the ideal Christ, namely, the eternal wisdom of God, which is manifested in all things, in the human mind particularly, and in a pre-eminent degree in Jesus Christ—that wisdom which alone teaches man what is the true and false, good and bad.'[14]

The idea of God offered by Goethe shows a direct relation with the thought of Spinoza. It is given in Eckermann's synopsis of Goethe's final statement on the subject:

Christ thought of a God, comprising all in one, to whom he ascribed all qualities which he found excellent in himself. This God was the essence of his own beautiful soul; full of love and goodness, like himself; and every way suited to induce good men to give themselves up trustingly to him, and to receive this Idea, as the sweetest connection with a higher sphere. But, as the great Being whom we name the Deity manifests himself not only in man, but in a rich powerful nature, and in mighty world-events, a representation of him, framed from human qualities, cannot of course be adequate, and the attentive observer will soon come to imperfections and contradictions, which will drive him to doubt, nay, to despair, unless he be either little enough to let himself be soothed by an artful evasion, or great enough to rise to a higher point of view.[15]

This higher view Goethe says he found in Spinoza, that it fortified him in youth, and, since it was not a subjective notion but an idea manifested in Nature, formed 'root and germ of a plant' which flowered into later knowledge. Not that this knowledge is or can be full: there remains always something inscrutable about the Highest Being: 'For the rest, nature and we men are all so penetrated by the Divine, that it holds us; that we live, move, and have our being in it; that we suffer and are happy under eternal laws; that we practise these, and they are practised on us, whether we recognize them or not.' This is definitely Spinozist pantheism. One may reasonably assume that from the time Arnold was

introduced to the philosopher Spinoza by the humanist and
scientist Goethe, their influence upon him was complementary and
harmonious, an assumption fully warranted by the nature of the
dual references in the essay on Spinoza.

It was inevitable that Arnold's adaptation of ideas derived
from these sources, and still more his search for a substitute
God, should have invited attack from those who demanded
precision and accuracy, as well as from the orthodox. Before
going on to consider some of these attacks, however, we may
notice briefly the reasons why Arnold's treatment of the idea of
God, and of the 'divinity' of Christ, owes less to other sources
than to those already discussed.

Coleridge can insist on the 'Eternal not ourselves' with more
than Arnoldian thoroughness: 'The law of God and the great
principles of the Christian religion would have been the same had
Christ never assumed humanity.' [16] But he adds to the Absolute
Will or moral law the idea of a 'super-personal' God 'having the
causa sui, or ground and principle of its being, in its own in-
exhaustible might', just the kind of metaphysical argument for
divine personality which Arnold rejects. He bases psychological
truths of religion on the appeal to experience—even the idea of
God 'can only be awakened and brought into distinct consciousness
by the appropriate experience'. But on the nature of God he
'reasons' from personal and emotional need. Though we cannot
demonstrate the existence of 'a good, wise, loving, and personal
God, there are so many convincing reasons for it . . . that for
every mind not devoid of all reason, and desperately conscience-
proof, the Truth which it is the least possible to prove, it is little
less than impossible not to believe'.[17] This emotional appeal to
the 'reason' reveals a temperamental bias towards belief common
to Coleridge and Newman. The belief in the existence of God
is to Newman irresistible, and the reason is frustrated in attempt-
ing to prove the opposite: 'The case is pretty much the same as
regards the great moral law of God. We take it for granted, and
rightly . . . how should we conduct ourselves, if there were no
difference between right and wrong, and if one action were as
acceptable to our Creator as another? Impossible! if anything
is true and Divine, the rule of conscience is such, and it is frightful
to suppose the contrary.' [18] On the question of the operation of
the moral law Arnold agrees with Newman and Coleridge,
because here is something revealed in human experience. To

argue from this to the existence of a personal God is unsound, however, because it involves what is by its very nature outside experience. Regarding such arguments as eloquent apologies for anthropomorphism, Arnold dismisses them as roundly as does his own Empedocles, though with less asperity of manner.

In the Cambridge Platonists, contemporary with Spinoza, Arnold found corroborative testimony to the truth of his poetic definition of God as 'wisdom and goodness', and a healthy contempt for inadequate and anthropomorphic definitions of the deity. Atheism, said Smith, resulted from rebelling against too low and superstitious a picture of God: 'So easy is it for all sects, some way or other, to slide into compliance with the Anthropomorphitæ, and to bring down the Deity to a conformity to their own image.' [19] The metaphysical aspect of their thought had no interest for Arnold, as it appeared in the writing of Cudworth, Smith, and More. What attracted him was their witness, like that of Coleridge, to the psychological truth of Christianity, and their practical moral religion, finding in goodness the distinctive mark of God's presence. This led them to differ from the Neo-Platonists, and to agree with Spinoza, in holding that the real knowledge of God was achieved through moral obedience rather than through ecstasy. The best way to know Nature and the existence of God, Smith stated, was to look within: 'God is not better defined to us by our understandings than by our wills and affections: He is not only the eternal reason, that Almighty mind and wisdom which our understandings converse with; but He is also that unstained beauty and supreme good to which our wills are perpetually aspiring: and wheresoever we find true beauty, love, goodness, we may say, here or there is God.' [20] In spite of a stress upon the natural truth of religion, and upon reason as the 'candle of the Lord', the Cambridge men never failed to make moral obedience, for all its naturalness and reasonableness, an obedience to a power greater than man. Yet the terms in which the relationship was stated were often unorthodox, and Arnold felt free to call on them for supporting witness to his 'not ourselves' in conduct. Hardly a day passed without 'suggestions and stimulations' from outside us impinging upon our experience, said Arnold, 'And so Henry More was led to say, that "There was something about us that knew better, often, what we would be at than we ourselves." ' [21]

What Arnold's religious thought owed to Butler and his

religious imagination to Newman has already been noted. But their line of argument he could not accept, as he made clear in a passage showing Newman picking up the 'analogy' from Butler, and carrying on from a justification of revealed religion to a justification of Catholic authority up to and including papal infallibility. On 'this line of hypothesis and inference', says Arnold, nothing can be proved or disproved. 'Only, there may come some one who says that the basis of all our inference, the Supreme Governor, is *not* the order of nature, is an assumption, and not a fact; and then, if this is so, our whole superstructure falls to pieces like a house of cards.' [22]

Passing to the other theological extreme, we find that Strauss 'applies a negative criticism ably enough, but that to deal with the reality which is still left in the New Testament, requires a larger, richer, deeper, more imaginative mind than his'. Pfleiderer bears out this criticism, finding it a defect in Strauss that he attempts at the end of the *Leben Jesu* 'to restore dogmatically what he had destroyed critically', by transforming 'religious faith in Christ into a metaphysical allegory' with talk of Absolutes and Infinites. 'In all this Strauss was led astray by the influence of the Hegelian philosophy, which looked for the truth of religion in logical and metaphysical categories instead of in the facts and experiences of moral feeling and volition.' [23] It is by 'facts and experiences', of course, not by definitions of essence, being, and substance, that Arnold claims to proceed. This preference he shares with Joseph Joubert. For the Catholic and Platonic affinities of this 'French Coleridge' and refined 'reactionary in religion', as Babbitt calls him, Arnold has a great deal of sympathy. His essay on Joubert consists largely of direct quotations. We may note what Joubert has to say on the nature of God:

May I say it? It is not hard to know God, provided one will not force oneself to define him. Do not bring into the domain of reasoning that which belongs to our innermost feeling. State truths of sentiment, and do not try to prove them. There is a danger in such proofs. . . . In things that are visible and palpable, never prove what is believed already; in things that are certain and mysterious by their greatness and by their nature,—make people believe them, and do not prove them; in things that are matters of duty and practice, command, and do not explain. 'Fear God', has made many pious; the proofs of the existence of God have made men atheists.[24]

Clearly the way is open here to mere individual intuition on the one hand and to authoritarian obscurantism on the other. Arnold ignores these dangers in Joubert; what gains his unqualified approval is the scorn for attempts to settle systematically and metaphysically such problems as the nature and existence of God.

His conviction that metaphysic and logic are inadequate to explain the larger questions in the religious experience of man does not, however, cause Arnold to regard with tolerance the doctrine of nescience advanced by Herbert Spencer, who seems to him to furnish proof that the dogmatizing scientific philosopher is as bad as the dogmatizing theologian. The gist of his attack is that the name Unknowable, being completely negative, can arouse none of the positive feelings of awe and reverence which men, as a fact of experience, have felt towards a Power of which they know little, but know at least that it is 'the Eternal which makes for righteousness'. This Power they call God, and the warmth and poetry of traditional usage reinforce the moral experience of the Power's operation in a way which makes the substitution of a meaningless negation indefensible.

The opposition to his abstraction Spencer finds quite natural; it is so with 'every change from a lower creed to a higher'. It is desirable, too, since men must live in terms of current thought, and conduct is always geared to the current representation of the unseen Reality. 'Even now, for the great mass of men, unable through lack of culture to trace out with due clearness those good and bad consequences which conduct brings round through the established order of the Unknowable, it is needful that there should be . . . pains and pleasures of a definite kind.' For a long time, the candid evolutionist admits, few will be able to live by his faith, and to find it operative in conduct (even fewer, one might say, than by Arnold's, in spite of T. S. Eliot's disparaging equation of the Unknowable and the Eternal). But he finds his safeguards in the cumulative force of habit, in the moral experience of the race, and believes in a kind of organic morality as a stabilizing force:

Indeed, were it not that throughout the progress of the race, men's experiences of the effects of conduct have been slowly generalized into principles . . . were it not that under [accompanying] potent influences, habits have been modified, and the feelings proper to them made innate—were it not, in short, that we have been rendered in a considerable degree organically moral; it is certain that disastrous results would ensue from the removal of those strong and distinct motives which the current belief supplies.[25]

In the appeal to the moral experience of the race, there is almost complete agreement between Spencer and Arnold. But the difference, again, is vital. Where Spencer finds this 'organic morality' a sufficient safeguard for ethical principles to justify the introduction of his Unknowable, Arnold fears the 'disastrous consequences' from relinquishing the old moral and imaginative certainties bound up with one name, God, and with one source, the Bible. The idealizing and imaginative power of man must be directed, in matters of religion and morals, towards something he knows, verified in his own experience, not to some intellectual abstraction which is by definition unknowable. Pringle-Pattison is in accord with Arnold on this point. The Spencerian reconciliation is, he maintains, really a *reductio ad absurdum*. All that can be known, though proximate and relative, is given to science. All that seems worth knowing must be regarded as a mystery, and treated as a symbol, with no attributes whatever. Spencer is right in condemning the positivist, finite God of the so-called Religion of Humanity, and in stressing the 'Great Creative Power', but 'he strangely fails to see that it is only because the character of that Power is to be revealed in the highest human qualities that it can call forth either veneration or gratitude'.[26]

In summing up Arnold's position, we may say that he was driven by a need for authority as urgent as that of Coleridge and Newman. His 'wisdom and goodness, they are God' and his 'stream of tendency by which all things fulfil the law of their being', could not remain in complete harmony with the thought of Spinoza and Goethe. He had to go on, in his objectifying of an immanent moral principle, to a non-pantheistic statement of a controlling Power outside man. His most complete statement is in *Literature and Dogma*:

We would not allow ourselves to start with any metaphysical conception at all, not with the monotheistic idea, as it is styled, any more than with the pantheistic idea; and, indeed, we are quite sure that Israel himself began with nothing of the kind. The idea of *God*, as it is given us in the Bible, rests, we say, not on a metaphysical conception of the necessity of certain deductions from our ideas of cause, existence, identity, and the like; but on a moral perception of a rule of conduct not of our own making, into which we are born, and which exists whether we will or no; of awe at its grandeur and necessity, and of gratitude at its beneficence. This is the great original revelation made to Israel, this is his 'Eternal'. [27]

This 'Eternal *not ourselves* which makes for righteousness' is expanded at the end of the book, in the interests of totality, to include the one-fourth in man not devoted to conduct, and becomes 'the Eternal Power, *not ourselves*, by which *all things* fulfil the law of their being'. Arnold has added something to the Goethe 'who once for all put the standard inside every man'; and in his desire for permanence in the flux of things and for what Trilling calls 'apodictic certainty', he has made his moral Power, whose only verification is human experience and testimony, the Reality behind the appearances. This Power is not actually called an absolute, but Jesus, in whom a larger share of the Power appears than in anyone else, is so described (that is, of course, relatively to human experience). To Arnold, the great superiority of this God-concept over the personified abstraction of Spencer is that it has a degree of concreteness, and is at least partially knowable in the light of our experience of our own moral natures. Compared with the idea of the Trinity, it has 'the obscurity of the immeasurable depth of air, the other the obscurity of a fog'. Compared with the Unknowable, it offers something positive as a guide, something authoritative which can be obeyed, an ideal which can inspire, and an object which the poetical imagination of humanity can in the traditional way of symbolism invest with awe and grandeur.

It was at this point, where Arnold was carefully putting a cosmological dome on his psychological edifice, and moving the divine upstairs, that F. H. Bradley fell on it with his logical sledge-hammer. Apologizing to his readers for wasting their time with such an intellectual butterfly as Arnold (his bothering to do so may be taken as evidence of the disturbing impact of Arnold's ideas and definitions), Bradley dismissed as a tautology the definition of religion as 'morality, touched with emotion', and described the 'Eternal not ourselves' as 'literary clap-trap'. These were weighty blows. Professor Trilling feels that Bradley pretty conclusively proved faulty logic, shallow reasoning, and a misuse of scientific and philosophical terms.

The fuller consideration of these questions, in their bearing on the relationship of morality to religion, must be left until the following chapter. Here we may notice Bradley's insistence that

an ideal of personal morality is not enough: the religious con-
sciousness must have a real object, however indistinct. 'Be
virtuous and you will be happy' may be a good copy-book
maxim, says Bradley; it is not a God. The point is, of course, that
Arnold never gets clear of the relative nature of his human
morality. The empirical experience of a moral power operative
in human life is too subjective to sustain the kind of objectification
he wants. Yet does Bradley offer anything more acceptable?
The object of the religious consciousness, he says, is this same
'ideal self of morality', only it *is*, not ought to be. Not finite, it
nevertheless exists: 'We find ourselves, as this or that will, against
the object as the real ideal will, which is not ourselves, and which
stands to us in such a way that, *though real, it is to be realized*,
because it is *all and the whole reality*.' [28] A staggering idea, Bradley
admits, but a fact, even if one chooses to call it a delusion, and
it cannot be got rid of by 'fine phrases'.

As a substitute or synonym for God, it is hard to see what
superiority can be claimed for this piece of logical scholasticism,
or what advantage the 'real ideal will' has over the 'Eternal not
ourselves' as a practical clarification of the object of religious
worship. Saying it *is* God does not simplify the metaphysics for the
man seeking an object towards which to direct his specifically
religious emotion—for, in other words, the doubting, thoughtful
people to whom Arnold was trying to offer an emotional and
imaginative reality. The affirmations of the culture-prophet may
be technically vague, but the definitions of the brilliant logician are
intellectually exclusive, to say the least. Pringle-Pattison rightly
refers to Bradley's 'way of criticizing human experience not from
the standpoint of human experience, but from the standpoint of
an absolute experience'. In his Absolute, it *may* be, it *must* be, it
is; but the *how* is ignored. Bradley rightly withdraws all predicates;
his Absolute 'is not personal, nor is it moral, nor is it beautiful
nor true'. Hence to Pringle-Pattison it is 'a cluster of negations,
which, though technically true,. . . are practically more false than
would have been the corresponding affirmations'. [29]

It was not only the logician or metaphysician who rejected
Arnold's God-concept. To many of the sincere and unsettled
souls for whom he wrote, whose need was personal and emotional,
his message of accommodated Spinozism was no more satisfactory
than Spinoza's intellectual absolute. R. H. Hutton summed up
their grievance against Arnold when he said: 'It is open to him

to maintain that the Bible is a dream, but it is not open to him
to maintain that it never seriously expresses faith in the personal
life and love and goodness of God, in the very same sense in which
it attaches the most intense moral significance to the righteousness
of man'.[30] It is true that Arnold occasionally recognized those
whom he could not reach. In the poem 'Pis-Aller', where the
speaker cries that all is dark without belief in the miraculous God
of revelation, Arnold replies 'For God's sake, believe it then!'
Yet the didactic tone of his religious criticism, and the contro-
versial atmosphere in which it was published, meant that his
strikingly phrased definitions and generalizations were received
as a challenge by all thinking men. Of those who protested not
all were as indignant as Hutton. Martineau, for example, mildly
pointed out that the essence of religious belief in both Judaism
and Christianity had been the belief in personal relations between
the human and the divine expressed through the medium of
prayer. Turning Arnold's habitual weapon of playful irony back
upon him, Martineau asked whether one could pray to an
abstraction, a stream of tendency, and implore, 'O thou Eternal
Not-ourselves that makes for righteousness, if it be possible, let
this cup pass from me.'

In his essay, 'Ideal Substitutes for God', Martineau is, how-
ever, concerned to do more than to poke fun at Arnold's defini-
tions. He contrasts the growing science(s) of religion(s), studying
what men have believed in, with the science of theology, studying
the object of belief as a Real Being, and puts Arnold high among
those ethical humanists who are trying to set up an ideal morality
as a focus of faith. Yet the important truth they emphasize is
'within the limits of Ethics', and 'Religion centres precisely' on
what these moralists discard. Like Bradley and other idealists,
Martineau insists that in religion the ideal is also the real. We
cross the line into religion 'when we affirm that over us and in
relation to us the All-perfect Mind exists. Devout faith is a belief
of *real Being* on the strength of *what ought to be*.' Now this view is
possible only to Theism without paradox, for one side reflects
eternal perfect Mind, the other, Nature as becoming. Take away
'this objective persistence of living Holiness' and moral idealism
loses its objective hold, and becomes dependent for witness upon
the marred and condemned reality of mere contingent existence.
In this way humanism can venerate only its own idea, which
becomes an exercise of the imagination, an æsthetic ideal. There

is a truth 'caricatured' in these new movements, 'that the *progressive element* of Religion is to be found in an ever-expanding moral ideal as human experience enlarges and the human conscience increases its refinement and range'. But, Martineau concludes, 'on the ontological side of Religion . . . there is no such process of advance . . . the Ideal which for ever grows must, in essence, be secured upon the Real'.[31]

I pointed out in the preceding chapter that had pragmatism achieved earlier formulation, Arnold would have found congenial philosophical expression for his ideas. Alternatively, he might have saved himself considerable embarrassment had he resisted his distaste for metaphysics and system sufficiently to base his appeal to experience on the concept of intrinsic value dominant in idealism since Kant. In other words, he should have recognized more explicitly his leaning towards idealism, permanence, and unity, as against materialism, flux, and multiplicity, a leaning apparent in his early desire for 'an Idea of the world, in order not to be prevailed over by the world's multitudinousness'. He might have keyed in with his belief that our moral endeavour is not limited to what we are, a vision of perfection, in more systematic terms, that transcended empirical or experiential fact. He might have said, as Pringle-Pattison does: 'The presence of the Ideal is the reality of God within us'; or, more directly: 'The presence of a [moral] life is explicable only through the actual presence within it, or to it, of the Perfection to which it aspires.'[32] That the transcendence of the divine negates the moral experience of man, where it assumes ontological separateness rather than distinctions of value or quality, is a philosophical statement of Arnold's position; it could be put, as it is in Pringle-Pattison, in terms of the reciprocal relationship between the 'Eternal' and man which Arnold considered to be an experienced fact: 'God has no meaning to us out of relation to our own lives or to spirits resembling ourselves in their finite grasp and infinite reach; and, in the nature of the case, we have absolutely no grounds for positing his existence out of that reference.'[33]

To all attacks and reproaches, however, Arnold replied that he was not at all interested in advancing or retaining a concept of God which would be satisfactory in a metaphysical, epistemological, theological, or indeed in any but a moral, sense. The object of his earnest effort was to unite in the name of God the human-divine perfection of 'wisdom and goodness' towards which our higher natures strive, with an eternal moral principle marked by permanence and incorruptibility and apprehended by the imaginative reason as the voice of authority. Withal as much of the rich symbolism of traditional worship should be preserved as possible in a purged, simplified, and universal religion. A humanistic ethic of this kind, maintaining itself against either a naturalistic or metaphysical monism, is, in effect, the position to which Pringle-Pattison comes. Finding Bradley's attempts to determine the Absolute barren, he concludes that agnosticism is 'the only healthy attitude' in some areas: 'Our statements about the Absolute—i.e. the ultimate nature of things—are actually nearer the truth when they give up the pretence of literal exactitude, and speak in terms (say) of morality and religion, applying to it the characteristics of our highest experience. Such language recognizes itself . . . as being "thrown out", as Matthew Arnold used to say, at a vast reality.' [34]

Many Victorians besides Arnold were speculating afresh upon this 'vast reality', and, as Martineau's essay suggests, offering variations of the humanist-ethical-scientific ideal as substitutes for God. The revolution in thought operated within theology as well, under the influence of men like Maurice, and J. S. Lidgett points to the 'change of temper' which 'caused men to turn from the abstract Divinity of the Incarnation to its humanity, as revealed in the character, teaching, and self-sacrifice of the historic Christ'. [35] Lidgett, of course, is concerned with the belief in the Father and the Son, in the personal relationship, but the language used could apply at times equally well to Arnold's idea of appealing to experience: 'It must be remarked that man's only means of interpreting the Universe is supplied by that which becomes manifest in his own nature as evolved and conditioned by the Universe itself.'

On the other hand was the Victorian thinker whose frame of reference was the Nature of physical science. To J. R. Seeley, 'that man believes in a God who feels himself in the presence of a Power which is not himself and is immeasurably above himself', and since all theologies have seen the laws of Nature as the laws of God, 'it is evident that in knowing Nature we do precisely to the same extent know God'. This natural religion is not the old eighteenth-century Deism, however: 'It must contemplate its God mainly in Nature and not mainly beyond it.' Seeley concludes that 'the Eternal Law of the Universe . . . equivalent to God might form the basis of a great religion if only it revealed itself by evidence as convincing to the modern mind as that of miracles was to antiquity'.[36] The hope and even the language remind us of Arnold, but Seeley does not venture upon prophecy, and the 'might' and 'if' showed an understanding of the new 'scientific' spirit lacking in Arnold's confident pronouncements.

Even the men most affected by the methods and spirit of science were, for the most part, anxious to avoid a sudden disloca-tion in the traditional sanctions for morality, much less to rush to the militant atheism of Clifford or Bradlaugh. Mill, like Spencer and Huxley, conceded the force of habit and association: 'The obligation of duty is both theoretically acknowledged and practically felt in the fullest manner by many who have no positive belief in God, though seldom, probably, without habitual and familiar reference to him as an ideal companion.' [37] At the other extreme from this cool if sociable concession, is Samuel Butler's hearty belief in gradualism or compromise. When Higgs is leaving Erewhon for the second time, heartsick at the discovery that he has been made the object of religious worship, he nevertheless advises against the destruction of the Musical Bank system, 'because . . . though false in the letter, if good counsels prevail, it may be true enough in spirit'. 'Then', says George, 'you would have us uphold Sunchildism, knowing it to be untrue?' 'Do what you will', Higgs replies, 'you will not get perfect truth. If you . . . get rid of cock-and-bull stories, idealize my unworthy self, and . . . make me a peg on which to hang your own best thoughts— Sunchildism will be as near truth as anything you are likely to get.'

There was great diversity of opinion between Arnold and his fellow 'liberals' from different camps on the value and strength of traditional religion and its symbols. But there was fundamental agreement on the main point, namely, that the development of moral idealism and stability was the most precious fact in human experience. Nor was it merely a question of holding any gains made in this direction by painfully evolving humanity; the creation of new and truer sanctions for conduct and the purifying and simplifying of old ones were urged in the name of ethical progress. Concern with moral stability did not keep these writers, or for that matter Arnold, from being 'dissolvents', exponents of the 'modern' spirit that widened a breach between religion and morals, and that carried to the limit the concept of man as the measure of all things. Maurice Guyau analysed the tendency at the time:

Side by side with its somewhat sentimental element the love of God contains a moral element, which is progressively detaching itself with the march of ideas. God being the very principle of goodness, the personification of the moral ideal, the love of God ultimately becomes a moral love properly so called, the love of virtue, of sanctity at its height. The subjective act of charity thus becomes the religious act *par excellence*, in which morality and subjective worship are identified; good works and the externals of worship are simply a translation into the outer world of the moral consciousness.[38]

This subjective and æsthetic morality, reinforced by a growing emphasis on social service and social reform, Guyau quite rightly read as a sign of the times, and of the future. He credited the author of *Literature and Dogma* with some share in this movement of thought, saying that 'Mr Matthew Arnold and the group of liberal critics, who, like him, are inspired by the spirit of the age (*Zeitgeist*), seem thus to have guided faith to the ultimate breaking-point beyond which nothing remains but to break definitively with the past and its dogmas.' To ignore Arnold's avowed conservatism to the extent of lumping him with the 'liberal critics' is hardly just to his purpose, nor in fact has Guyau's prophecy been entirely borne out. But he correctly indicated the direction of Arnold's idea that Israel, while apparently worshipping 'a magnified, non-natural man', was unconsciously deifying a natural law. At the same time he expressed the usual criticism that Arnold read Israel wrongly: 'The believer of other times affirmed the existence of God first, and then made His will the rule of conduct; the liberal believer of today affirms the existence, first of all, of the moral law, and cloaks it in divinity afterwards. He, like Matthew Arnold, treats with Jahveh on equal terms.'[39] This describes the process, but makes no allowance for the great emphasis Arnold put upon the retention, for the emotions and imagination, of the awesome name of God, and of the spiritually enriching symbolism of communal worship.

It was characteristic of Arnold that, while he tried by radical opinions to bring ideas of God into line with modern thought, and so angered the orthodox, he followed his conservative temper in trying to retain them in purified form as sanctions for conduct, and so ran foul of the secularist. It was inevitable that he should fall between the two stools. But that it was not sheer blundering the interest in his ideas testifies. With his eye on a throne for the human spirit in the prophetic distance, he posited a compromise on which the human spirit might, in his opinion, relax with some sense of security. Bearing in mind the audience he was consciously addressing, Arnold emphasized caution in forsaking the old and tried sanctions for moral behaviour. As man progresses, runs Arnold's significantly relativist argument, he may suceed where the Greek humanist failed.

The clearer our conceptions in science and art become, the more will they assimilate themselves to the conceptions of duty in conduct, will become practically stringent like rules of conduct, and will invite the same sort of language in dealing with them. . . . To treat science with the same kind of seriousness as conduct, does seem, therefore, to be a not impossible thing for the Aryan genius to come to.[40]

But there is a reservation; and it furnishes the motive in Arnold's religious writings: 'For all this, however, man is hardly yet ripe. For our own race, as we see it now and as ourselves we form a part of it, the true God is and must be pre-eminently the God of the Bible, *the Eternal who makes for righteousness*, from whom Jesus came forth, and whose Spirit governs the course of humanity.'

I

CHAPTER VI

'Morality, Touched with Emotion'

In the place of all other delights, substitute this, that of being conscious that you are obeying God, that not in word, but in deed you are performing the acts of a wise and good man.

EPICTETUS, *Discourses*

Conceive universal order! Everything that conforms to it in ideas, in imagery, in opinions, in institutions is beautiful; everything which conforms to it in action, in scheme, in enterprise is good. There you have the criterion.

JOUBERT, *Pensées*

THERE was much in the writings of Matthew Arnold to make some of his contemporaries look dubiously upon his claim that he was a serious friend of religion; there was nothing to make them doubt his serious concern with the problem of conduct, and the fundamental seriousness with which he viewed the whole business of living. This concern and seriousness were present from the beginning. Especially revealing are the letters to Clough and the *Note-books* in which the critical religious essayist quotes with increasing frequency passages full of the consolations and solemn warnings of Christianity from such sources as St Augustine, Thomas à Kempis, Lacordaire, Pascal, Barrow, and Jeremy Taylor. The largest number of quotations is from the Bible; the second largest, from *De Imitatione Christi*. Ranging from Epictetus to Vauvenargues, these quotations illustrate the conscious and unremitting search for self-mastery and moral perfection. Arnold's fondness for moral maxims and aphorisms is reflected in the extent to which he quotes from Bishop Wilson, and in the gnomic utterance characteristic of his own verse. The worthy Bishop was a comfortably pious man whose moralizings strike us as rather obvious, but Arnold prized him for his 'practical religious sense' and derived much satisfaction and many moral 'touchstones' from Wilson's *Maxims of Piety and Christianity*. In 1849 Arnold wrote to Clough: 'As I get more awake to this [need for self-mastery] it will I hope mend for I find that with me a clear almost palpable intuition (damn the logical senses of the word) is necessary before I get into prayer: unlike many people who set to work at their duty self-denial, etc. like furies in the dark hoping to be gradually illuminated as they persist in this course.' [1] Later in the same letter he stated positively, 'That which is morally worthless remains so, and undesired by Heaven, whatever results flow from it.'

Three major developments occur in the maturing of Arnold's ethical ideal. The first may be described as the addition, under the pressure of the desire for order and permanence, of an external authority to the inner standard furnished by Goethe and the Stoics. This has been discussed. The second is the addition of the positive psychological sanction of joy, and finds expression as the earlier religious nostalgia yields to the claims of extrovert activity in domestic and professional life. The third is an increasing cultural and religious interest in the family of man, in solidarity, what today we should call the social consciousness. The last two developments again reveal the influence of Spinoza's *Tractatus*, and of the various sources which encouraged Arnold in his naturalistic and psychological treatment of the teachings of Christ.

The combined influence of Dr Thomas Arnold and the four 'voices' of Oxford days, and his own moral earnestness, meant that the un-Victorian frivolity and the romantic *Weltschmerz* apparent in the life and poetry respectively of the young Arnold were never more than superficial. He read Béranger, even attempted to sing snatches of him, but could say to Clough in 1848, 'I have with me only Béranger and Epictetus . . . of the former I am getting tired . . . with all his genius, there is something "fade" about Béranger's Epicureanism.' But Epictetus remained a lifelong friend and counsellor. This was the period of Senancour's *Obermann*, with its charm and its inadequacy. Years later Arnold stated wherein *Obermann* satisfied, and wherein it came short. What attracted him, and remained attractive, were the sincerity, the inwardness, the self-renouncement, the exquisite feeling for Nature. What repelled him were the discouragement, the ennui, the powerlessness. For the young man there was a fascination in the Byronic pessimism of 'Why is earth thus stripped of illusions in my eyes? Satiety I have in nowise known, the void I find everywhere'; in the longing for mountains, forest, evening and romantic solitudes; in the 'sensibility' which represented the author's emptiness and wretchedness as playing a fugue with external Nature. But the futility, apparent even in 1849 when Arnold bade a poetical farewell to Obermann, was clearly set forth in the course of the essay on Emerson over thirty years later: 'The forlorn note belonging to the phrase, "vast debility", recalls that saddest and most discouraged of writers, the author of *Obermann*, Senancour, with whom Emerson has in truth a certain kinship. He has, in common with Senancour, his pureness, his passion for nature, his single eye; and here we find him confessing, like Senancour, a sense in himself of sterility and impotence.' [2]

The strength of Senancour is recalled with equal decisiveness: 'He was born with a passion for order and harmony, and a belief in them.' Added to this was 'a concern for the state and prospects of what are called the masses', a concern the result of 'singular lucidity and plain-dealing' and a hatred for 'flagrant inequality and injustice'. 'Arrange one's life how one will,' Arnold quoted approvingly from Senancour, 'who can answer for its being any happier, so long as it is and must be *sans accord avec les choses, et passée au milieu des peuples souffrans?*' This was the Obermann who found the truly good man marked by balance, control, and rational action: 'He is virtuous, not, however, through fanaticism, but because he is desirous of order.' His analysis of his own ethical position, terminating with a quotation from Montaigne, was expressed with a secularist and psychological emphasis which must have struck the young Arnold forcibly:

Morality would be substantially the gainer by abandoning the support of an ephemeral fanaticism in favour of dignified dependence upon indisputable evidence. If we would have principles which appeal to the heart, let us recall those which are in the heart of every well-organized man. Let us say: 'In a world of mingled pleasure and sadness the vocation of man is to increase the consciousness of joy, to stimulate overflowing energy, and combat, in all which feels, the principle of degradation and of sorrows.' [3]

Neither in Senancour nor in the Stoics, however, did Arnold find more than passive moral virtues for the most part, nor any sanction for conduct in joy or hope. This was to come later. Meanwhile he preached his austere doctrines of centrality and self-mastery to Clough, and let his emotional and imaginative dissatisfaction find its outlet in his poetry, where, under the images of nostalgia and frustration and yearning, the moral imperative was often simply, 'Endure!' The titles of many of the poems—'Consolation', 'Resignation', 'Self-Dependence'—

are themselves indicative of the bleakly stoical basis from which Arnold started.

Nowhere is the need and desire for adequate self-knowledge more poignantly expressed than in 'The Buried Life'. The Arnold who hears the 'Know thyself!' of Socrates, the 'Trust thyself!' of Emerson, and the austere words of Epictetus and Marcus Aurelius, here cries out that man, forced to 'obey even in his own despite his being's law', yearns for the knowledge of his 'genuine self':

> There rises an unspeakable desire
> After the knowledge of our buried life;
> A thirst to spend our fire and restless force
> In tracking out our true, original course;
> A longing to inquire
> Into the mystery of this heart which beats
> So wild, so deep in us—to know
> Whence our lives come and where they go.
> And many a man in his own breast then delves,
> But deep enough, alas! none ever mines.

Occasionally, as when love stimulates the feelings and imagination, the insight comes, and with it the calm and peace of understanding:

> A man becomes aware of his life's flow,
> And hears its winding murmur; and he sees
> The meadow where it glides, the sun, the breeze.

The 'unwonted calm' of this imaginative insight may even bring with it the illusion of knowing the before and after, but as in 'The Future', it is an illusion only:

> And then he thinks he knows
> The hills where his life rose,
> And the sea where it goes.

One aid to man in his search to find his 'hidden self', the self which in Spinozist terms fulfils 'his being's law' and is, in the idiom of Arnold's later praise of culture, man's best self, is Nature. Not the evolving living Nature around us, of which we too are a part, and which is cruel and fickle, but the grand cosmic Nature of time and space, of which our higher selves are emotionally and imaginatively aware. The former is the Nature which man must surpass; the latter is the Nature from which he must learn. One lesson, as the invocation to the 'untroubled and unpassionate' heavens in 'A Summer Night' makes clear, reveals to man, 'madman or slave' as he is, his own spiritual possibilities:

> You remain
> A world above man's head, to let him see
> How boundless might his soul's horizons be,
> How vast, yet of what clear transparency!
> How it were good to abide there, and breathe free;
> How fair a lot to fill
> Is left to each man still!

The other lesson, reinforcing that of the sages, is that if man would achieve the serenity of the stars he must achieve their self-sufficiency. He must '*live* as they', Arnold tells us in 'Self-Dependence':

> 'And with joy the stars perform their shining,
> And the sea its long moon-silver'd roll;
> For self-poised they live, nor pine with noting
> All the fever of some differing soul.
>
> 'Bounded by themselves, and unregardful
> In what state God's other works may be,
> In their own tasks all their powers pouring,
> These attain the mighty life you see.'
>
> O air-born voice! long since, severely clear,
> A cry like thine in mine own heart I hear:
> 'Resolve to be thyself; and know that he,
> Who finds himself, loses his misery!'

Now this adequate life of self-realization, to which joy, or at least loss of misery, is possible, suggests again the reading of Spinoza. Additions to the basis of stoical acquiescence are being made, and we are prepared for the later discovery that even the finest stoicism must yield to Christianity, in which right conduct is definitely associated with happiness. There is another addition to endurance and self-knowledge, however, and that is the demand for helpful activity. The voices of Carlyle, Goethe, and Dr Thomas Arnold sound strongly here, and the tribute in 'Rugby Chapel' is to men who translate moral insight into beneficent action. They, sons of God, rather than servants, would not 'alone be saved'. They, like Dr Arnold,

> Move through the ranks, recall
> The stragglers, refresh the outworn,
> Praise, re-inspire the brave!
> Order, courage, return.

Matthew Arnold was not the zealous crusader depicted in these lines; although he heard Carlyle's call to duty he did not share Carlyle's admiration for men of action. But there is no doubt that Arnold felt himself, in his social and religious criticism, to be doing something for humanity in a much-needed critical way, the way of intelligence, a way which he considered to be much more practical than most of the activity advocated and indulged in by his disparagers and opponents. It is a kind of self-realizing activity in line with the active stoicism of Spinoza, so attractive to both Goethe and Arnold, rather than in the line of Dr Arnold's militantly Christian call to action. What Spinoza offers, Arnold tells us, is 'a moral lesson not of mere resigned acquiescence, not of melancholy quietism, but of joyful activity within the limits of a man's true sphere'.

There are three important practical conclusions to be drawn from Spinoza's application (and accommodation) of his general postulates to specifically human nature, and these serve as leading principles in Arnold's thinking. They are that in following virtue man is simply fulfilling the law of his own being, that true happiness accompanies this attempt at self-realization, and that this in turn is the richer for sharing, for being construed as a social and objective good. The emphasis in Spinoza is positive; rigorous asceticism and self-mortification are of no value, except as means to a higher end (that is, positive moral good). Vices, misery, sorrow, death, are all negative emotions and facts (that is, inadequate ideas). Man is driven to seek his *utile*, and 'nothing that is for a man's advantage can be at variance with morality'. But the self-regarding utilitarianism indicated is not that of Mill or Spencer. Pleasure is not the end, but self-realization. A quotation from the *Ethics* covers adequately the first two points: 'As virtue is nothing else but action in the laws of one's own nature, and as no one endeavours to preserve his being except in accordance with the laws of his own nature, it follows, *first*, that the foundation of virtue is the endeavour to preserve one's own being, and that happiness consists in man's power to preserve his own being.' [4]

Happiness, then, is to be associated with right conduct,

which is the reward of following out a self-realizing search for the good which is man's perfection. But that good, while a moral absolute in terms of God's (natural) law, is also relative to man's understanding. Difficulties arise, from each individual's seeking 'to make his idea of good and bad into a universal law, and to impose his will upon all the rest. The result can only be strife, confusion, and hatred.' The clash comes, to Spinoza, between adequate and inadequate conceptions of good, the latter making for excess, present good, or blind and ungoverned action. A real good can be achieved only on a basis of a better understanding. This suggests many aspects of Arnold's thought: the danger of inadequate conceptions of what is good or needful, the walking by the best light we have, the being sure that our light is not darkness, the need for cultural self-development commensurate with the fullest capacities of the individual, the positing of a moral absolute.

To Spinoza, part of man's adequacy is to see himself as one with nature and other men, as, at the simplest level, his body is one with external things by virtue of its dependence on food. The reason which shapes man's activities is immanent, but the external exercise of these activities constitutes his happiness, and is a natural necessity of his moral life, the achievement of his highest *utilitas*. As Duff says, this 'idea of the essential solidarity of men in virtue of their moral nature is one of [Spinoza's] leading principles'.[5] It is worth having the fullest statement of Spinoza on this point: 'As every man seeks that which is most useful to him, so are men most useful to one another. For the more a man seeks what is useful to him and endeavours to preserve himself, the more is he endowed to act according to the laws of his own nature, that is to live in obedience to reason; therefore men will be most useful to each other, when each seeks that which is most useful to him.'[6]

I think one may see throughout this precise reasoning a possible basis for Arnold's earlier emphasis on individual culture, which is 'to make an intelligent being yet more intelligent'; for his insistence when culture deepens into religion that the aim is 'to make reason and the will of God prevail', and that solidarity marks the highest human good; for his pleading for a 'collective best self'. The 'parmacetti and moonshine' gibes at Arnold ignored the elements derived from the 'strong thought of Spinoza'; the religion of culture had a solid basis in Spinozist ethics.

Spinoza would not dispense with the terms 'good' and 'bad' (though rationally these are only modes of thought), since he wishes to frame an ideal of human nature, an exemplar. It is reason itself (adequate knowledge) which gives validity to this good (which is relative to individual human nature) and objectifies it. And in so far as this objectified good is perceived, it becomes 'an ideal of human nature to which we may approach ever nearer, and we shall call men more perfect or more imperfect according as they approximate more or less to this exemplar'. With the Christian religion as the objectified good, and Christ as the exemplar, the accommodation of the 'strong thought' in the *Tractatus* to the needs of the many is complete. Turning to Arnold we find emotion touching (and imaginative reason idealizing) the moral good rather than logical reason objectifying it, and, with an historical rather than a philosophical method, a proof offered on the basis of cumulative human experience rather than immanent necessity.

It was pointed out that Spinoza found merely power and desire in the 'natural' state, but that man, by the necessity of his nature, which had the potentialities of morality and reason, was enabled to work towards a moral, social and religious happiness, to obey the divinely implanted impulse, to fulfil, in other words, 'the deepest law of his being'. This Duff considers to be Spinoza's greatest ethical idea. It has the corollary that men, starting from a similar basis of desires and powers, develop differently, for example, with regard to ideas of justice. Hence we find a peculiar genius for religion in the Hebrew people; in their imagery everything is of God. And so it is to Spinoza, only rationally, not emotionally: 'Spinoza's great principle, then, is that there is nothing secular in the universe, nothing common or unclean, nothing that does not reveal or express God.' [7] This inclusiveness is not found in Arnold. Whether because of a persistent intellectualism colouring his values, or because of something as irrelevant as personal fastidiousness, Arnold's religion of culture laid itself open to the charges of critics as diverse as Henry Sidgwick and Walt Whitman, the former of whom observed that culture, if it is to succeed, must learn 'to call nothing common or unclean', while the latter uttered a barbaric yawp against the effeminate æsthete who could see nothing in 'people —just people!' The charge has truth in it, yet it was for 'the masses' that Arnold was striving to preserve the moral teaching of the

Bible; it was for them that he emphasized, in diluting the 'strong thought' of Spinoza, the doctrine that following the teachings of Christ made for social as well as private good, that only through the 'religion of sorrow' was possible a joy commensurate with the dignity of human nature at its higher levels.

This higher nature, or distinctively human nature, *our* human nature as Arnold calls it, is the level at which the self-realization of which Spinoza speaks is operative. It reflects as well the Stoic and Christian teachings on the two selves in man, and in that form is central to Arnold's ethical thought. To the explicit statements given in chapter II we may add a further passage in which the thought of Spinoza and the Stoic (and Christian) teachings are fully harmonized:

To serve God, to follow that central clue in our moral being which unites us to the universal order, is no easy task; and here again we are on the most sure ground of experience and psychology. In some way or other, says Bishop Wilson, every man is conscious of an opposition in him between the flesh and the spirit. *Video meliora proboque, deteriora sequor*, say the thousand-times-quoted lines of the Roman poet. The philosophical explanation of this conflict does not indeed attribute, like the Manichæan fancy, any inherent evil to the flesh and its workings; all the forces and tendencies in us are, like our proper central moral tendency the desire of righteousness, in themselves beneficent, but they require to be harmonized with this tendency, because this aims directly at our total moral welfare,—our harmony as moral beings with the law of our nature and the law of God,—and derives thence a pre-eminence and a right to moderate. But though they are not evil in themselves, the evil which flows from these diverse workings is undeniable.[8]

Here Spinozist idiom is virtually reproduced—the central moral tendency linking us with the universal order, the beneficence of all impulses when properly harmonized with this central tendency. It is clear why Arnold can describe Christianity and moral perfection as both natural and unnatural. They are natural to that level of man's nature where his proper development is to be realized. Whichcote can say of this, 'Whoever finds not within himself a principle, suitable to the *Moral Law*; whence of Choice he doth comply with it: he is departed from himself, and has lost the natural perfections of his being.'[9] Or, conversely: 'What is Morally Filthy, should be equivalent to what is naturally impossible; we should not, is morally we cannot.' On the lower level, virtue and religion are not natural. This scheme of things represents the frank dualism which probably impressed Arnold most forcibly first in Epictetus, who says, 'It is shameful for man to begin and to end where irrational animals do; but rather he ought to begin where they begin, and to end where nature ends in us; and nature ends in contemplation and understanding, and in a way of life conformable with nature.' [10] What Arnold added to the inward and rational discipline by which men should control the animal self and live at the level of the best self, was the attractiveness of Christianity. The naturalistic teachings of Goethe and Spinoza and the Stoics both supported and were superseded by the teaching of Jesus:

Jesus made his followers first look within and examine themselves; he made them feel that they had a best and real self as opposed to their ordinary and apparent one, and that their happiness depended on saving this best self from being overborne. *To find his own soul*, his true and permanent self, became set up in man's view as his chief concern, as the secret of happiness; and so it really is. 'How is a man advantaged if he gain the whole world and suffer the loss of *himself*?'— was the searching question which Jesus made men ask themselves. And then, by recommending, and still more by himself exemplifying in his own practice, by the exhibition in himself with the most prepossessing pureness, clearness, and beauty, of the two qualities by which our ordinary self is indeed most essentially counteracted, *self-renouncement* and *mildness*, he made his followers feel that in these qualities lay the secret of their best self; that to attain them was in the highest degree requisite and natural, and that a man's whole happiness depended upon it.[11]

The sanction of happiness here added to Arnold's stoicism was anticipated by the joyful self-realizing activity he found in the morality taught by Spinoza, and by Goethe, although Goethe speaks on the subject more as an artist than as a moralist:

A consciousness of the worth of the morally beautiful and good could be attained by experience and wisdom, inasmuch as the bad showed itself in its consequences as a destroyer of happiness, both in individuals and the whole body, while the noble and right seemed to produce and secure the happiness of one and all. Thus *the morally beautiful could become a doctrine*, and diffuse itself over whole nations as something plainly expressed.[12]

The æsthetic overtones are absent from Arnold, whose emphasis is more exclusively ethical, but the rooting of happiness in right conduct by the appeal to experience is precisely reflected in Arnold's thinking on the subject. This emphasis on the joy or happiness which is the reward or sanction of right conduct is the most positive of the developments in Arnold's ethical thought, that which merges it with religion. It has nothing to do with rights. Arnold is completely opposed to the idea of 'natural rights', which is to him pure theory. Nor is there any guarantee of material rewards, nor of the avoidance of suffering. The benefits visualized both in popular Christianity and in Benthamite Utilitarianism are to Arnold crassly materialistic. What he has in mind is the satisfaction which comes from obeying the voice of conscience, in spite of all difficulties and hardships; the joy which comes from translating the (symbolic) death and resurrection of Christ into a sacrifice of the lower nature and a living in the higher nature of man: in Spinozist terms, the happiness attendant upon self-realization in the direction of moral perfection as an end proper to the reason and the nature of man. This inward 'doing' is to Arnold the most 'practical' thing in life, the object of morality and religion, the richest fruit of experience. It is the great achievement of Israel, 'happiness being man's confessed end and aim, to have more than any one else felt, that *to righteousness belongs happiness*'.[13] The authority of Quintilian, Bishop Wilson, Thomas à Kempis, and St Augustine is appealed to as witness that to right conduct belongs happiness, though the words these men actually used may be joy, peace, calm, or gratitude.

It is when Arnold calls upon history and experience for evidence that he runs into trouble, and is posed by Bradley with his own use of 'verification'. For in his anxiety to lay down a general rule for human conduct, guaranteed efficacious by reciprocal action between the moral inner self and the 'Eternal not ourselves', Arnold makes the reward for righteousness something more than a self-realization independent of external circumstance. Men and nations, he says, are shipwrecked on conduct. One after another they fall—Babylon, Greece, Rome —and, he prophesies, France will inevitably pay the penalty for her worship of the goddess Lubricity, her adherence to the standards of the *homme moyen sensuel*. But questions inevitably arise, as Professor Trilling says. Where are the nations which stood through righteousness? What complex of forces actually caused the downfall? Are there not cases, both with men and nations, of unrighteousness triumphant over righteousness?

It was pointed out earlier that the difficulty is indicated by Bradley's use of the word 'ordinarily'. Arnold translated those moral and spiritual values operative at the level of human nature on which moved the philosophy of Spinoza and the exaltation of à Kempis into the sphere of historical human experience and literary language. That he had a notion of what he was doing we may infer from a remark in the preface to his *Last Essays on Church and Religion*: 'As a matter of experience . . . it turns out that the only real happiness is in a kind of impersonal higher life, where the happiness of others counts to a man as essential to his own.' A remark by G. E. Moore would suggest that Bradley's attack on Arnold's use of 'to verify' points to a semantic as much as a logical carelessness, and extends the criticism to the whole idea of the true or best self. Having exposed as a 'naturalistic fallacy' the hedonistic equation of pleasure and good and the metaphysical equation of real and good, Moore goes on to say that such an assertion is made by 'modern writers who tell us that the final and perfect end is to realize our *true* selves—a self different both from the whole and from any part of that which exists here and now in Nature'. Here the fallacy comes in. For 'if ideal consists in the realization of the "true self", the very words suggest that the fact that the self in question is *true* is supposed to have some bearing on the fact that it is good'.[14]

It is, as Trilling suggests, Arnold's hatred of system which betrays him, allowing him to use with confidence, in an approximate and pragmatic setting, words and facts which are restricted, by the nature of the truth they proclaim, to areas of experience above the distorting influence of ordinary human nature, its activities, its motivations. Spinoza could exemplify his doctrine that virtue is its own reward; he could also narrowly escape death at the hands of a murderous mob which was not punished for the outrage it committed. Christ could symbolize in his life and death the moral and spiritual regeneration of man; the fact remains that he suffered persecution and a lingering death at the hands of intolerant fanaticism. What Arnold does not clearly see is that the sphere of the 'ought-to-be' is where the truths of teachers like Spinoza and Christ are 'facts' of (ideal) human experience; or rather, he sees this but does not admit that when the sphere is expanded to include the course of human history, the appeal to experience in the association of happiness with righteousness becomes both subjective and relative. Empirical science, with which Arnold claims kinship by virtue of his pragmatic appeal to experience, will not accept this. Huxley can declare, as we have seen, that the gravitation of sin to sorrow is as sure in operation as a natural law. He can also say, however, of the ethical process which in its use of 'self-restraint' is in opposition to the natural process, 'But the practice of self-restraint and renunciation is not happiness, though it may be something better.' [15] The last clause contains a thought which Arnold sometimes overlooked in his anxiety to make the human desire for happiness dependent upon right conduct.

A closer reading of Coleridge, whose emphasis upon the 'natural' psychological truth of Christianity Arnold so highly praised, might have given him the clue to what he was trying to say himself, what he was, indeed, saying in his more consistent utterances. Coleridge sees in stoic morals the nearest approach to Christian morals, yet at the same time a psychological basis opposite to that of Christianity. The Stoic attaches honour solely to 'the person that acts virtuously in spite of his feelings. . . . Christianity instructs us to place small reliance on a virtue that does not *begin* by bringing the Feelings to a conformity with the Commands of the Conscience. Its special aim . . . is to moralize the affections.' [16] Something of the same distinction is made, more loosely, by John Smith: 'Religion is no sullen Stoicism, no sour Pharisaism: it does not consist in a few melancholy passions, in some dejected looks, or depressions of mind; but it consists in freedom, love, peace, life, and power; the more it comes to be digested into our lives, the more sweet and lovely we shall find it to be.' [17]

The moralizing of the affections, as Coleridge has it, is the clue, even if Arnold reverses it to the emotionalizing of morality. Indeed, Arnold's own comments on his stoical teachers make clear their (comparative) inadequacy, as it appears to his maturer experience. Christ is superior to Epictetus as a moral teacher by virtue of his warmth, his feeling, not by virtue of superior reasons given for good conduct. It is the difference between character and soul, and upon this discernment rests a moralist's claim to true greatness: 'It is because Mr Mill has attained to a perception of truths of this nature, that he is,—instead of being, like the school from which he proceeds, doomed to sterility,—a writer of distinguished mark and influence, a writer deserving all attention and respect.' [18] Yet Mill is not 'sufficiently leavened' with them, and hence falls short of being a 'great writer'. So it is with Marcus Aurelius, a difficult case to judge. He can say, 'If thou workest at that which is before thee, following right reason vigorously, seriously, calmly, without allowing anything else to distract thee, but keeping the divine part pure . . .; if thou holdest to this, expecting nothing, fearing nothing, but satisfied with thy present activity according to nature . . . thou wilt live happy.' [19] Where Seneca has intellect, and Epictetus character, this man has soul, he has something of Christian sentiment, he is a great example for goodness. But one thing is missing. Add the Sermon on the Mount, says Arnold, and the result is perfection. Marcus Aurelius could save his own soul, but—and here we have a reminiscence of 'Rugby Chapel'— he could do no more. For the whole point of the warmth, the feeling, and the positive sanction of joy far removed from mere hedonism, which are the distinguishing marks of Christianity, is that they make for solidarity, for obedience to the practical injunction, 'Love thy neighbour!' 'Truth illuminates and gives joy,' says Arnold, 'and it is by the bond of joy, not of pleasure, that men's spirits are indissolubly held.' [20]

As social service or political programme, Arnold's culture did not function. It was not intended to. With what he considered hasty and ill-advised action going on all about him, the one thing needful seemed to him to be the movement of individuals, of a whole nation of individuals, towards a higher degree of enlightenment, at which level less hasty and ill-advised action would be possible. In spite of some of the problems pressing for attention, this emphasis seemed to him the one to make, at that time, and for the English people. In the ordinary sense of the word, of course, he was not 'practical'. He saw his own function as that of a critic, especially of the schemes and reforms and 'isms' that in his view over-simplified the problem. Comte's religion of Humanity he considered quite inadequate, and communism disturbed him because of what he considered to be its blindness to other than material standards of well-being. But he approved the general thought of putting communal well-being first as 'a witness to the infallibility of the line of Jesus. We must come, both rich and poor, to prefer the common good, . . . the body of Christ of which we are members, to private possession and personal enjoyment.' [21] His culture, that panacea which shunned all panaceas, could at least point the way to a practical application of the Christian principle of solidarity, or the brotherhood of man. It poured scorn on the canting practitioners who would have the slum children of London 'succour one another, if only with a cup of cold water', and insisted that the causes of suffering could be eradicated only by adequate ideas and widespread enlightenment:

> Surely, so long as these children are there in these festering masses, without health, without home, without hope, and so long as their multitude is perpetually swelling, charged with misery they must still be for us, whether they help one another with a cup of cold water or no; and the knowledge how to prevent their accumulating is necessary, even to give their moral life and growth a fair chance! [22]

The other principle of Christian morality which Arnold came to insist on was that of chastity, or pureness. Professor Trilling suggests that Arnold's real concern was with something more like 'innocence', and that this, a question of style in morality, is more the concern of the psychological novelist than of the moralist. To Arnold it was definitely a moral problem, with psychological and social implications. He found the principle exemplified, as well as laid down, by Christ, taught by all the great moralists, and a subject of concern to our (higher) human nature. It became virtually an obsession with him in his later warnings to France, the tone of which deepened from critical friendliness into severity. All the grace, politeness, refinement, and lucidity of France were not regarded as adequate compensations for her worship of the goddess Aselgeia, her addiction to the moral standards of the *homme moyen sensuel*.

In part this is merely a reflection of Arnold's favourite critical doctrine of 'a return upon oneself'. A nation is truly civilized or cultured only by virtue of the power to recognize and correct its own excesses. The English have moral earnestness and energy, but want lucid intelligence; the Italians have refinement and taste, but want energy; the French have logic and lucidity, but want moral earnestness; and so on. But the reproach to France becomes sharper as time goes on, until in 1882 Arnold can tell the boys at Eton that they are superior to their French counterparts by virtue of their Puritan heritage. This is not a complete *volte-face*. Arnold had always insisted on the virtues of Puritanism, even while he attacked its uglier manifestations. Yet there is certainly a shift in critical emphasis. In the more considered arraignment in the essay 'Numbers' the reason for the added emphasis is made clear. Renan, in spite of his unconcern for chastity, Arnold had always found fundamentally safe on matters of conduct. He praised Michelet for his discernment in seeing that what France needed most was a *moral* reformation. But now the goddess Aselgeia had 'a whole popular literature, nay, and art, too, in France at her service!' The average sensual man was triumphant, and 'in M. Zola we have the average sensual man going near the ground'. It was an ominous symptom: 'The Eternal has attached to certain moral causes the safety or the ruin of States, and the present popular literature of France is a sign that she has a most dangerous moral disease.' [23]

If ever Arnold seemed to speak as the typical Victorian of later caricature, it was here. Yet he was merely emphasizing his belief that moral values had the glow of vitality only from inward pureness. He never tired of reiterating that Christ's most important message was 'Cleanse thou the inside of the cup', that for 'every one to mend one' was the best and surest way to social reform. A Frenchman later came independently to conclusions that made Arnold sound like a prophet. 'O incurably frivolous people of France!' cried André Gide in 1940, 'You are going to pay dearly today for your lack of application, your heedlessness, your smug reclining among so many charming virtues.' Two months later he wrote, 'The sort of Puritan rigor by which the Protestants, those spoil-sports, often made themselves so hateful, those scruples of conscience, that uncompromising integrity, that unshakable punctuality, these are the things we have most lacked. Softness, surrender, relaxation in grace and ease, so many charming qualities that were to lead us, blind-folded, to defeat.' [24] In deploring a lack of moral fibre, Gide, if no Arnold, was yet discovering in the unattractive Puritan tradition a power and a value that men neglect at their peril.

Arnold put at least as much emphasis on charity, or the brotherhood of man, as on chastity, or inward pureness. But to move from inwardness to solidarity, from stoical self-sufficiency to active selflessness, required a belief in something larger than oneself, required too an emotion directed towards that object of belief, or at least towards those manifestations of that not ourselves that come within human experience. In other words, morality must become religion. Even the language of Spinoza, adequate for the moralists, was not quite adequate in speaking of religion:

K

Why should it be one thing, in its effect upon the emotions, to say with the philosopher Spinoza,—'Man's happiness consists in his being able to preserve his own essence', and quite another thing, in its effect upon the emotions, to say with the Gospel, 'What is a man advantaged, if he gain the whole world, and lose himself, forfeit himself?' How does this difference of effect arise? I cannot tell, and I am not much concerned to know; the important thing is that it does arise, and that we can profit by it.[25]

Experience tells us, then, that though religion and morality are so closely identified in their nature and object that we cannot define the difference, there is nevertheless a difference. The burning candle placed in oxygen has in nowise changed, but it burns with a brighter flame. 'The paramount virtue of religion is, that it has *lighted up* morality; that it has supplied the emotion and inspiration needful for carrying the sage along the narrow way perfectly, for carrying the ordinary man along it at all.' The final statement of this point of view is in *Literature and Dogma*:

But is there, therefore, no difference between what is ethical, or morality, and religion? There *is* a difference; a difference of degree. Religion, if we follow the intention of human thought and human language in the use of the word, is ethics heightened, enkindled, lit up by feeling; the passage from morality to religion is made when to morality is applied emotion. And the true meaning of religion is thus, not simply *morality*, but *morality touched by emotion*.[26]

It is this definition which Bradley (and Professor Trilling follows him) pounced on as a tautology, saying that an emotion which would transform morality into religion must be, not *any* emotion, but one specifically religious. This is the case, Trilling points out, with regard to the series of parallel pagan and Christian maxims quoted by Arnold, where the emotion in the latter is directed towards a transcendent external power. Now it is apparent that up to a point Bradley's attitude is also Arnold's: 'Religion is essentially a doing, and a doing which is moral. It implies a realizing . . . of the good self.'[27] The religious consciousness has only the moral ideal as content. 'Apart from duties, there is no duty; and as all moral duties are also religious, so all religious duties are also moral.' Religion cannot collide with morality. 'In order to be, religion must do.' The difference comes in considering what constitutes the superiority of the religious state over the moral. Reflection on morality, says Bradley, shows us that it is imperfect, in a way which implies something higher. This something higher is religion, relieved from the inadequacies of an ideal which remains at the level of ought-to-be: 'The main difference is that what in morality only is to be, in religion somehow and somewhere really is, and what we are to do is done.' Morality survives within religion, but not as mere morality.

We may now state the nature of the disagreement. Bradley postulates an Ideal or Absolute which can be the object of systematic thought, a Reality which can be the object of belief because it is independent of contingent experience, and which frankly requires the attitude of faith. Arnold postulates an Eternal moral law as a parallel to man's experience of the need for conduct, and the recorded witness of man's feeling about this 'not ourselves' is taken as evidence that it works around us and in us. The element of faith is here disguised, the pragmatic justification for morality being illogically extended to an absolute sanction that is outside the world of experience, even though it depends upon that world for its (partial) verification. To Bradley, justification is possible only by faith, a doctrine which he finds to be the glory of Protestantism. The will must be present as well as belief—there must be both the object to believe in and the will that it be real. To Arnold justification is by works: 'The noblest souls of whatever creed, the pagan Empedocles as well as the Christian Paul, have insisted on the necessity of an inspiration, a joyful emotion, to make moral action perfect; an obscure indication of this necessity is the one drop of truth in the ocean of verbiage with which the controversy on justification by faith has flooded the world.' [28]

When we read Arnold's tribute to the 'immense emotion of love and sympathy inspired by the person and character of Jesus', it becomes clear that the emotion intended by Arnold in his definition is not *any* emotion. It is that of love, the positive emotion which makes for the joy sanctioning conduct, the happiness attendant upon right living. It is love for wife and children; it is love for one's neighbour (as Spinoza too sees it); it is, in its highest form, love for Christ who exemplifies human nature moving on a level of moral perfection which we may call divine.

Faith, then, is this 'moralized affection', which stimulates to action, if the rational grounds for right conduct are of themselves insufficiently persuasive. And it operates, not because it satisfies the logician, but because it is a matter of experience. The moral perfection of Christ and the awesome vastness of the 'Eternal making for righteousness' may be only partially realizable in experience, but their truth depends upon that power in us to realize them, not upon their possession of an absoluteness beyond even the imaginative experience of mankind. The emotion which lights up morality, or heightens it, into religion, is then something positive, something which is a matter of experience, something which assists man in the process of self-realization by 'cementing the alliance between the imagination and conduct'. Love is the readiest illustration from experience, and the most inclusive term, but the emotion is present in other forms:

> The power of Christianity has been in the immense emotion which it has excited; in it engaging, for the government of man's conduct, the mighty forces of love, reverence, gratitude, hope, pity, and awe,— all that host of allies which Wordsworth includes under the one name of *imagination*, when he says that in the uprooting of old thoughts and old rules we must still always ask:—

> > Survives *imagination*, to the change
> > Superior? Help to virtue does she give?
> > If not, O mortals, better cease to live! [29]

It is significant that the emotional overtones which for Arnold separate religion from morality suggest the poetic imagination, which is not likely to employ its terminology in a way satisfactory to either the orthodox believer clinging to his creed or the logician demanding precise definition.

Arnold's emotional sanctions for conduct must inevitably be the expression of individual human experience, and leave untouched, as Bradley saw, the virtual synonymity of his religion and his morality, so far as a philosophical or cosmological statement is concerned. This emphasis upon morality as the essence of religion, or even as a substitute for it, was not uncommon amongst Arnold's contemporaries. Huxley offers Arnold's idea exactly, even to the accompanying emotion, but without the concrete symbolism furnished by devotion to Christ the exemplar. He says of religion that 'it ought to mean, simply the reverence and love for the ethical ideal, and the desire to realise that ideal in life, which every man ought to feel'.[30] It was the austerity of such idealism that moved Arnold to seek the sanction of happiness attaching to love for the highest form of life embodied in human experience.

Perhaps the contemporary moralist whose position most resembled Arnold's was Edmond Scherer. He was a singularly fine, but never popular, critic, who admired Arnold and was admired by him. His inward development and critical ideas on all subjects showed an interesting if not exact parallelism with those of Arnold and he expressed, effectively and beautifully, though perhaps with a touch more of traditional religious feeling, much that Arnold felt and said about the source and founder of Christianity:

Jésus s'est offert au monde dans la pureté de son caractère morale: voilà quelle a été son œuvre. Il n'est pas venu révéler des mystères, enseigner une doctrine, fonder une Église, constituer un clergé, établir des rites; mais ayant vu Dieu dans le miroir de son âme limpide et profonde, le Dieu qui est esprit et amour, il a redit aux hommes ce qu'il avait vu. Uni avec le Père celeste par la vertu d'une affinité native, il a montré en sa personne tout ce qui peut paraître de la divinité sur la terre. Ses paroles mêmes n'ont été que la manifestation de ce qu'il portait au dedans de lui, et leur prix vient de la fidélité avec laquelles elles traduisent ce qu'il était. Puissance de la beauté morale! Jésus est apparu aux siens sous les traits d'une si ineffable grâce, que le souvenir s'en est gravé à jamais dans la mémoire de ceux qui l'avaient contemplé, et que, dans ce souvenir, l'humanité a vu se lever un idéal nouveau, commencer pour elle une vie meilleure et divine.[31]

What we may take to be the final expression of Arnold's belief in the reality and meaning of Jesus for humanity, and in his power to lift morality into religion, occurs in the preface to the popular edition of *Literature and Dogma* in 1883:

Jesus himself, as he appears in the Gospels, and for the very reason that he is so manifestly above the heads of his reporters there, is, in the jargon of modern philosophy, an *absolute*; we cannot explain him, cannot get behind him and above him, cannot command him. He is therefore the perfection of an ideal, and it is as an ideal that the divine has its best worth and reality. The unerring and consummate felicity of Jesus, his prepossessingness, his *grace and truth*, are, moreover, at the same time the law for right performance on all man's great lines of endeavour, although the Bible deals with the line of conduct only.[32]

The use of 'absolute' here is not a concession to traditional orthodoxy, under pressure from Arnold's growing conviction that

Christianity is irreplaceable. He can never, as Seeley does in *Ecce Homo*, speak of Christ's other power, 'the power over nature', for to him moral power as supported by 'natural truth' is *the* claim to permanence in Christian example and thought. Indeed, some of Arnold's most interesting criticism is his naturalistic explanation of the seemingly miraculous. With regard to the cures effected by Jesus, he says:

To what extent, or in how many cases, what is called *illness* is due to moral springs having been used amiss, whether by being overused or by not being used sufficiently, we hardly at all know, and we too little inquire. Certainly it is due to this very much more than we commonly think; and the more it is due to this, the more do moral therapeutics rise in possibility and importance. The bringer of light and happiness, the calmer and pacifier, or invigorator and stimulator, is one of the chiefest of doctors. Such a doctor was Jesus.[33]

Yet the Jesus who remains the 'perfection of an ideal' somehow suggests an absolute to the 'struggling, task'd morality' of mankind. Arnold knows that ethical codes are in themselves insufficient. He knows, too, that 'it is as an ideal that the divine has its best worth and reality'. In the same way that, in his search for authority, he set over us an Eternal moral law not ourselves, he comes to invest Jesus the exemplar with a human-divine perfection that is and will probably remain unique, yet is sufficiently realizable in human experience to offer humanity an ideal in the reality of which they can believe, and a star towards which they can rise in the hope of arriving at least at a nearby planet. Both his God and his Christ reveal a kind of 'relative absolutism', and the fact that this is a contradiction in terms leaves Arnold vulnerable.

Arnold's whole line raises the interesting question of whether a psychological analysis, divorced from a philosophically systematic exposition as well as from theological dogma, can yet have sufficient pragmatical truth to warrant its being offered as a guide to a higher form of life and a better world. In spite of the Newmans and Bradleys and Harrisons, he was sure that it could; he was also sure that he was offering just such an experiential truth. His argument is not dismissed by T. S. Eliot's criticism that Arnold's advice is 'to get all the emotional kick out of Christianity one can, without the bother of believing it', nor by Eliot's deliberately provocative remark that 'the spirit killeth, but the letter giveth life'. Belief for Arnold is independent of dogma, and of ritual or form, though he would retain the latter as the poetry of religion, elevating communal morality by its power and dignity and uniformity. It is bound up with an inherited way of life, which verifies by experience a developing human, as against a static animal, nature, and is objectified in a body of moral judgments whose validity is established to the point of their being recognized as a law of that human nature's adequate self-realization. The rationale and norm are represented in an ethical humanism; the evidence is furnished by the pragmatic test of results; the emotional sanctions are the joy and sense of elevation, far removed from mere psychological hedonism, which accompany the dying to selfishness and animality as symbolized by the death and resurrection of Christ; the stimulus to the imagination is the rich glow which suffuses the 'human-divine ideal' of moral perfection exemplified in reality by all the great moral and spiritual figures of the past, and uniquely by Jesus Christ. To say that this lacks intellectual system and logical definition is a fair criticism; to say that there is here no 'law' of sufficient authority to compel uniform obedience is again a fair criticism; but to say with Eliot that here is only an 'emotional kick', or with Bradley that here is only a 'thin abstraction', is to utter criticism which is unreasonable to the point of being perverse.

It is true, as John Holloway says, that Arnold 'had no metaphysics which might form apparent premises for the moral principles he wished to assert'.[34] Whether this is a damaging criticism is another matter; to Arnold it was not. We have noted the kinship with William James. F. C. S. Schiller, while patronizingly noting that Arnold 'was not a philosopher', went on to declare that the logical idealism coming into vogue at the turn of the century was the death of morals, that the metaphysics of transcendent reality as seen in Bradley was 'pulverizing to ethical aspiration' by raising the All above 'ethical valuation and moral criticism'. The reaction was setting in, said Schiller, pointing to James and pragmatism, and 'Conduct is reinstated as the all-controlling influence in every department of life.'[35] The fact is that Arnold has continued to worry both the theologian and the philosopher, turning up all over again after he has been put in his place or disposed of for the last time. He sinned by trespassing on their preserves, and the irritating currency of his ideas and

definitions meant that he had to be dealt with. Roped in by
dogma, padlocked by logic, and shut up in a dark metaphysical
cupboard, he would always escape Houdini-like, stroll back to the
footlights, and urbanely tell the audience that such conventional
bonds were child's play to a supple man of culture.

Not only is a truce with philosophy possible, through prag-
matism. In theology the definition of religion by the *Lux Mundi*
essayist Aubrey Moore allows Arnold to be a fellow-traveller
all the way up the mountain, leaving him only at the point of
transfer for the flight through interstellar space: 'The test of
fitness is the power to assimilate and promote intellectual truth,
and to satisfy the whole man. An ideally perfect religion is not
"morality touched with emotion", but a worship which reflects
itself in the highest known morality, and is interpreted and
justified to itself by reason.' [36] Even with science peace could
be made, certainly on the basis of such conclusions as arrived
at by C. S. Pierce. Disposing of those forms of 'thinking' which
arose from *a priori* reasoning, authority, and the tenacity of
irrational habit, Pierce sternly limited belief in reality and the
growth of logical conscience to the use of the scientific method.
But going on to the idea of probability, involving a transfer of
logicality to a larger context of social principle, Pierce found
'three sentiments, namely, interest in an indefinite community,
recognition of the possibility of this interest being made supreme,
and hope in the unlimited continuance of intellectual activity,
as indispensable requirements of logic'. What was involved here
was a scientific restatement of charity, faith, and hope, 'in the
estimation of St Paul, the finest and greatest of spiritual gifts.
Neither Old nor New Testament is a text-book of the logic of
science, but the latter is certainly the highest existing authority in
regard to the dispositions of heart which a man ought to have.' [37]

In all these approximations to, or partial recognitions of,
the essentials of Arnold's position, it is important to remember
that Arnold sought no philosophically coherent system of
religion. Yet he was concerned to formulate a philosophy of life,
humanistic and ethical in content, and touched into religious
warmth by the devotion of men to the highest they had known or
could know in experience. One may feel at times that Arnold's
hopes for his cultural religion tend to develop into a too credulous
faith, as one may also feel when Bishop Butler says that all that
is needed for the spread of true Christianity is the 'laying it

before men in its divine simplicity, together with an exempli-
fication of it in the lives of Christian nations'. But the stress is
on 'practical religion', and the appeal is to experience.

Arnold offers at least two important reminders to a twentieth
century experimenting with 'isms' and 'services' and legislation.
One is that 'the kingdom of God is within you', that inward
transformation is a preliminary or corollary to really effective
solidarity, to love of one's neighbour. Commenting on the appli-
cation of this text, Arnold says:

It is undeniable that whoever thinks that virtue and goodness will
finally come to prevail in this present world so as to transform it, who
believes that they are even now surely though slowly prevailing, and
himself does all he can to help the work forward,—as he acquires in
this way an experimental sense of the truth of Christianity which is of
the strongest possible kind, so he is, also, entirely in the tradition and
ideas of the Founder of Christianity.[38]

The other reminder is that of the importance of conduct. Inter-
preted in the larger sense, as Arnold in his *Study of Poetry* interprets
the word *moral* in the larger sense, it expresses his conviction that
personal integrity and moral standards are of supreme importance
in every department of life. One may in the following passage
subtract the emotion which, in the form of the word 'Christianity',
has heightened morality into religion, and insert Arnold's earlier
word, conduct. In either case, there is apparent the ethical
centre of his humanism, the ethical basis of his idealism, the
issue which was of major concern to Arnold all his life: 'What-
ever progress may be made in science, art, and literary culture,
—however much higher, more general, and more effective than
at present the value for them may become,—Christianity will
be still there as what these rest against and imply; as the indis-
pensable background, the *three-fourths of life*.' [39]

CHAPTER VII

Church and Dissent

If men be disposed to find faults, no Church can be pure enough;
for something will be amiss either in doctrine, or discipline or
ceremonies, or manners; but if they be disposed to peace and
union, then Charity will cover a multitude of failings.

BISHOP STILLINGFLEET, *The Mischief of Separation*

I regard the Church of England as, in fact, a great national
society for the promotion of what is commonly called *goodness*,
and for promoting it through the most effectual means possible,
... the means of the Christian religion and of the Bible.

Last Essays on Church and Religion

IN claiming scientific verification for the findings of his human-
istic criticism, and for his deifying of the moral law, Arnold
lays himself open to the charge of being illogical and inconsistent.
In his plea for preserving a comprehensive and progressively
enlightened national church, however, his line of reasoning is
perfectly consistent, granting his sense of the overwhelming im-
portance of conduct, and granting as his premises the two main
principles of his religious psychology. These, as we have seen, are
a need for inward pureness and for the solidarity of man. The
Spinozist view of man's nature as compelled by inner necessity to
seek its own adequate self-realization acts first as a philosophical
reinforcement to both the stoical and the Christian teachings on
self-mastery and spirituality. But such inwardness as the sole end
would become a sterile asceticism, and so would defeat full self-
realization, which seeks happiness through a joyful activity in
right conduct. Both the Christian gospel (self-renouncement,
salvation for all) and humanism (social as well as individual
enlightenment) have the ideal of a realized Kingdom of God.
Now a Spinoza may rationally convince us of our proper nature
and destiny, and a Senancour may sting the conscience with his
'we cannot be happy in the midst of people who suffer'. But it is
Christ, appealing to our imaginative reason with a beauty of
moral perfection we call divine, who uniquely succeeds by teach-
ing and example in rousing us to a sense of the paradoxical truth,
that man's profoundest happiness lies in a selfless doctrine of
brotherhood.

On this line of reasoning, we conclude with the thought of a community sharing ethical ideals of inward purification and outward solidarity, 'a society for the promotion of goodness'. In the Western world this has taken the visible form of a Church, the Christian Church, with the power over the emotions and imagination of its historic continuity, its poetry and æsthetic beauty, and its help to the individual who would transcend his limitations through communal worship. Not only is such an organization or institution the reasoned conclusion to a line of thought; it is for Arnold a natural growth, an expression of men's needs. We recall his insistence on the importance of conduct, his view of Jesus as 'restoring the intuition' and 'lighting up morality', his reiterated belief in 'the natural truth of Christianity', and his definition of Christianity as 'the happiest stroke ever made for human perfection'.

To many readers there was nothing of religion in all this, much less of the true Christian faith. To Arnold these were the essential religious facts that remained when the withering breath of the scientific *Zeitgeist* had consumed the non-essential accretions, and if they were to continue to elevate and console humanity, it was necessary that they should continue to be the special care and study of an institution devoted to their preservation, development, and transmission. This institution could only be the national and established Church, the function of which would be not to exalt a priestly caste or to speculate about the supernatural, but to treat the Kingdom of God on earth as a partially realizable ideal, by helping men to live as moral and spiritual beings on a level above that of their blind unregenerate selves.

To fulfil this function there must be peace and unity. Here Arnold turned on the Dissenters whom he had already identified with the middle classes and castigated as Philistines whose dogmatic Hebraism interfered with cultural totality. Like the heretics who separated from the early Church on points of discipline or dogma, these are 'separatists for the sake of opinions'. They are wrong, 'because the Church exists, not for the sake of opinions, but for the sake of moral practice, and a united endeavour after this is stronger than a broken one'. Arnold agrees with Newman and 'the great Anglican divines' that the idea of development must be applied to the Bible and to the doctrines and disciplines derived from it. In his view this means that fuller and sounder formulations are yet to come, as philosophical and critical ideas filter slowly into the Church, which must retain a comprehensive outlook and an open mind. This is far more the mark of the historic Church than of separatist bodies, Arnold maintains. Separatism can be justified only on moral grounds, like those which were the real cause of revolt at the time of the Reformation, and to confuse matters of intellectual opinion with matters of moral principle is to dissolve the very basis of the Christian religion. What this basis is we have seen, and Arnold uses the twofold teaching as a reproach to Nonconformity:

> If, in order to gratify in the Dissenters one of the two faults against which Christianity is chiefly aimed, a jealous, contentious spirit, we were to sweep away our national and historic form of religion, and were all to tinker at our own forms, we should then just be flattering the other chief fault which Christianity came to cure, and serving our ordinary self instead of annulling it.[1]

As evidence both for the Church's powers of comprehension and for the needlessness of separation, Arnold points to the Evangelical party, a powerful force in the Church for the past hundred years. Holding as strongly as the Dissenters to a belief in predestination and justification by faith as the fundamental doctrines of Christian faith, the Evangelicals found scope for their ideas and their services within the Church. The weakening hold on these ideas under the impact of sceptical criticism would compel them to explore the ground held in common with the rest of the parent Church, perhaps even to develop a liberal temper under the influence of the growing Broad Church movement. But the Dissenters, keeping alive the memory of their very real historic grievances and fiercely maintaining the 'fractious mixture' of religion and politics, were increasingly forced to find the ground of disagreement in a third doctrinal issue, the question of Church discipline and government. To make episcopacy and priesthood a permanent stumbling-block to reunion, even with the scandal of Ritualist excesses, was to Arnold a clear case of separatism on a secondary matter, of confusing form and substance. Using cajolery as well as attack and satire, Arnold pleaded for concessions on both sides that would make for healing measures, and assured Nonconformists that their fine qualities—independence, conscientiousness, vigour—were exactly what the Church needed to resist encroachments by the State, to carry out her evangelistic mission, and to preserve her Christian soul while opening her mind to the influences of modern thought. All they had to do was to accept the State connection and episcopal rule as witness to historic continuity, in a Church which neither would nor could compel uniformity of belief in these secondary matters.

In so far as the views here outlined are not simply an extension of his earlier criticism into the field of religious controversy, they may be attributed to the influence of Thomas Arnold and Coleridge, and of the whole tradition running back from them to the 'latitude men' and other Anglican divines of the seventeenth century. Coleridge distinguishes three levels of religious being. There is the level of true Christian faith, of Christianity in its pure form, where the individual soul and God are the only realities. There is the Church visible and militant, the Church against the World or against the State as State, the Church Catholic and Apostolic, free to work in its own way and owning no head but Christ, no power but the spiritual. Finally, there is the national Church of paid officials and functionaries, the Church which is merely the State in another aspect, the Church to which Christianity is in a sense 'a happy accident', the Church whose object is 'to secure and improve that civilization, without which the nation could be neither permanent nor progressive'. To this institution belong all the learned and professional people, the 'clerisy' as Coleridge calls them, including those in theology. Of the Church in this State capacity 'the proper object and end . . . is civilization with freedom', the preserving of morality and the bringing of a germ, a nucleus of civilization to the remotest village. Anticipating the comment that all this has little to do with religion, Coleridge says, 'The morality which the State requires in its citizens for its own well-being and ideal immortality, and without reference to their spiritual interest as individuals, can only exist for the people in the form of religion.' [2]

Arnold in effect accepts this moralizing and civilizing function of the Church, and, by virtue of his more rationalistic and sociological interpretation of the New Testament, makes the State Church the vehicle also of Christ's distinctive teaching. This extension both Coleridge and Thomas Arnold would have rejected with horror as not only illegitimate but also irreligious. Yet his view of the Church and State as expressions of our 'collective best self', and of the established Church as the active source of moral enlightenment, clearly derives from them. To Thomas Arnold the Church is 'a society for the putting down of moral evil', for 'the moral improvement of mankind'. To him this means that 'the clergy of a national Church are directly called upon to Christianize the nation', which is identified with the Church only when the government is 'avowedly and essentially Christian'. Doctrine has disappeared and evangelism been transformed in the son's writing, but the basis or guiding principle in the father's churchmanship is carried forward by the son. To Thomas Arnold 'the great philosophical and Christian truth, . . . [is] that Christian unity and the perfection of Christ's Church are independent of theological articles of opinion, consisting in a certain moral state, and moral and religious affection, which have existed in good Christians of all ages and all communions, along with an infinitely varying proportion of truth and error'.[3] Another passage makes clear the elevated, almost mystical, view of the State involved in identifying it with the Church as a power for good. 'The ἔργον of a Christian State and Church is absolutely one and the same; nor can a difference be made out which shall not impair the Christian character of one or both; as, e.g., if the ἔργον of the State be made to be merely physical or economical good, or that of the Church be made to be the performing of a ritual service.'[4] Here is anticipated Matthew Arnold's recurring theme addressed to the middle-class Philistine and to his *alter ego*, the Puritan Dissenter, of the need for State action and for a fresh and fruitful idea of the State.

Dr Arnold's view of the Church and State, at once mystical and rational, may not have been in itself Erastian, but to the Tractarians it was bound to lead to Erastianism, to a return of the eighteenth century, when under Walpole the Church was regarded as 'a useful State engine', and when worldly and self-seeking prelates were responsible for 'a grovelling instead of a noble conception of the nature and function of the Church as a Christian society'.[5] True, not all Church historians declare of this period that 'a lover of the English Church cannot study it without a blush'. A later and balanced study by Norman Sykes shows that much better work was done than one might assume from the one or two cases always held up for censure by writers 'not uninspired by a desire to discredit the episcopate of the pre-Tractarian epoch',[6] and that even the much-decried bishops Hoadley and Watson were at least consistent liberals. This liberal and latitudinarian temper was of course as suspect as any Erastian taint, and, when exhibited by men like Thomas Arnold, was as

hateful to Tractarian zeal as time-serving complacency and aridly
rational piety had been to Evangelical zeal.

The protesting wave of Evangelical enthusiasm and spirituality
(with its extreme forms of fanaticism and doctrinal narrowness)
had carried over from the eighteenth into the nineteenth century
within as well as without the Church, when the fresh wave of
protest, both reinforcing and conflicting with the first, arose in
the form of the Oxford Movement. It was no time to advance a
theory that in any way permitted State control in church affairs,
even one that dealt only with an established Church as the off-
spring of the mystical union of Church and State. The suspicion
of Dr Arnold felt by Tractarian and Evangelical became certainty
in the response to Matthew Arnold by High Churchmen and by
Nonconformists. One of the latter called him 'a pure Erastian',
and warned those who would preserve the Establishment that
whereas the Ritualists would make it a 'handmaid of Rome',
Arnold would have it serve 'rationalism and unbelief'.[7]

Arnold's view of the Church and State relationship was,
however, less irritating to the Nonconformist than his continually
putting the Puritans and their Dissenting successors in the wrong
for separating. Some replies, like those of R. W. Dale and
Edward Miall, were both able and dignified, establishing the
right and duty of separatism on grounds of moral principle and
giving historical as well as theological reasons. Others indulged
in *tu quoque* arguments or imputed unworthy motives, like the
author of a slashing sixty-four-page attack in the *British Quarterly
Review*. The writer manages to keep his temper while analysing
and refuting Arnold's interpretation of Pauline Christianity, but
loses it, understandably enough, over the reiterated charges
against Puritan contentiousness and Philistine vulgarity. 'Wild,
shrieking declaration', 'Pharisaic self-complacency', 'Hotspur
shall speak for us'—after a barrage of such phrases the conclusion
seems mild: 'Mr Arnold condemns Nonconformity, not upon high
principles of intrinsic wrong and right, but upon the low and
selfish ground of injury to his own Church.'[8]

The charge that Arnold was unfair and irritable in his treat-
ment of Dissent did not enough allow for his avowal that he
based his approach upon a fresh reading of seventeenth-century
history. Historians having, in his opinion, unduly favoured the
Puritans as the party of civil liberty, it was time to remind his
readers that exclusion from the national church had not been the

result merely of a rigid and vindictive demand for conformity by a triumphant party. It had been due in large measure to the Anglican refusal to reinterpret the articles of faith to meet the uncompromising demands of Calvinistic Puritanism. Writing to Gladstone in 1870, Arnold says that, unlike the Puritans, 'the Church has in this way been extremely favourable to the development of thought and philosophy in connection with religion'. It is a bad thing for the Church that 'she has not been on the side of civil liberty', but a philosopher will see that this is due less to servility than to attending to New Testament injunctions to stay out of 'political agitations, without which, it seems, civil liberty cannot well be had'. This reflection leads Arnold on to a distinction which he states more clearly than in his essays. The conduct of human affairs may need 'a supplementing of religion by something besides, a taking another order of wants and ideas into account, along with man's religious wants and ideas'. One would not then say that 'a body specially charged with serving man's religious wants and ideas did wrong in not mixing other things up with them. Certainly the Puritans, who were impelled to try the mixture, and to get civil liberty by and through the Bible, made a mess of it, and, in my opinion, make a mess of it still.' [9]

Arnold believed that the zeal of the Puritan side in gaining (ultimately) constitutional liberty obscured the fact that the Church of England stood for a true spiritual freedom. Certainly Hales of Eton, taking a grave view of schism and schismatics, nevertheless adds: '. . . were liturgies and public forms of service so framed, as that they admitted not of particular and private fancies, but contained only such things, as in which all Christians do agree, Schisms on opinion were utterly vanished.' [10] And Chillingworth can say that 'if instead of being zealous papists, earnest Calvinists, rigid Lutherans', men would 'become themselves, and be content that others should be plain and honest Christians', if men would believe the Scripture and live by it, since 'all necessary truths are plainly and evidently set down in scripture', then would follow 'unity of opinion', and 'notwithstanding any other differences that are or could be, unity of communion, and charity, and mutual toleration'. [11] If there is a naïve confidence here that anticipates Thomas Arnold, in the matter of simple truths on which all Christians can agree, there is also a tone and temper and freedom from institutional bigotry that justify Matthew Arnold's admiration and the perceptive tribute of a modern scholar: 'In addressing themselves to the individual, both Hales and Chillingworth were offering a broader and more permanent solution to the problem of persecution than could be achieved by any oaths of allegiance, or mechanical separation of Church and State.'[12] That a theme of moderation was not always expressed in moderate terms, however, is evident in Simon Patrick's 'Account of the New Sect of Latitude-Men', where he praises the golden mean of the Anglican Church in language hardly calculated to conciliate schismatics of any sect: 'As for the Rites and Ceremonies of Divine Worship, they do highly approve that virtuous mediocrity which our Church observes between the meretricious gaudiness of the Church of Rome and the squalid sluttery of fanatic conventicles.'[13]

Rather than a jealous clinging to prerogative or a vindictive and revengeful spirit, the proposals for union by these churchmen show often a large-minded concern for the future of religion in the nation, along with a turn for searching out the hidden or unconscious motive. The Calvinists, Chillingworth declares in his dedicatory epistle to King Charles I, surely cannot, at least the wiser among them, believe 'their own horrid assertions'. But 'this they must say, otherwise their only great argument from their damning us, and our not being so peremptory in damning them, because we hope unaffected ignorance may excuse them, would be lost'.[14] And Stillingfleet, fearing an 'infinite divisibility in churches' if current grounds for separation are admitted, concludes an analysis of the Puritan claims by saying 'it is not uniformity they dislike, but that they do not prescribe the terms of it'.[15]

That the terms proposed by Tillotson and Stillingfleet for union were generous, as Arnold maintained, and that they were wrecked by such stiff-necked Anglicans as Dr Jane, a fact he admitted, is borne out by the letter of a Presbyterian in 1689: 'Dr Tillotson was one that would have granted us all that we could have wished for both in the alteration of the liturgies, prayers, ceremonies, and all; but this Jean [Dr Jane, Canon of Christ Church, Oxford, chosen prolocutor of Convocation] is so stiff for the Church of England that he will grant nothing.'[16] What Tillotson had to contend with in drawing up his proposals is clear from an outburst in his *Argument for Union* in 1683. He was willing to include Presbyterians, and some of the Independents,

L

but as for 'Arians, Socinians, Anabaptists, Fifth-Monarchy men, sensual Millenaries, Behmenists, Familists, Seekers, Antinomians, Ranters, Sabbatarians, Quakers, Muggletonians—they may associate in a caravan, but cannot join in the communion of our Church'.

A study of such men as these, and still more of the 'latitude men', tends to give one the impression that sweetness and light did in the main pervade the Anglican hierarchy, even touching the austere portrait of Laud with a belated glow. But there were many Dr Janes, and it is well to listen to a historian from the other camp. John Stoughton was a Nonconformist theologian whom Arnold admired and with whom he was personally friendly. He was impartial and objective in a way that is not easy for religious historians, and reminded the reader, as Arnold tells us in a footnote, to 'bear in mind this circumstance', that in 1660 both Anglicans and Puritans (Presbyterians) 'were advocates for a national establishment of religion'.[17] In the see-saw battle of late 1660, he declared, and in the unequal struggle from then on, 'more of Christian consideration and charity is discernible on the Puritan than on the other side', and he added that 'in none of the Nonconformist publications of that day, have I ever seen anything like the scurrility poured upon them by their opponents'. Stoughton, who placed Richard Baxter above any of the Caroline bishops and divines in spiritual stature, quoted Baxter to the effect that Whichcote, Tillotson, and Stillingfleet were men who, had they been given control, could have healed matters in a short time. But theirs were not the voices that prevailed.

Despite his attacks on Dissenters for preventing the Church by separatism from fulfilling the law of her being, and his re-reading of religious history to show that largeness of mind and a true feeling for liberty were mainly found among Anglicans, Arnold did not find the Church faultless. In his address to the London clergy at Sion College, he hinted gently that they would do well to keep abreast of the times, to open their minds: 'There are times when . . . the very object of the Church and of the clergy, —the promotion of goodness through the instrumentality of the Christian religion and of the Bible,—is endangered, . . . from the want of a new and better construction . . . to put upon the Bible.'[18] Not only must they move with the times intellectually, they must move with the nation socially, which meant making common cause with the working classes, whose ideal, and rightly, was social transformation, the Kingdom of God on earth.

Leslie Stephen had described the Church of England as fashionable, privileged, entrenched, adding social contempt for Dissenters to theological hatred: 'In the Church of England you can always ask your spiritual pastor to dinner without fear of his using his knife in place of a fork, or enquiring into the welfare of your soul. This is a very great comfort, and implies freedom from many annoyances.'[19] As the novels of Trollope show, there was plenty of truth behind Stephen's sarcasm. Arnold insisted that alliance with wealth and power was not the 'authentic tradition' of the Anglican Church, not 'the line of her great men', but felt the sting of such attacks enough to spend a large part of his lecture warning the clergy that they must not only labour for the improvement of the working class, they must also feel 'a positive sympathy' with its ideal, which was the ideal for which the Church was founded. He agreed with Renan that 'the future will belong to that party which can get hold of the popular classes and elevate them', and for Arnold the last three words were as important as the rest of the sentence, if not for us as prophetic. That his advice in general was prophetic is clear enough. Bishop Henson tells us that 'when the twentieth century opened, the neo-Tractarians were still gaining ground', but that among the Anglican clergy at large 'traditional conservatism had largely given way to sentimental socialism, more ardent than intelligent or practical, but always highly exciting'.[20] This was not the earlier Christian Socialism of Kingsley and Maurice; it was rather a form of labour for social justice that accompanied the highest of Church doctrine.

Leaving to one side the effect of the growing secularism which was later to alter drastically the very field of conflict, we may ask why Arnold's proposals for comprehension, reasonable and practical and coherent, met with so little favour from either side. The trouble lay with his premises, or rather, it lay with his purely ethical and humanistic interpretation of those premises, and with the development of a national or even universal Church from them. For him the importance of conduct, and the need for unity and peace in the Church so that the higher self could work for the good of the people as a whole, made all other matters of little or no significance. This conviction made him overlook the continuing power of the doctrine of justification by faith, resting as it did on the individual's right to seek out, interpret, and serve his God by the promptings of a free conscience. In fact, he over-looked, or denied, the power of the voluntary principle, and so failed to see, or refused to admit, that Dissent was not so much a matter of theological doctrine as of human nature. As W. H. Dawson points out, it was part of the political instinct and education of the English, grown into a cherished right to in-dependence and liberty of choice.[21]

Replying to Arnold, R. W. Dale made a strong case for regard-ing Nonconformity rather than the Establishment as exhibiting development, as having great and original minds in spite of the restrictions imposed, as showing a better record of toleration, though he admits the force of much that Arnold says on these counts. But his main point was that the need and desire for the contact of the individual soul with God, the dynamic spirituality of justification through faith, was really the inspiration of Luther rather than moral grievances, and that this had been 'the true aim of every religious reformation'.[22] To urge the Dissenter to dismiss this belief, and the anti-State, anti-Catholic sentiments that went with it, was to ask him to disregard his conscience and deny his liberty of soul. Arnold was ironically informed that he should rather honour these men for fidelity to righteousness, and that Evangelicals must feel as the keenest censure his praise of them for staying in the Establishment with Ritualists whose practices and beliefs they detested as Romish and un-Christian.

Though Arnold had not been addressing himself to Uni-tarians, it was Martineau who put his finger on the really sore spot, in a letter to Arnold in 1871. Agreeing on the need for unity, and a 'natural' level of authority, he said, 'But the moral weight of such consent to a common worship depends on its inward reality; and it is fatal to demand for its sake sacrifices which carry with them a consciousness of radical insincerity.'[23] The fact was that comprehension was becoming less rather than more possible, and Dale put the matter bluntly and accurately, when the furore over disestablishment was at its height: 'It may be assumed . . . that whatever the legislature may attempt in the way of reorganizing the Church of England, the religious com-munities which are outside the Establishment will remain so.'[24]

If Arnold outraged zealous Nonconformists (and Evangelicals) with his confident assertion that the very essence of their faith, 'the Protestantism of the Protestant religion', was a mistaken

notion blindly held, he outraged High Churchmen by his treat-
ment of the Catholic elements of faith as mere poetry and illusion.
Puzzle at their champion changed to alarm as his opinions on
supernatural and revealed religion were more fully expressed, and
Dissenters noted with glee that even *Blackwood's*, not too unhappy
over laughs raised at Mr Miall or Mr Winterbotham, were
indignant at satirical allusions to a venerable nobleman and two
bishops. It was a critic of Anglo-Catholic sympathies, R. H.
Hutton, who saw the significance of Arnold's earlier religious
essays and the disturbing question they raised. He was attacking
Dissenters, said Hutton, 'on grounds which appear to mean that
they were wrong because there was nothing worth dissenting from
in the creeds of the Church. Have not such doctrines, casually
thrown out, a great deal more tendency to dissolve all Christian
Churches than to convict the Dissenting Churches of self-will?' [25]

Arnold's view of the Church as 'a great society for the pro-
motion of moral goodness' harmonized well enough with the vague
ideas and sentiments of many in the large and ill-defined middle
party to make them no more than uneasy at his grounds for
preserving and extending the Establishment. It was this party that
Newman satirically described in giving his later view of Anglican
Orders:

> As the matter stands, all we see is a hierarchical body, whose
> opinions through three hundred years compromise their acts, who do
> not themselves believe that they have the gifts which their zealous
> adherents ascribe to them, who in their hearts deny those sacramental
> formulas which their country's law obliges them to use, who con-
> scientiously shudder at assuming real episcopal or sacerdotal power,
> who resolve 'Receive the Holy Ghost' into a prayer, 'Whose sins ye
> remit are remitted' into a licence to preach, and 'This is my Body,
> this is my Blood' into an allegory. [26]

But if Arnold's view of the Church was only an uncomfortably
secular one to this broad middle party, it was worse than Pelagian
heresy to the growing Anglo-Catholicism which found in the
creeds and sacramental mysteries the treasure committed to the
Church's keeping by her Lord, to be cherished and interpreted by,
at the worst a faithful, at the best an inspired, apostolic succession.
The fervent conviction and sense of vocation motivating High
Anglicanism is summed up half a century later: 'It is because
Catholicism is credal that it has been able to safeguard the

worship of Christ in the modern world in a way in which Liberal Protestantism does not.'[27] Even the liberal and modernist Bishop Henson stated that 'the humanitarian view of Jesus, however disguised by devotional laudation, will work out in the decay and ultimate disappearance of the Christian Religion'.

There are two points to note about Arnold's proposals. One is that to him the English Church, being the nation in its religious aspect, must have comprehensiveness as its primary feature. Such an attitude was anathema to the sectarian or party spirit: to the Anglo-Catholic party taking its stand on the supremacy of the Church (the creeds and the apostolic tradition), and to the Evangelical party and Dissenters taking a stand on the supremacy of Scripture as interpreted in the free light of individual conscience. The second point is that to Arnold order came before liberty. This did not mean that one principle should be sacrificed to the other; it meant rather that the freedom worth having was a concomitant of order rather than of anarchy. He was insistent that class distinctions must dissolve, that property rights must give way to human rights, that there was in human nature an instinct for equality, an irresistible urge towards expansion of powers. But he was as firmly insistent that order came first, in the interests of reason, justice, and intelligible standards.

This preference is clear in his literary criticism when he praises the French Academy and says that provincialism in English prose shows the lack of any source of authoritative judgments. It is clear in his social and political criticism when he calls for State control of middle-class secondary education, and urges that concessions to solve the Irish problem be made in an atmosphere of calm and order, not of riots and threats. It is equally clear in his religious criticism, where his institutional view of the Church is reinforced by his view of human psychology: 'Obedience, strange as it may sound, is a real need of human nature;—above all, moral and religious obedience. . . . There are in the popular classes of every country forces of piety and religion capable of being brought into an alliance with the Church, the national society for the promotion of goodness.'[28] Arnold did not agree with the Wordsworth who placed 'one impulse from a vernal wood' above the sages, but rather with the Wordsworth who said, 'me this uncharter'd freedom tires'.

If Arnold was conscious of his preservative purpose, he was unconscious of the full effect of his dissolvent powers. How commonplace certain of his critical ideas were to become is remarked by H. L. Stewart, commenting on the infiltration of modernism even into the Anglo-Catholic citadel: 'Surely Matthew Arnold would have stared in amazement if he could have foreseen at least one group by whom his audacious speculations would so soon be taken as too obvious even for advocacy.' [29] But at the time, the radical and destructive features of his religious essays were what struck critical readers most forcibly and caused them to see his influence as part of the broadening stream of humanistic and scientific secularism. A *Quarterly* reviewer condemned the 'philosophers of culture' for their air of 'patronizing friendship' to Christianity, found that Pater followed Arnold in exhibiting an 'art of spiritualizing language' that degraded criticism through impressionism into poetical prose, and concluded that a spirit of liberalism was at fault throughout, manifested in 'a principle of self-worship' and in 'private and impossible ideals'.[30] When a critic whose ideas affected his contemporaries in this way urged the union of Protestants in 'a moral society for the promotion of goodness', it is little wonder that he seemed blind to the meaning of religious experience for either Dissenter or Churchmen.

Perhaps Arnold was attempting the impossible. He tried to direct the river of religion so that it would receive every tributary of thought, yet, with institutional marges uncrumbled, keep its moral current flowing clear and pure and strong from sources both lofty and profound. Certainly he was plain enough about the Church and its reason for existing. As a great society for the promotion of goodness, it lived by communicating the primitive gospel, which was 'the good news of an immense renovation and transformation of this world'. For, he believed, 'this was the ideal of Jesus:—the establishment on earth of God's kingdom, of felicity, not by the violent processes of our Fifth Monarchy men, or of the German Anabaptists, or of the French Communists, but by the establishment on earth of God's righteousness'.[31]

3. INFLUENCE AND RELEVANCE

CHAPTER VIII

A Summary of Arnold's Position

Man muss sich immerfort verändern, erneuen, verjüngen, um
nicht zu verstocken.

GOETHE, quoted in *Note-books*

It may well be that for harmonizing Hebraism with Hellenism
more preparation is needed than man has yet had. But failures
do something, as well as successes, towards the final achieve-
ment.

St Paul and Protestantism

A: The Basic Principle

THE Victorian conflict, the Victorian dilemma, the Victorian
compromise—critic after critic has summed up the Victorian
age as one of conflicting issues for which the major figures tried
to find a synthesis, a middle way, or a hierarchy of values. They
are seen as having failed, and the failure is variously attributed
to timidity, inconsistency, a biased approach, or a basic confusion
as to the real nature of the issues involved. We have considered
Arnold's attempt to be 'a healing and reconciling influence' in the
warfare of science and religion (or of naturalism and super-
naturalism). His ideas met with interest and sympathy from many
readers, but received rough treatment from those who found him
a shallow or inconsistent thinker and from those who, more
emotional in their response, saw his criticism as a force destructive
of their belief in a loving and personal God. The diversity of
response is more fully examined later in this chapter. That there
was a conflict in his thinking has been shown. The late E. K.
Brown's thesis of a heavily damaging psychological fracture
maintains that this conflict, productive of irritations and contra-
dictions, crippled the critic in his efforts to be disinterested and
objective. But it may rather be seen as a fruitful interplay among
ideas, a philosophic polarity of attitudes that ensures continuing
vitality and relevance. In any case, the basis of the conflict, or
tension, needs closer investigation before we attempt a summary
of Arnold's religious and ethical position.

The key essay to an understanding of Arnold as critic, and,
if no philosopher, as a man with a philosophic turn of mind, is

The Function of Criticism at the Present Time. Coming after the attack on Colenso for confusing the spheres of science and religion, at a time when Arnold was shaping his own ideas on man as a social and religious being, the essay is a manifesto of method and principle. The main ideas are well known—that there are alternating epochs of concentration and expansion, that the important function of the critic is to prepare for the next expansive epoch by knowing and propagating the best that has been thought and said in the world, that such an endeavour must be disinterested, aloof from the sphere of practice. We are told that the literary critic must know foreign thought and foreign literature; that the political critic, if attached to no party, is free to meet dithyrambic fatuity with a reminder of ugly conditions and needed reforms; that the religious critic will expect modern scholars to understand the nature and needs of the religious spirit before advancing their fresh interpretations. With all partial achievement criticism will be patient but firm, for its business is 'to be perpetually dissatisfied with these works, while they perpetually fall short of a high and perfect ideal'. Above all, the critic must be flexible and open-minded. He must avoid any commitment to a system of ideas, as he does to a school in literature, a party in politics, a sect in religion. He must always, like the statesman Burke on the subject of revolutionary activity, be capable of making 'a return upon himself'.

That this phrase points to the fundamental principle in the whole of Arnold's criticism is suggested by his ringing the changes upon it. Puritanism must learn to make 'a return upon its own thoughts'; the Liberals fail to make a 'return upon their own minds'; it is a merit of St Paul that 'he goes back upon himself again and again'; we should, he says in his essay on Emerson, 'return upon' the friends of our youth, and surrender our illusions. Now this is in part the classical doctrine of the golden mean, the Aristotelian avoidance of extremes, and in part the example of Sainte-Beuve, whose signal merit it was to oppose the medium in which he was whenever 'the currents of that medium' seemed 'excessive and tyrannous'. Effective as a principle in giving balance and flexibility to the critic, it was effective also as a critical method in dealing with the experiences and ideas receiving his attention. It was not only to Greek flexibility (*eutrapelia*) and to the lucid disinterestedness of Sainte-Beuve that Arnold owed his sense of the importance of this capacity to 'make a return upon oneself'. Strange as it may seem, the vigorous and hard-hitting Dr Arnold was fully aware of it, even if his convictions were of a kind to make partisanship irresistible. He lamented the difficulty of speaking out when congregations were of mixed social classes. We should dwell on our own faults, 'not that the poor have not theirs also, but because it does *us* nothing but harm to think of those, as it seems to afford a sanction to our own'. In attacking Newman and his friends for exalting the mediæval church at the expense of Protestantism, Dr Arnold was quite clear on the nature of their historical bias: 'There are few stranger and sadder sights than to see men judging of whole periods of the history of mankind with the blindness of party-spirit, never naming one century without expressions of contempt or abhorrence, never mentioning another but with extravagant and undistinguishing admiration.' [1]

If *The Function of Criticism* is the essay most clearly setting forth the critical principle which governed Arnold's approach and shaped his recommendations, *Pagan and Mediæval Religious Sentiment*, also of the year 1864, is the essay in which the application is most perfectly illustrated. Arnold gives a delightful picture of a happy, sensuous pagan world at its best, and points to Pompeii as witness of the ennui and surfeit that must come. He then gives us the mediæval St Francis accepting the whole of life, 'transfigured by the power of a spiritual emotion', but sees the self-torturing doubts as a sign that 'the measure of spiritualism had been overpassed'. Life needs both: 'Human nature is neither all senses and understanding, nor all heart and imagination.' True, the 'religion of sorrow' has a great advantage over the 'religion of pleasure'; not even the Renascence revival of paganism nor the 'sinister mockery' of a Heine can alter its superiority as 'a stay for the mass of mankind'. Yet at this point Arnold turns back upon himself to give the old pagan world, the Greek world, its due recognition, and finds that the modern spirit is best expressed by the fusion of Greece and Judæa, the reason and the imagination, summed up for us by the phrase he coins, the 'imaginative reason'. Sophocles is as great a figure as Dante, and if in him the 'thinking-power a little overbalances the religious sense', in Dante 'the religious sense overbalances the thinking-power'. Poetry is 'the priestess of the imaginative reason', and no poets have so fully shown and so well satisfied this blend of powers as the poets from Pindar to Sophocles.

In all its operations this principle of redress and restraint, of balance and flexibility, is in a tradition of humanistic writing which, as I suggested with reference to biblical criticism, looks back to Erasmus and forward to Edmund Wilson. Described as one of 'the absolute idealists who, at the same time, are thoroughly moderate', Erasmus offered an 'imagined world' that was 'an amalgamation of pure classicism . . . and pure, biblical Christianity'.[2] His own critical principles reflect a philosophy that reveals, not logic and system, but rather a set of attitudes that are eclectic in allegiance and tolerant in application: 'This sort of philosophy is rather a matter of disposition than of syllogisms, rather of life than of disputation, rather of inspiration than of erudition, rather of transformation than of logic. . . . Moreover, though no one has taught us this so absolutely and effectively as Christ, yet also in pagan books much may be found that is in accordance with it.'[3] This humanizing of Christ into a reasonable being and ethical teacher, the attempt to make sweetness and light prevail in regions full of the conflict of passions and superstitions, suggests a 'philosophy' of middle principles akin to what Arnold was trying to work out for himself.

A clearer parallel to his method, however, may be seen in Edmund Wilson's interesting tribute to the Jewish ideas about morals, which as principles of rectitude and justice and human fellow-feeling have resisted changes in time and locale. After all the criticism, and all the difficulties of language and of time sense, something remains, 'something that has done a good deal to sustain the morale of the Gentile as well as that of the Jew through the strictly historical happenings . . . of the last three thousand years'. Yet the prophetic tone and the 'prophetic verb', giving hope by the escape from historical time, may bring something obsessive and, as all four religions have shown (Judaism, Christianity, Islam, and Marxism), a suicidal intolerance, suicidal because productive of mutual hate: 'This sense of transcendent principle has always had to be corrected by the realistic observation, the practical worldliness, of the Græco-Roman tradition. It is the reciprocal relation of the two that has made up what there is of our civilization.'[4]

When Arnold fuses this 'reciprocal relation' by means of 'the imaginative reason', he reaches the climax of his endeavour, the completion of his critical doctrine. The synthesis has been achieved, the dialectic successfully resolved. The phrase is persuasive and challenging. Yet it is a phrase that defies precise definition, that vaguely suggests transcendent mysteries, a departure from the horizontal to the vertical. The critic has left the plains and foothills of historical experience and humanistic judgment and for the moment stands tip-toe on the misty mountain-top. Long before, he had written to Clough that he was not one for 'profound thoughts' and 'mighty spiritual workings', but for 'a distinct seeing of my way as far as my own nature is concerned'. And he had also said of his search that he would plant no post not 'perfectly in light and firm'. But the contemplation of human nature as revealed in himself, in literature, and in the behaviour of social, political, and religious man, led him to set up as facts of experience what could only be objects of speculative thought, uncertainly distinguished in the shadowy world beyond the last well-lighted post. When the reconciling and synthesizing power of Arnold's critical principle was extended to operate between the known and the unknown, it was asked to do a work for which its fluid and humanist character was necessarily inadequate. Introducing the ideal and eternal in reciprocal relation to the pragmatic and historical, Arnold set up a tension of opposites that could not, and perhaps should not, be reconciled. No amount of appeal to verification could hide the fact that an act of faith, or at least an hypothesis, was called for in postulating a metaphysical or irrational element of experience. And one return upon himself that Arnold would not make was to recognize, and admit, that he had added just such an element.

What happened in his case is in fact what can also happen in the thinking of the strict rationalist, if we are to accept the verdict of J. M. Keynes on the limitation of certain philosophical techniques:

The rationalist is always faced by the same dilemma. . . . In spite of his attempts to be empirical, to return to experience, . . . an unwanted constant is forever appearing in his equations; a joker keeps on turning up in the pack, placed there unwittingly by himself; it is a hypothesis which he has made, which unconsciously he has converted into an ideal or an absolute, and which destroys the empirical nature of his work.[5]

Keynes directs his criticism to a philosophically systematic rationalism as applied to ethics, without, let it be added, coming to the conclusion that a rational approach can be dispensed with in questions of value. Yet the intellectual shift or turn described is akin to that of Arnold, who retains his humanistic criteria, but appeals to an eternal or constant principle that is neither fully realizable in experience nor clearly demonstrable in Nature or history. A generation later he might have been content with an 'as if' formulation on a pragmatic basis, but he belonged to a generation which, though learning to do without God, could not do without absolutes, especially in the moral sphere. Speaking of Stephen's attempt to find in evolution a God, 'a law which will govern the moral relations of the individual to society', Noel Annan observes, 'This desire to find metaphysical sanctions gives Victorian agnosticism the appearance of a new nonconformist sect.'[6]

Another way of putting it is that Arnold followed the natural direction of a sensitive and thoughtful mind in exploring both the psychological and the cosmological areas beyond the boundaries of the self-evident and the verifiable, yet claimed for his intuitions a consenting witness from general human testimony, uniform enough to be 'scientifically' valid. This, in effect, is to equate the findings of the poet and humanist with those of science, not merely as equally important truths, which is one thing, but as truths similarly verifiable, which is quite another thing.

We see this extension of experience in Arnold's psychological dualism, which functions in two ways, as a distinction between the higher and lower natures, and as a distinction between the apparent and the true or real self. The former is a relatively simple matter, and the extension is the hypothesis of a cosmic moral law. Up to that point the dualism merely affirms moral values, which can be pragmatically tested in behaviour and judged by accepted standards. As an explanation this stoical-Christian dualism may seem naïve and unrealistic to modern psychological and anthropological science, but its frame of reference is experiential and normative. When we turn to the other form of psychological dualism, however, we find the extension of experience operating within the psyche itself. An element not merely of complexity but of mystery has been added in the interpretation of experience offered by intuition or imaginative insight. What is this 'true self' of which Arnold speaks so often, this buried or hidden self of which a man becomes aware in moments when a power like love has heightened his perception, or the busy world has ceased to distract him at the level of his superficial self?

> Deep and broad, where none may see,
> Spring the foundations of that shadowy throne
> Where man's one nature, queen-like, sits alone,
> Centred in a majestic unity.

The contrast between the distracted superficial self and the true and profound self is a more elusive idea than the moral contrast of the higher and lower natures. In Bosanquet we get a metaphysical and idealist formulation of such a doctrine, the true self shown as striving to transcend the world of appearances, into a reality free of the limitations of the finite. Arnold's distaste for metaphysics prevented any such formulation. In effect, he preferred a poetic if variable statement of what he felt to be a profound truth about the self to a logically convincing philosophical statement remote from experiential emotion. What he himself meant by the buried self is never quite clear. Sometimes it seems to be soul, sometimes a stern and stoical power by which man keeps his integrity, sometimes the Spinozist stream of tendency by which he fulfils the law of his being, a definition which shows Arnold passing through metaphor into metaphysics without admitting it. But whatever it was, to Arnold it was the compelling object of man's lifelong search, the sense of which filled him often with a strange loneliness that reminds us of De la Mare's poem 'Haunted'. Expressed in his favourite imagery of water, it seems to be a subterranean current reached only by the imaginative piercing of more than one layer of consciousness:

> Below the surface-stream, shallow and light
> Of what we *say* we feel—below the stream,
> As light, of what we *think* we feel—there flows
> With noiseless current strong, obscure and deep,
> The central stream of what we feel indeed.

Arnold had both the philosophic mind which seeks to reconcile and to synthesize, and the poet's imagination which prefers intuited findings to an orderly philosophic solution. The 'imaginative reason' is one of those happy but arbitrary turns of phrase that light up experience and literature for us without being really clear. There is no similar phrase resolving the other polarities of his critical thought. We must have equality, but also the saving remnant; we must make reason *and* the will of God prevail; our freedom is meaningful only if it is freedom in obedience to the best. Sometimes the tension resolves itself in our minds, as reason

M

and the will of God will do in a Platonist or Spinozist line of thought. But sometimes it remains, a polarity of experience that may be in itself a condition of dynamic life. With a philosophical aim ethically controlled, Arnold was neither content to sacrifice humanistic sanctions, and so gain a metaphysical transcendence free of limitations and contradictions, nor willing to forgo his longing for absolute and eternal truth and remain content with a solution for the human problem at a purely human level. It is because he did neither that he remains of such challenging interest. The tension remains between the idealistic challenge to humanity to live at the highest attainable level, and to strive ever higher, and the realistic knowledge that this is a slow and painful achievement which, since it assumes a partial realization of the divine in man, is virtually impossible.

Between some of Arnold's polarities the return upon one's self or the pointing of the middle way is simple enough; in other cases it is difficult to the point of paradox. But the paradoxes, like the Christian paradoxes, are fruitful. The very condition of development, of life, is the unremitting effort to resolve the unresolvable conflict, to seek to reduce a tension that by its very nature is permanent. Only by accepting the very tension he struggles to reduce can man ensure himself a continuing hope and vitality. 'Liberalism', says Lionel Trilling, 'does not fail because it follows Arnold's idealism; rather, it fails because it does not follow his realism.' A comment by H. J. Muller points up the value of the paradox involved in Arnold's continued search for a synthesis. Finding in Arnold a diverse ideal, a non-partisan attitude, and a capacity always to return from his absolute or eternal to the world of man, Muller concludes: 'If, in an age of violence, the attitudes he engenders cannot alone save civilization, it is worth saving chiefly because of such attitudes.' [7]

B: Arnold's Ethical Idealism

The distinguishing marks of Arnold's religious thought may be seen as eclecticism and an individual use of the principle of accommodation, accommodation to a large middle range of religiously inclined but dissatisfied people and, some of his critics would insist, to his own limitations. His position in his early poems and letters is compounded of religious agnosticism, philosophical tentativeness, and moral certitude. The changes are rung on moods of spiritual despair, romantic nostalgia, and intellectual uncertainty. Yet the influence of writers like Senancour is countered from the beginning by the powerful combination of the Stoics, Carlyle, Emerson, Thomas Arnold, and Goethe, and it is the moral purposiveness of life, never once doubted, which more than any philosophical urge drives Arnold in his search for 'an Idea of the World'.

Here Goethe becomes the guiding star, with his naturalistic and cultural norm, his humanism which puts the standard 'once for all inside every man', and his emphasis on morality as the main part of religion. He in turn leads Arnold to Spinoza, the source of a non-teleological view of the universe, an active stoicism, and a stress on adequate ideas, a trinity of teachings which had attracted and held Goethe himself. In Spinoza Arnold discovers a philosopher to whom he can pay unreserved tribute, one who, with his 'positive and vivifying atmosphere', can satisfy both his reason and his imagination, both his religious sense and his moral determinism. It is not the mathematical rationalism of the *Ethics* which attracts Arnold, however. It is rather the practical teaching of the *Tractatus Theologico-Politicus*, where religion, the Bible, and Christianity are interpreted in the light of human nature and human experience, purified of irrational excrescences, and justified as a permanent contribution to the adequate realization of man's distinctively human nature, a nature whose goal is the achieving, as fully as possible, that moral perfection which is one aspect of God.

In progressively developing his moral stature, then, man is not only obeying the omnipresent God of Spinoza, but is following the dictates of his own higher nature, that level of his being at which reason is operative. Here Coleridge's stress on the natural truth of Christianity, and the devotion of the Cambridge Platonists to reason as the 'candle of the Lord', come in to reinforce the teaching of Spinoza and the psychological dualism which Arnold derived in part from Epictetus and Marcus Aurelius. The reason, difficult to define because of the lack of theoretic distinctions in Arnold's usage, is no philosophic rationalism, but a faculty akin to intuition, touched with the imagination, and dependent upon the historical witness of experience which Arnold calls upon for verification. He follows Butler and Vinet in finding Christianity and religion eminently reasonable, and finds the distinctive and necessary mark of 'the modern spirit' to be the 'imaginative reason'.

This phrase anticipates the high place Arnold later assigns to poetry as the main part of religion; the best poetry, like Christianity, satisfies the thinking-power (reason) and the religious sense (imagination and feeling). The imaginative reason, then, is for Arnold the power by which man is able to comprehend moral and religious truth, and, since the findings are subjective, agreement must be assumed by an appeal to what man's higher nature has always found and still finds to be reasonable, by an appeal, in other words, to history and experience. Arnold not only makes this appeal confidently, but he finds scientific certainty in these subjective facts of experience; he tries to give permanent validity to their moral authority by regarding them as a law and calling the law God.

Arnold is met here by Huxley, who accepts the moral imperative and even the religious sense as facts of experience, capable of verification. This does not mean an identity of point of view. Huxley admits the existence of certain feelings as facts, but this is not to say that they are susceptible of proofs sufficiently rational or empirical to permit of objectification. A comment by Gilson is suggestive. After pointing out that feelings about God 'are not proofs but facts', Gilson continues:

> Whether we make it the result of spontaneous judgment of reason, with Thomas Aquinas; or an innate idea, with Descartes; or an intellectual intuition, with Malebranche; or an idea born of the unifying power of human reason, with Kant; or a phantom of human imagination, with Thomas Huxley, this common notion of God is there as a practically universal fact whose speculative value may well be disputed, but whose existence cannot be denied. The only problem is for us to determine the truth value of this notion.[8]

Huxley, we may say, is in agreement with Arnold on this finding of the 'imaginative reason', that the necessity for right conduct and the existence of a religious sense are experiential facts of distinctively human nature, but the agreement does not extend to the objectifying and idealizing by Arnold of these experiences in religious and even Christian terms.

In this steady moving away from his earlier agnostic and stoical naturalism, Arnold not only leaves Goethe and Spinoza, but reveals wherein he differs from Renan, to whose psychological and historical interpretation of Christianity he owed something, and with whose emphasis on the importance of conduct he was in complete accord. His objectifying of moral power in a law to which he gives the name of God reveals an idealizing tendency absent in the more thoroughgoing rationalism of Renan, and his exalting of Jesus from an oracle of 'sweet reasonableness' into a moral absolute is very different from Renan's romantic and thoroughly human conception of Jesus. In his search for stability and authority, Arnold develops the Spinozist 'law of being' which informs his earlier definitions into an objectified moral principle which man obeys and which, by virtue of clothing it in the poetic symbolism of traditional religion, he may even worship. Now it is true that this principle is an extension of man's higher (rational) self and preserves a reciprocal relationship with the moral experience of man, but it is also true that something of the Ideal and the Absolute has been erected on a humanistic basis. This confusing of two spheres of being and two sets of values is what motivates Bradley's attack. In substance, Bradley asks how a moral 'absolute', which is offered as a projection of man's necessarily limited, tentative, and various experience, and for which only empirical verification is admitted or adduced, can be regarded as, in effect, an object of faith.

The criticism is just. Arnold is trying to have the best of two worlds. Having jettisoned the whole of orthodox dogma and belief, Arnold finds his 'Idea of the World' in the stoical naturalism and scientific humanism of Goethe, while his 'imaginative reason' discovers, in the accommodation of Spinozist rationalism to human nature, its needs, and experiences, the clue to the restoration and preservation of moral and religious values. But this position does not content him. Whether it is because the voices of his father and Newman continue to sound in his ears, or simply because of temperamental bias, Arnold imposes upon his humanist and naturalist creed a kind of imaginative and emotional dualism for which there is no intellectual basis in his religion of historical and psychological experience. To Arnold the resultant lack of philosophical system, inviting attack from the logician, is more than compensated for by what he considers the adequate psychological analysis and the accurate reflection of man's emotional and imaginative experience. To one who believes in logical reasoning (as opposed to something called the 'imaginative reason') or in the authority of intellectual dogma (as against the appeal to relative human experience), the whole direction of Arnold's religious thought appears irritatingly confused or dangerously subversive, according to the emphasis of the critic. T. S. Eliot not only repeats Bradley's indictment, but makes the further charge that *Marius the Epicurean* and even Wilde's *De Profundis* may be regarded as lineal descendants of *Culture and Anarchy* and *Literature and Dogma*: 'The total effect of Arnold's philosophy is to set up Culture in the place of Religion, and to leave Religion to be laid waste by the anarchy of feeling. And Culture is a term which each man not only may interpret as he pleases, but must indeed interpret as he can. So the gospel of Pater follows naturally upon the prophecy of Arnold.' [9]

Difficulties that arise are mainly due to Arnold's descriptive, rather than definitive, method and his failure to discriminate between a loose literary and an exact philosophical use of terms. The empirical verification so often claimed by him really consists of the subjective findings of humanistic culture. His failure at times to establish clearly his own meaning for the word 'nature' forces the reader to do his own clarifying. The reason, as Arnold uses it, is often intuition, imaginative insight, or experiential memory. It is akin to Newman's 'implicit' reason, as he defines it in one of his University sermons. Having developed the analogy of a mountaineer scaling a steep cliff by a unique combination of powers blended of instinct, unconscious memory, and practised skill in exploring terrain, Newman concludes:

It is not too much to say that the stepping by which great geniuses scale the mountains of truth is as unsafe and precarious to men in general, as the ascent of a skilful mountaineer up a literal crag. It is a way which they alone can take, and its justification lies in their success. And such mainly is the way in which all men, gifted or not gifted, commonly reason,—not by rule, but by an inward faculty. Reasoning, then, or the exercise of Reason, is a living spontaneous energy within us, not an art. [10]

It is not easy to classify Arnold as a religious teacher. Even to those who found him stimulating and helpful, he was something of a puzzle, in spite of his saying that our first concern is to keep our religious ideas 'clear of puzzle'. Some modern readers, like the radical and positivistic among his contemporaries, have found his culture academic and his religion thin. But this is to ignore the practical human emphasis emerging at the most significant points in his work and his ability to make a 'return upon himself'. To his conviction that the kingdom of God, a reflection of the higher nature within man, is a kingdom to be established on this earth, and that to follow Christ is to assist in this end, we may add one of his most measured and judicious humanistic utterances, in a preface pleading for the continued study of biblical as well as of classical literature:

Our acts are, it is most true, infinitely more important than our thoughts and studies; but the bearing which thoughts and studies may have upon our acts is not enough considered. And the power of animation and consolation in those thoughts and studies, which, beginning by giving us a hold upon a single great work, end with giving us a hold upon the history of the human spirit, and the course, drift, and scope, of the career of our race as a whole, cannot be over-estimated. Not pathetic only, but profound also, and of the most solid substance, was that reply made by an old Carthusian monk to the trifler who asked him how he had managed to get through his life:—'*Cogitavi dies antiquos, et annos aeternos in mente habui.*' [11]

Using the classification in E. A. Burtt's *Types of Religious Philosophy*, we may now attempt to analyse Arnold's position with relation to some of the larger movements in religious thought. With neither Catholic nor Protestant theology, it is clear, has Arnold anything in common. He rejected both metaphysical knowledge and literal inspiration. Yet his religion, despite his appeals to observation and experience, is no more in line with the materialism of empirical science than with the older rationalistic science. Nor is his humanism the same thing as the philosophy of religion going by that name, although this more radical development is in many ways a logical outcome of teachings like his. For the radical humanism of today, which can take the extreme forms of a sentimental humanitarianism and a completely secular and even dialectical movement such as communism, goes far beyond the limits set by a humanism like Arnold's. It would dismiss the name 'God', since such a term is apt to be misleading in a religious philosophy which rejects theism. It refuses devout allegiance to a religious teacher of two thousand years ago, many of whose teachings, it alleges, are inadequate to solve the problems of modern industrial and urbanized society, and finds dangers in preserving 'the Jesus stereotype'. It rejects the idea of a moral absolute or law, on the grounds that new situations and conditions arise which demand a fresh orientation even of moral attitudes.

The moral humanist of Arnold's type can associate himself, as Paul Elmer More did, with a religious philosophy like that of

Anglo-Catholicism. Or he can follow Santayana in regarding
Christianity as a beautiful myth, 'an imaginative interpretation
of the moral quest of mankind', the beauty and sweetness of which
must be preserved to the enrichment of our better natures, at least
until art and science can furnish us with effective substitutes in
the way of forms, symbols, and moral affirmations. It is in fact
this very flexibility of humanism as a creed which makes it, in the
opinion of T. S. Eliot, a moral and spiritual menace. He blames
Arnold, and Babbitt, for hastening the disintegration of distinc-
tively religious values. A 'pure' humanism he can tolerate, as the
mark of a few valuable individuals (like Babbitt), and even of an
intellectual aristocracy. But it can never be the bond in a society
nor, as it attempts to be in its 'impure' forms, a substitute for
religion.

There is no such thing as 'just morality', in Mr Eliot's opinion.
Faith must precede morals, and the richer and fuller life belongs
to the Christian who accepts dogma and the supernatural.
'Christian morals gain immeasurably in richness and freedom by
being seen as the consequence of Christian faith, and not as the
imposition of tyrannical and irrational habit.' [12] A restored faith,
then, must replace such sanctions for conduct as Arnold's 'best
self' and 'cumulative human experience', Babbitt's 'inner checks',
and Bertrand Russell's 'gospel of happiness', all of which, diverse
as the opinions of the writers in question may be, are taken by Mr
Eliot to represent the dangers in a humanistic norm capable of
degenerating into, or allying itself with, humanitarian sentimen-
tality, hedonistic materialism, or mere moral anarchy. It is the
point of view of those who, appalled at the prospect of moral
and spiritual chaos, and critical of persisting attempts to replace
religion by morality, science, or socialism, advocate the return to
a Church, a body of religious dogma, and a philosophical dualism.

Another movement, equally elastic and diverse, and described
by Burtt under the rather capacious title of Modernism, comes
close in essentials to Arnold's position. The modernists differ from
the fundamentalists in accepting the findings of science and the
Higher Criticism and in feeling that whatever is of enduring
significance in religion and in Christianity is untouched by the
dissolution of theological orthodoxy. They differ from the radical
humanists in being concerned with a specifically religious ex-
perience and in regarding Jesus as eternally supreme among
religious and moral teachers. Fusing the emotional subjectivism

of the Schleiermachian tradition with a 'scientific' recourse to empirical verification, the modernist achieves a point of view blended of the traditional and the revolutionary, a position fluid, relative, and adaptable and, of course, condemned by Catholic, fundamentalist, and radical humanist as muddled and inconsistent.

There is much in Arnold, however, that does not suit with the doctrines of the modernist, for instance his humanistic admission that science and art may some day take the place of traditional religious sanctions for morality and his equating of God with moral law. In the one case the modernist is less, in the other more, revolutionary than Arnold. The modernist, applying the evolutionary concept to the religious experience itself, contemplates a God who is the object of progressive discovery and redefinition by the religious consciousness. Arnold's definition may have helped to initiate this tentativeness, but his own 'not ourselves' at least was consistently a power making for righteousness, and a force recognized by the rationally governed power for conduct in man himself, not a cosmic shadow cast by the personality and consciousness of man.

The remaining major movement in religion is described by Burtt as ethical idealism, and in its modern form takes its rise in the philosophy of Kant and his successors. Allowing a few concessions to modernism and humanism, I think we may say that Arnold belongs here. The distinguishing features are the grounding of religion itself in ethics, and the denying or ignoring of metaphysical knowledge:

> To take this position is to make a daring assertion of man's moral competence. It means claiming the right to reinterpret the nature of God in terms of our moral experience, instead of humbly submitting that experience to the judgment of a God believed to possess moral character and authority independent of our interpretations. It is to say: God must be what man's moral insight demands that he be; if not, he is no God.[13]

This is not only, as Burtt suggests, a reconstruction of religion from the autonomy conferred on morals by agnosticism. It is also the translation of a personal need into a moral certainty, which is felt to be necessary to the living of a full, good, and distinctively human life. As such it reflects Arnold's attempt exactly. Pfleiderer has no doubt as to Arnold's proper category. 'Matthew

Arnold', he tells us, 'has advocated, as a substitute for supernatural religion, an ethical idealism very much of the same nature as that of Fichte.'[14] He is not much impressed by the 'Eternal not ourselves'. Since it might be either a real, efficient power, which would suggest a theistic point of view, or a merely operational natural law, which would reflect a scientific positivism, Pfleiderer concludes that the whole idea is 'a remnant of mystical speculation' and a further proof that Arnold was quite right to disclaim any aptitude for philosophical thinking.

On the whole process of ethical idealizing, however, Burtt makes favourable comment. It is merely a 'conscious recognition of a fundamental aspect of religious progress frequently exemplified'. The changes in the Hebrew God from a jealous, martial chieftain to a just and merciful ruler, then to a father tenderly caring for the individual soul looking to him, themselves reflect the tendency to objectify and idealize man's highest moral development. This is essentially what Arnold does when he ignores the basis of empirical relativism and exalts the moral imperative into an absolute, the Eternal not ourselves.

A would-be 'practical' movement emerged from the general current of ethical idealism in the form of ethical culture societies. In an address outlining the ethical religion he wishes to see, Felix Adler spoke as follows:

It differs from orthodoxy in the fact that the sting that gives us no rest is the torment of being in the wrong relations [i.e. to one another, to society]. It differs from practical reform movements, in that the question they answer is 'How can society be made different?' whereas our question is, 'How can we be made over by the introduction into our life of a regenerative principle?' And thirdly, it differs from the ethics of liberal churches, in that the liberal movement in a certain sense is bound to ethics of the past, while we would look into the future unhampered and free.[15]

The fusion at the end with radical humanism is noticeable, but the significant emphasis is on the 'regenerative principle' and the practical relationship which yet is not the busy practicality of social activity. Such aims are in line with the recurrent moral and cultural emphases in Arnold's writing. Indeed, another address in the same series, entitled 'Forerunners of our Faith: Matthew Arnold and Ethical Clarification', suggests a degree of conscious discipleship. The speaker finds that Arnold not only announces 'a religion of pure morality and ethics', but surpasses Emerson and Carlyle in his stress upon the principle of continuity in human development and achieves his main service in the redefinition and clarification of the ethical ideal. In this way Arnold avoids the 'freakishness' of much contemporary culture and is a great help in satisfying religious needs, for example, in his dictum that 'man philosophizes best alone; he worships best with the community'. He is, the speaker concludes, with an obvious reminiscence of Arnold's own comment on Emerson, a friend to those who would live in the spirit.

A more perceptive tribute is contained in Professor Lowry's reminder, that Arnold presents us still with 'a living faith in what is excellent'. For Arnold's message, in spite of its appeal to ethical culture societies, is not the blend of easy moral optimism and mystical utterance which produces cults. The 'walking by the best light we have', as he knew, is not easy. He tried to ease the shocks and pains of a 'period of transition' by offering an ethical ideal suffused with emotion as a substitute for dissolving dogma, and he insisted that the only psychologically sound sanction for right conduct lay in the positive end of happiness, and conversely, that only by following right conduct did we achieve this happiness. By the standards either of dogmatic orthodoxy or of a hedonistic calculus such reasoning is unsound; by the standards of Arnold's ethical idealism, seeking conformity with the highest and best self in man, it is a profound truth taught by all the great teachers of morality who were his masters. The kind of happiness he meant, the priority of inwardness over 'the social idea', and the simplicity and sincerity which marked the deepening of Arnold's culture into religion through an ethical centre common to both are all best expressed for us in his own words:

I have always insisted that the only right way to an outward trans-formation was through the inward one, and that the business for us and for our age was the latter. In *Literature and Dogma* I have pointed out that the real upshot of the teaching of Jesus Christ was this: 'If every *one* would mend *one*, we should have a new world.' . . . To insist on this new world, on felicity, as the result of the widespread cultivation of personal religion, and as the goal for mankind to have in view, is most important, and, I think, is overlooked by many who insist on personal religion.[16]

C: A Survey of Critical Opinion

On the question of institutional religion nothing need be added to
the points of view given in the preceding chapter, except to
suggest why it is that the exasperated and partisan response to
Arnold's ideas on Church and Dissent was no sign of continuing
vitality. One reason is that the removal of legal and civil dis-
abilities took the aggressiveness out of Dissent, while at the same
time the aggressiveness of Anglo-Catholic doctrine made com-
prehension impossible. Indeed the spirit of sectarianism increased
within the Church itself, until Bishop Henson could say that,
whereas Arnold's claim for the superiority of the Establishment on
the grounds of intellectual distinction and leadership might have
applied from the seventeenth to the nineteenth centuries, 'the
clergy are now largely severed from the main stream of English
life'.[17] The larger reason is, however, the general loss of interest
in the question itself, whether the division is seen as due to forms of
worship or to differing dogmatic beliefs. It is simply a part of the
whole fundamental shift to an increasingly secularized world. As
T. S. Eliot says in The Idea of a Christian Society, the problem is no
longer one of the Established Church against Dissent, but one of
living the Christian life in a society increasingly de-Christianized
by a number of steadily mounting pressures.

In the matter of biblical criticism or interpretation there is
more to say, even though a secular industrial society may be as
indifferent to the Higher Criticism as to the problems of Non-
conformity. Arnold's achievement here was of two kinds. In
the first place, his interpretation of Pauline teaching as primarily
ethical and psychological was sufficiently original and challenging
to receive serious scholarly attention. In reviews of St Paul and
Protestantism, even those by doughty Nonconformist critics, there
was a marked difference in tone between the response to Arnold's
views on Dissent and the consideration of his Pauline exegesis.
Secondly, there was his larger critical principle that the Bible
should be read as a literary not a scientific statement of man's
moral and religious experience. Even reviewers who disparaged
his scholarship, describing Literature and Dogma and God and the
Bible as a popular summing-up of theories and discoveries already
advanced, admitted the power and influence of his main teaching,
and the recognition of this influence became virtually unanimous
following his death in 1888. W. C. Brownell expressed the general

verdict in 1901: 'No commentator on the Scriptures has ever
accomplished a more cogent and seductive work than his showing
of the *use* to which the truly religious soul may put [the Bible]. . . .
He brought out its general interest and rescued it from the hands
of the specialist. He treated it properly as a branch of culture.' [18]
The fact that the interpretative ideas Arnold advanced or cham-
pioned have become commonplaces of modern thought has
obscured the freshness and force with which they appealed to a
large number of his contemporaries. In September, 1902, *The
Times* prophesied this absorption: 'Fifty years hence . . . we may
even have a theology which . . . will have learnt . . . the central
doctrine, unquestionable in itself, but sometimes very question-
ably developed, which lies at the root of all his theological writing
—the doctrine that the books of the Bible are literature.'

The severest of the strictures against Arnold faded during the
eighties and nineties, and against them may be set a diversity of
favourable comment. In 1888, 'a kind of *plébiscite* recently taken
by a democratic newspaper brought out *Literature and Dogma* as his
most valued work'. [19] The late Principal Jacks testified to the
decisive influence of *Literature and Dogma* on him as a young man,
especially of the 'Power not ourselves' idea, which 'sank deep into
the substance' of his mind, 'where it has remained ever since,
uneffaced by the subsequent experience of life'. [20] In his preface
to *The Religious Experience of Saint Paul* Percy Gardiner stated in
1911 that after wide reading for this essay, begun in 1909 as a
contribution to *Cambridge Biblical Essays*, he found that 'the best
short account of the Pauline theology known to me is still Matthew
Arnold's essay of forty years ago: so greatly does insight surpass
learning'. [21] In 1927, Percy Houston discussed Arnold's 'God of
experience' as a modern concept and added: 'It has been said
that our theological schools are turning for guidance and inspira-
tion to these three books [*Literature and Dogma, God and the Bible,
St Paul and Protestantism*] composed by a layman in the face of
active opposition by the churchmen of his time.' [22]

The major objection made against Arnold's 'literary' reading
of the Bible was that he tended to read his own modern views not
only into the utterance but into the very thoughts of Paul and of
Jesus. It was a fair criticism. Arnold tried to guard against it by
reminding his readers frequently that Paul, and even Jesus,
naturally spoke as men and as Jews of that era, but he was con-
tinually turning his insights into certainties and telling what this

'figurative' or 'affirmative' language really was intended to convey. Maurice Vernes amused himself with Arnold's 'spiritualizing' of concepts, asking what kind of exegesis it was that preferred a single text—'the Kingdom of God is within you'—to twenty which had to be interpreted materially, and assigned only the former to Jesus. To his religious idea or formula of the Eternal not ourselves (a dogma!) Arnold compelled the Bible to conform as narrowly and mistakenly as theologians, whose dogma after all was there in the germ. No doubt the serene self-confidence and lack of philosophic mind were necessary if these fine things were to penetrate English intellects, and the book must be judged as an English rather than as a 'human' work. In all this M. Vernes was having his French fun with the scourge of the Philistines, and he concluded with a sincere tribute to the book's well-merited influence. *Literature and Dogma* was 'une des manifestations les plus remarquables de la pensée religieuse contemporaine', a highly original work and no mere echo of Germany.[23]

When we place these questions in a larger context of ethical and religious ideas the pattern of Arnold's impact and influence becomes clearer. At the turn of the century there was a strong tendency to deprecate his theological writing; this was followed by a period of indifference, when a dearth of articles and commentary showed him a victim of the general reaction against the Victorian era; from the 1920's on there has been a steady revival of interest in his ideas, with Arnold, as E. L. Hunt said in 1936, still the object of dissent, still needing to be seen as he really was.[24] Nor has this revived interest been merely a recognition of the continuing usefulness of his distinctions and definitions, of their being woven into the very fabric of twentieth-century criticism and civilized discourse.[25] It is simply that Arnold, yearning for an absolute but always turning his gaze back to the complexity and relativity of experience, was far ahead of his time, writing for those who would come to see that the extreme positions taken up in his day were indefensible. His agnostic attitude to the divine and supernatural repelled the orthodox; his transcendent ethic was a mere metaphysical remnant of speculation to the secularist. But Arnold was 'writing and working for something beyond the horizon of his critics and his friends—a natural development of historical Christianity which should, not grudgingly, but eagerly, include all the knowledge that true science had to offer, as a necessary deepening of its own Christian discipline'.[26] If this 'dream of a new birth of a new Catholic and Christian faith, and a new European unity based naturally upon it' points to the sources of continuing dissent, rather than of revived interest, there is an equally forceful secular comment upon his prophetic vision and continuing relevance. Arnold, we were told in 1941, 'was more radical in his criticism of human nature and human society than those who denounce him for not being radical enough'. He diagnosed today's problem while it was yet in germ: 'The problem with which he confronted the 1860's—how to moralize the coming mass-State—is the problem of the 1940's.'[27]

How to preserve individual morality and to develop social ethics—this in effect was the problem as Arnold saw it and the task to which he set himself. It is understandable that many of his contemporaries saw him as trying to construct a new religion and brought a passionate partisanship into play.[28] But the novelist J. H. Shorthouse, in a letter of extravagant adulation of Arnold as poet and philosopher, comparing him with Plato and Cervantes, saw clearly in 1871 that the attitudes indicated in Hebraism and Hellenism called for a synthesis 'by which men may be at once aroused to a sympathetic perception of their daily life, and at the same time perceive on such perception, as on a stage, the divine excellence at work'. Arnold's modest reply shows, in the simplest terms, his sense of purpose in his work and his sense of its difficulty:

I recognize in what you say notions and aims that have long been present to me, and which I should rejoice to satisfy; but one does what one can, rather than what one will, and the passing day and what it develops raise up for me work which I had never intended for myself, but which I cannot help doing. Of what I am capable of doing, you judge far too favourably and speak much too warmly; but it is a great pleasure to me to find what I have done meeting with so much sympathy and understanding from you. To any one who labours to change the current modes of thinking which he finds around him the task he has set himself must often seem hopeless.[29]

Hebraism and Hellenism, idealism and realism, conservatism and liberalism, religiosity and rationalism—there are many pairs of contrasting terms that suggest the polarity of the attitudes between which Arnold oscillated in the hope of achieving a synthesis, or at least pointing the need for one. In an age of discredited extremes and absolutes, his attempt, informed, sincere and flexible, continues to challenge those who believe, from the standpoint of humanism, science, or religion, that a working balance can be struck between the claims of what is and what ought to be. But the logically consistent critic, whether naturalist or supernaturalist, remains dissatisfied. From R. H. Hutton to T. S. Eliot, the critics of Arnold for whom there can be no church and no religious truth without dogma would agree with an anonymous writer of 1888, that the ardour of faith in an agnostic cause is 'an impossible combination'. In an obituary on Cotter Morison, an 'extremer Arnold', the writer says: 'You cannot advocate the service of a limited posterity of mortal beings with the passion which is due to the regeneration of a world of immortal beings; and though here and there . . . the paradox may seem to be achieved, we may be quite sure that either the agnostics of the future will cease to be ardent, or that the ardent devotees of the future will cease to be agnostic.' [30]

Similarly the more complete rationalists or naturalists, determined to base their ethics, like their reason and logic, entirely in science and demonstrable fact, have shown impatience with the conflict or polarity of values in Arnold, but for the opposite reason that he is too prone to introduce the transcendental, to establish a hierarchy of values that takes him out of the realm of experience altogether. Abraham Flexner in 1895 accused Arnold of being cold to the idea of democracy, and of trying to impose the 'dream of an absolute and unrelated ideal' on the 'necessities of society' and the 'imperious demands of life'.[31] Critics who speak from a background of sociology or science or humanistic philosophy have, however, increasingly tended to be both just to Arnold and sympathetic to his ideas, with H. J. Muller offering perhaps the most balanced critical estimate of Arnold's sociological significance today. An interesting essay is that of C. V. Boyer in 1923. Writing from the vantage-point of later research, he finds in Arnold a falsely dualistic psychology that sets up an arbitrary scale of values, conflicting with his objectivity as a thinking man who, sensitive to social well-being, takes his criterion from the social fact. On the one hand a standard is applied by reference to an abstract law of truth or righteousness, on the other judgment is given in a concrete situation. On the one hand is a dualism of values that sees only some powers as beautiful or worthy, on the other a comprehensive demand for the harmonious development of all our capacities. Boyer comes to the conclusion that 'if we take over this second standard, making no exceptions on the basis of intrinsic worth, but regulating the development of all by the ideal of harmony, we reject only that which is confusing, and retain that which is most illuminating in Arnold's criticism'.[32]

A selective judgment of this kind, not the demand for a consistent naturalism or supernaturalism, will find continuing relevance in Arnold's message. But there is a more judicious estimate, a more sensitive insight, that perceives both the delicacy and the depth of the balance Arnold was trying to realize, and perceives also the humanistic faith that underlay his attempt. From this point of view the essay by Lewis Gates in 1899 remains unsurpassed. For all his sympathy with the intuitions and aspirations of romantic and idealistic poetry, Arnold 'came to regard its underlying conceptions of life as inadequate and misleading, and to feel the need of supplementing them by a surer and saner relation to the conventional world of common sense'. His spiritual Hellenism, his philosophy of 'Goethe tempered by Wordsworth', accepted the 'wise limitations of the scope of human endeavour to this world', with a 'sane and uncomplaining acceptance of fact' and a 'pursuit of tangible ideals of human perfection'. His is 'a worldliness that holds many of the elements of idealism in solution', elements derived from the ideals, especially the Christian ideals, of former generations, and exhibiting his belief in 'the continuity of human experience'. His exacting temperament finds a good deal of crudeness and disorder. 'But he has faith in the instincts that civilized men have developed in common, and finds in the working of those instincts the continuous, if irregular, realization of the ideal.'[33]

N

CHAPTER IX

A Glance at the Contemporary Scene

Humaneness consists in never sacrificing a human being to a
purpose.

ALBERT SCHWEITZER, *Civilization and Ethics*

There are two and only two finally tenable hypotheses about
life: the Catholic and the materialistic.

T. S. ELIOT, *Selected Essays*

Catholicism is inadmissible. Protestantism is intolerable. And
I feel profoundly Christian.

ANDRÉ GIDE, *Journals*

Altruism as passion; that would seem as yet Nature's noblest
product; the greatest contribution made by man to life.

SIR CHARLES SHERRINGTON, *Man on His Nature*

THE quotations above suggest the diversity of moral and
spiritual statement that can be heard today, when the modern
and challenging formulations of a scientific humanism coexist
with, even at times intermingle with, the religious or rationalistic
strains that carry us back to the mediæval era and beyond. In
my first chapter I dealt with the questions most agitating to the
religious world of Arnold's controversial prime. The question of
continuing importance, and of continually shifting lines of attack
or defence, has been the humanistic secularizing of ethics, together
with the ever-increasing extension of scientific method into the
nature and sources of the moral life itself. The foregoing chapters
dealt with Arnold's attempt to pour old wine into new bottles, to
preserve and adapt and modify. I propose now to glance at some
of the contemporary approaches to this question, made in the
name of religion or science or humanism, in an admittedly tenta-
tive and superficial way that yet may be useful for purposes of
comparison. The conclusion will discuss a possible harmonizing
of points of view, not a soaring synthesis, but a humble lowest
common denominator of practical co-operation. In such a
conclusion, a reminder of Arnold's contribution will have its
place.

Of the many signs of the times that might serve to introduce
such a survey and discussion four must suffice. There is first the
variety of ways in which the basic conflict is now seen, in contrast

to the oversimplified picture of a struggle between a pugnacious natural science and a dogmatic supernatural religion. Often the conflict is expressed in political or economic or social terms, most impressively in Karl Popper's analytical study, *The Open Society and Its Enemies*, where the interweaving of these forces is set against their historical and philosophical background. Metaphysical idealism and historicism, from Plato to Marx encouraging the 'closed society', are seen as the reactionary or stultifying enemies of the expanding spirit of man. Popper's belief in a modified rationalism and in 'piecemeal social engineering' is of course diametrically opposed to the traditional religious faith demanded by Christopher Dawson: 'We are faced with a spiritual conflict of the most acute kind, a sort of social schizophrenia which divides the soul of society between a non-moral will to power served by inhuman techniques and a religious faith and moral idealism which have no power to influence human life. There must be a return to unity—a spiritual integration of culture—if mankind is to survive.'[1] This plea is echoed by Toynbee, when he says that 'the spiritual side of man's life is of vastly greater importance for man's well-being (even for his material well-being, in the last resort) than is his command over non-human nature'.[2]

Sometimes this form of the conflict is a familiar one, as when our 'neo-scholastics' are attacked by Miss Kathleen Nott for setting up the idolatrous and talismanic in opposition to the forces of science and humanism. Certainly it is anticipated by Pater's acceptance, in quoting from *Robert Elsmere*, of 'two estimates of life—the estimate which is the offspring of the scientific spirit, and which is for ever making the visible world fairer and more desirable in mortal eyes; and the estimate of St Augustine'.[3] Perhaps, after all, the variety of ways in which the conflict is expressed—economic and sociological, or religious and scientific—is illusory. For what really are opposed are two ways of viewing experience. The question is whether or no human nature and human behaviour require for explanation and motivation a belief in a transcendent reality, a reality which will serve as an object of faith and a source of controls or sanctions. This reality may assume a secular superhuman form, as in the concept of the State, rather than the divine transcendent form. In this case the conflict is the only too familiar one today of totalitarianism, with or without benefit of clergy, against individualism, with or without a conscious adherence to Christian values. Karl Mannheim stresses the

need for a third way between regimentation and a disintegrated
laissez-faire liberalism, the way of a planned and militant demo-
cracy, in which 'group existence, loyalty to common issues
and emotional solidarity will not be in contradiction to the
emergence of an independent personality with critical powers of
judgment'.[4]

As another sign of the times, the attempt to reconcile, or syn-
thesize, contrasting philosophies has been noticeable for decades
in the religious writing of scientists, especially of physicists. From
Whitehead's *Religion in the Making* to C. A. Coulson's *Science and
Christian Belief*, to select at random, books have been written to
prove that the telescope and the microscope are after all but two
of the paths to God, and even to specifically Christian belief.
These statements have in the main been eagerly welcomed by
churchmen as evidence that a triumphantly materialistic phase of
scientific thinking is passing away. To recognize relativity, un-
certainty, and probability as scientific principles seems somehow
to open the way to reinstating theology as the queen of the
sciences, or at least to confess that a religious answer to ultimate
questions is a necessity of human nature.

Not all are equally enthusiastic, however, about these new
evangelists bearing gifts from the world of Greek endings, and a
student of Arnold may be pardoned some amusement at the
spectacle of Arnold's successors in amateur theology taking knocks
from both sides. In 1931 the Anglo-Catholic Eliot found some-
what naïve the grateful recognition of the new climate in science
and philosophy, hailed in the Report of the Lambeth Conference
of 1930 as favourable to faith. These 'scientists should be received
as penitents for the sins of an earlier scientific generation', not as
friends and allies. They may remove some prejudices, but they
have no confirming value in matters of religion. The humanistic
thinker H. J. Muller is inclined to regard this idealistic urge to
restore the Divine Mind to power as a regrettable lapse into
anthropomorphism. 'Eminent physicists', he remarks, 'seem to
have a natural inclination to idealism, and the rarefied materials
they now work with leave them wide open to intimations of
immortality.'[5]

A third question, one of the widest possible interest, is that
with which one writer began a review of 'Three Existentialists'.
He referred to 'the currently fashionable problem, "Can there be
morals without religion?" '[6] That it would be more realistic to

speak of a recurrent problem is evident from Macaulay's essay on 'The Utilitarian Theory of Government' in 1829, and from the numerous nineteenth-century attempts to separate ethics from religion. Disposing of the 'greatest happiness' principle as either a truism or a contradiction, Macaulay said of the Utilitarians:

They have taken the precept of Christ and left the motive; and they demand the praise of a most wonderful and beneficial invention, when all that they have done is to make a most useful maxim useless by separating it from its sanction. On religious principles it is true that every individual will best promote his own happiness by promoting the happiness of others. But if religious considerations be left out of the question it is not true. If we do not reason on the supposition of a future state, where is the motive? If we do reason on that supposition, where is the discovery? [7]

Oversimplified as this distinction will seem to most modern readers, it still points up the basic issue for a great many thinking people, whose anxiety finds expression in certain questions. Is autonomy possible, or desirable, in ethics? Are our moral values simply part of our cultural heritage, especially of Christian teaching, and will they suffer progressive attrition with the weakening of religious belief? Can a scientific attitude, operating in a purely humanistic and naturalistic context, with special application in the areas of psychology and sociology, furnish the needed sanctions for desirable moral behaviour? It is not only in the realm of mechanical invention that the pace has been bewilderingly rapid since Arnold's day; his prophecy of a distant time when the arts and sciences might replace biblical religion as a source of ethical norms is already upon us in the form of these urgent questions.

The mention of prophecy brings me to the last of these arbitrarily selected issues, for the united and universal Christian Church Arnold hopefully foresaw, the 'Catholic Church transformed', is as far from realization as ever. There are two questions here: the decline of interest in religion as such, and the inability of the various segments of the Christian Church to compose their differences. The former question is difficult to treat statistically: a statement that church attendance in York fell from 35 per cent of the adult population in 1901, to 18 per cent in 1935, to 13 per cent in 1948, is countered by the claim that a similar survey in Derby 'revealed that a majority of the population do listen to religious broadcasts at some time or other', and by a suggestion that such changes in actual churchgoing merely reflect an up-heaval in 'our social living'.[8] Certainly the late Bishop Henson outdid the 'gloomy Dean' when, after a visit to an old parish with its evidence of a time when religion dominated life, he remarked, 'Who wants Religion now? It is at the best the amiable hobby of eccentric individuals.'[9] Another theologian refers unhappily to the 'empty churches and full cinemas, and questioning of funda-mentals in conduct as well as creed',[10] with a resultant loss of influence among the workers. These complaints are not new, but they are uttered against a background of unresolved conflict between a modernist and 'socially conscious' view of Christian teaching and the endeavour, Catholic and non-Catholic, to maintain or restore a doctrinal and dogmatic Christianity. 'Too many Christian Socialists', said Egerton Swann, 'think of the Kingdom of God as merely a human society in which perfect justice rules and whose members are bound together by perfect human love. It is simply the apotheosis of humanitarianism.' But an editorial in *Theology* for October 1946 suggests that the recoil from this view can go too far:

It is credibly reported now that Christian students in our univer-sities and colleges, unlike their predecessors a generation ago, are eager to study the Bible and dogma, but display little, if any, interest in the discussion of social and political questions. This change may at first sight gratify the theologian, but it ought not to do so for long. There is something radically wrong with Bible study that induces pietism or absorption in religious interests.[11]

The two questions are of course linked together, since it may reasonably be argued that any general decline of interest is at least partly due to the failure of the churches to achieve unity. The rapprochement between the Anglican Church and the Eastern Orthodox Churches is a small gain beside the continued refusal of the nonconformist churches to accept episcopal rule as the price of union, and the continuing strain of divisive forces within the Church of England represented by modernist liberal-ism and Anglo-Catholicism. The œcumenical movement of the World Council of Churches at Amsterdam in 1948, representing all bodies except the Roman Catholic, was unable to translate good will into action. They were in 'agreement only on the con-fession of Christ'. They were in disagreement not only 'on the

Church, on the Priesthood, on the Sacraments, on the veneration of the Saints, on the conception of the future life', but also on fundamental questions of 'the being and character of God and the nature of His purposes for men'.[12]

The writer adds that for the Roman Catholic 'observer' whose findings are reported, and accepted, the thinking has been done already, and the final object of study is not God but the 'nature of authority'. Certainly, when one considers the unyielding opposition to modernism that expressed itself in the condemnation of Loisy and the excommunication of Tyrrell, the unchanged reply to Anglo-Catholic manœuvres for reconciliation that the only acceptable condition is the submission of penitent heretics to papal authority, the dogmatic formulation as an Article of Faith in 1951 of the doctrine of the bodily Assumption of the Virgin Mary —when one considers the consistency of this whole course of action, one is bound to find a complete lack of realism in Arnold's vision of a 'transformed' Catholic Church of the future as the probable form of a truly universal Christendom.

Of the possible approaches by religion and science and humanism to these issues of the day—the variety of conflicting forces, the attempts at reconciliation, morals without religion, and religion without ecclesiastical unity—obviously the simplest and safest approach for religion is that of a traditional dogmatic authority demanding unquestioning obedience. Only the Roman Catholic Church has effectively resisted the dissolvent action of liberalism and humanism upon absolutism and dogma, though post-Tractarian Anglo-Catholicism preserves an uncompromising purity in one wing of the Church of England. The basic beliefs and mediæval spirit of Catholicism make no other course possible. As Santayana says, 'The supernaturalism, the literal realism, the other-worldliness of the Catholic Church are too much the soul of it to depart without causing its dissolution.'[13]

There are many reasons for Catholicism's appeal to others than those born into its communion. In Rose Macaulay's *The World My Wilderness*, young Richard Deniston, trying to pick up the pieces after three years of war and barbarism, 'was impelled sometimes beyond his reasoning self, to grasp at the rich, trailing panoplies, the swinging censers, of churches from whose creeds and uses he was alien, because at least they embodied some continuance, some tradition'. Against raw mass newness and 'frightening evanescence' they 'kept their improbable, incommunicable secret, linking the dim past with the disrupted present and the intimidating future'. Richard, however, became not a Roman Catholic but an Anglo-Catholic—there was 'less to believe'. Another reason for the appeal of the whole Catholic tradition is evident in T. S. Eliot's disparaging comments on the humanistic and socialistic 'religions', all 'cheerfully plodding the road from nowhere to nowhere'. He remarks, 'These changed conditions are so prevalent that anyone who has been moving among intellectual circles and comes to the Church, may experience an odd and rather exhilarating feeling of isolation.' [14] It is only fair to add what he says in another essay: 'The World is trying the experiment of attempting to form a civilized but non-Christian mentality. The experiment will fail; but we must be very patient in awaiting its collapse, meanwhile redeeming the time: so that the Faith may be preserved alive through the dark ages before us; to renew and rebuild civilization, and save the World from suicide.' [15]

In this view the only alternative to 'totalitarian democracy' is a religious control and balance. 'The Christian can be satisfied with nothing less than a Christian organization of society—which is not the same thing as a society consisting exclusively of devout Christians.' [16] And when Eliot points to the alternative secular 'religion' (as he says, it is trite now to speak of Communism as a faith) we are reminded of the confessions of disillusionment in *The God That Failed*. The seeker for relief from the heavy burden of moral responsibility finds it lightened for him only by a dogmatic formulation of total truth, infallible even when it changes. Recognizing the nature of the appeal in Communism for what it is, the Catholic critic is more likely to fear, and respect, the power of this rival totalitarianism than he is the scattered forces of a liberal and individualistic humanism. Marxist Communism, de Lubac tells us, 'offered itself as the only concrete realization of humanism; it quite deliberately claimed to be a total solution for the whole human problem; moving to the plane of reality, it did not propose to figure there only as a social phenomenon but as a spiritual phenomenon also. This is what gives it greatness but this is also the radical flaw in it; it is this that bathes even its sound elements in a baneful atmosphere and it is this that chiefly arouses Christian opposition.' [17]

For religion in general the problem is one of preserving a moral code without a compelling creed, and neither the Barthian theology of the Word nor Niebuhr's theology of transcendence can offer the Protestant and 'liberal' world a power equivalent to dogmatic authority. The one would restore faith in a living God who has spoken his will through the Bible, with obedience the point of departure. The other postulates a fundamental need in man to believe in something 'larger and more inclusive than himself'; in *The Nature and Destiny of Man* Niebuhr interprets Christian teaching as showing that redemptive forces reside only at the eternal level of being above the level of history and rationalism. It is doubtful that a merely biblical theology can ever again have authority, so thoroughly has sceptical criticism done its work; and metaphysical idealism is not only little in vogue, but commands at the most intellectual assent to its propositions, whether in Bosanquet or Niebuhr. 'I understand and I accept' is a humanistic or scientific response at the natural level; it is only the priestly interpreter of a sacramental mystery who can expect the reply, 'I hear and I obey'.

We may say that whereas ethical idealism has a problem— how to make the individual moral will responsive to an Eternal Moral Will—modernism in religion is faced with a dilemma. Should it emphasize the divinity in Christ and call for obedience, or emphasize his humanity and call for emulation? The first alternative is close to orthodoxy, as an analysis by H. D. A. Major shows. The three essentials of modernist faith (hopefully advanced as a basis of agreement with the scientific humanist) are 'faith in the One Divine Creative Father; faith that we have the spiritual and moral nature of the Divine Father enshrined for mankind in the personality and Gospel of the Jesus of History; faith that by divine communion those who seek it are enabled to receive spiritual and moral strength and guidance to enable them to learn and carry out the Divine Will'.[18] An emphasis on Christ's humanity, on the other hand, may carry the modernist into ethical idealism, but is more likely to take him on to some misty middle ground indistinguishable from socialist or sentimental humanitarianism, and so virtually out of the Church. Such modernism tends to reject dogma and doctrine, to turn into a sort of moral pantheism, and even, as Santayana says, to find official Christianity 'offensive just because it presupposes that Christianity is true'. Of such a separation of morality and religion, beginning in late Victorian times, Elliott-Binns fears 'terrifying consequences;

. . . for without religious sanctions the masses of the people, who have no intellectual interest in ethical questions and little moral training, may so easily lose their grip on morality, and with it the love of truth and honesty. The modern idea of subjective freedom, then gaining force, can provide no secure basis for man's moral life, or even for his intellectual being.' [19]

Arnold's own fear of these dangers motivated his attempts to preserve both Bible and Church for their power over the emotions and the imagination, and to 'verify' as scientific truth an abiding power outside ourselves towards which our best selves move in obedient recognition. Yet his ethical idealism carries a corresponding danger, or at least difficulty, in the demand it makes on the individual moral will. This is implied by McGiffert, to whom the position is 'a species of pragmatism, a testing of religious truths and religious values by their workableness'. Finding Arnold, like Ritschl, to be in the line of Kant and Fichte, and quoting from *Literature and Dogma* on 'verification' through Jesus, he concludes, 'The great significance of this whole line of thought is that God is found in the realm of values; that he is interpreted primarily as moral purpose and influence rather than as substance; and also that he is reached neither by theoretical demonstration nor by mystical vision, but by exercise of the moral will.' [20] Such a view of moral life involves both testing by results and a disciplined approach to experience.

On this note we may turn to ask how science looks at the questions we have been considering, or rather at the problems of moral and religious experience contained in them. It must be said that in spite of essays in religious philosophy by Eddington, Jeans, and others, relations with theology continue to be set forth in terms of co-existence rather than of co-operation. Vitalisms and spiritualisms and pantheisms are still regarded with suspicion by most scientists (by 'scientists' I mean not merely trained technicians, but men with a capacity for conceptual thinking). The aggressive phase of purely mechanistic materialism seems to be over, but there is no retreat from the position that the straightest road to the most certain truth is by the experimental method working from reasoned hypotheses in a material medium. That is how discoveries have been made, and continue to be made.

An earlier generation was inclined to find any sort of experience not open to the strictly scientific method, if indeed there is such, comparatively unimportant. Facts were facts, and, as

A. J. Ayer says, could not be subordinated to logically necessary propositions even to make metaphysicians like Bradley happy in a Transcendent Reality. But now the scientist seems to recognize other kinds of fact, and their claim upon him as a moral being and citizen. The new modesty was the theme of an essay by Joseph Needham in 1929: 'What has happened now is not that the scientific view of the world has been shown to be baseless, still less that reason or knowledge has been argued out of existence, but that science has ceased to pretend that it is religion, philosophy, or art. These forms of experience are autonomous.' [21] This recognition by the scientist of claims upon his humanity has been most clearly and forcibly expressed by Sir Charles Sherrington:

Granted the scope of natural science be to distinguish true from false, not right from evil, that simply makes the man of science as such, not the whole man but a fractional man; he is not the whole citizen but a fraction of the citizen. The whole man now that his mind has 'moral values' must combine his scientific part-man with his human rest. Where his scientific part-man assures him of something and his ethical part-man declares that something to be evil it is for the whole man in his doing not to leave it at that. Otherwise in a world of mishap his scientific knowledge and his ethical judgement become two idle wheels spinning without effect, whereas they have been evolved and survive each to give the other effect. [22]

As Jacques Maritain has told us, the radical sentence passed by Marx on idealism as a metaphysical doctrine need occasion no regret, but that on the value of the immaterial in general is quite another matter. In Sherrington's recognition of the value of the immaterial we have an example of the fruitful thinking that has gone on about science and its implications, as we have in the admission that 'presuppositions underlying all scientific effort', for instance, a belief in 'the universal character of truth', are often 'unexamined by the scientist'. [23] This does not mean a confusion of two spheres of being. 'Remembering that science has not the words "suffering" or "good" or "bad",' Sherrington continues, man must, 'to secure his programme, yoke science to his own anthropisms'. Nor does it mean any loss of faith in the validity of the scientific method as a means of exploring the origins of moral values and the whole inner world of psychological experience. It means rather that the moral and religious thinking of man is itself admitted to be a necessary form of his (human) experience.

The distinction is carefully preserved with regard to religious beliefs in an essay by H. D. Roelofs. He points out that the essence of the experimental method is to establish constant correlations, by manipulation or observation, on a basis of repetition. The experimental attitude may be expressed thus: 'I *believe* Galileo dropped such and such weights, and I *know* that, *if* he did, the rest of the story is true.' But with the story of the Resurrection (and without the supernatural, Roelofs agrees, there is no Christian *religion*) the elements of the experimental method are missing. Not the uniqueness of the event is against it, but probability. Here faith is of the essence, for the merit consists in believing without proof from demonstration. Now the scientist, without believing, can yet take the supernatural elements seriously as the sign of a religious faith. The experimental challenge lies in 'By their fruits ye shall know them', but this is 'not a test to determine whether there is a god; it is a test for those who believe in God'.[24]

This returning recognition of significance in forms of mental activity other than those pursued within the stricter limits of science strikes us in considering the human studies, individual and social, to which the experimental method was enthusiastically and even aggressively extended. The spectacular success of the method in the physical sciences inevitably stimulated its use in economics and sociology, in psychology and anthropology, subjects which had felt the restraining effects of *a priori* and idealistic and teleological forms of thought derived from philosophy and theology. It was inevitable too that mechanistic explanations and environmental factors should have been given increasing, even exclusive, prominence, and that man should be studied as a material object in a material world.

Yet, the fact that man is the one creature with the power to control, shape, and explore both his total environment and himself keeps perennially fresh a speculative interest in the nature and sources of that power. The experimental method remains supreme but its success is seen as due in some measure to its taking a one-dimensional view of man, abstracting from a complex whole a particular aspect for specialized study. It is not a question of replacing the methods and aims of science, but of recognizing in the whole range of the relations of mind and matter that 'complementarity' which in physics permits the dual functioning of the corpuscle and wave theories of light. The Economic Man is now a nineteenth-century myth; the 'Nature red in tooth and claw' view of evolution has had to move over and make room for the facts of altruistic impulse and behaviour; the growing interest in ethical questions reflects the conviction that political science is inseparably bound up with them, an interdependence examined for the general reader in Walter Lippmann's *The Public Philosophy*.

In some quarters this turn for diversity and complementarity is taken as evidence that vitalist and even transcendentalist thinking has been re-established with respect to man and his place in Nature. A sounder judgment would be that the empiricist has himself come to conceive of a wider meaning for experience than strict materialism permitted, and has with Canon Raven found it ironical that 'the scientific interpretation of nature should after four centuries of effort have replaced the hieroglyphs of medieval Catholicism by the robots of modern Behaviourism'.[25] Commenting on the unnecessary muddle of affairs in 1931, Keynes stated his belief that a time was coming when 'the Economic Problem will take the back seat where it belongs, and that the arena of the heart and head will be occupied, or re-occupied, by our real problems—the problems of life and human relations, of creation and behaviour and religion'.[26] Observing that 'methods of impartial inquiry were developed' by such Renascence humanists as Montaigne, Ruth Benedict confessed her debt to Santayana, to Lovejoy, and to Furness and Dover Wilson among Shakespearian critics: 'If we are to use life histories for more than items of topical ethnology, we shall have to be willing to do the kind of job on them which has traditionally been done by the great humanists.'[27] The anthropologist will not change his own approach as a social scientist, but he 'can use both approaches'.

We may be sure that sociology will continue to follow the scientific thinking of a Durkheim rather than the philosophical thinking of an Urwick, but the artificial lines set up are fading. The social anthropologist Evans-Pritchard does not believe there can 'ever be a science of society which resembles the natural sciences' rather than the humanities. No sociological laws have yet been established. Yet applied anthropology, after the use of the scientific method, can help in many ways: for example, in the administration of primitive peoples and in meeting the problems of adolescence. His pragmatic conclusion is to approve the saying of Pasteur Junod, a saying which also brings the many-sided Albert Schweitzer to mind: 'To work for science is noble; but to help our fellow men is nobler still.'[28]

Of all the fields to which the scientific method was extended, psychology is perhaps the one in which practitioners still tend to assert with truculence or complacence the superiority of experimental techniques and materialistic hypotheses. The complacence is understandable in view of the achievements; the truculence reflects the opposition and criticism encountered. To a generation bred in traditional religious beliefs it was alarming to contemplate the degeneration of soul into mind, and of mind into matter, and the alarm was intensified by Freud's revelations of the importance of sexuality and the unconscious. To many of their descendants there still is, on the one hand, a flavour of the impious or the absurd in exploring the mind and personality as a team of geologists and speleologists explore terrain, and, on the other hand, a suspicion that it is impossible to achieve the same 'objectivity', to make sufficient allowance for the fact that the experimenter is part of the total experiment, whether the specimen is himself or another. Consequently there is a tendency to accept any vitalistic, holistic, or archetypal theories expounded, partly as a relief to resentment, partly as an expression of the usually unanalysed but powerful conviction that there is more to inner experience than meets the psychoanalytical eye. The favourable reception given Jung, especially by the religious, moves Edward Glover to reassert in strong terms the supremacy of Freud, and to find in Jung's 'monistic *élan vital*' and Collective Unconscious the evidence that he is merely a *conscious* psychologist, whose interpretations evoke the old obstructionist beliefs in the mystical and transcendental: 'The most comforting theories of mental function resume their earlier sway.' [29]

Yet even psychologists can concede the usefulness of 'conscience' and 'instincts' as concepts to work with and can speak with critical common sense of other psychologists who believe that a difficulty 'can be overcome by changing the name of instinct to propensity or drive or appetite or erg, as if a change of name could effect an alteration in the character of the phenomenon'. [30] J. C. Flugel can go further. He admits that psychology's failures are due to those (including psychologists) who see nothing in it but pure science as well as to those who fear tampering with 'values'. The layman will at least feel himself on familiar ground, where co-operation is possible, when he reads, 'It is pretty generally agreed that the problem of rebuilding our tottering society upon a sounder basis . . . to some extent a moral problem, . . . depends upon an appeal to the moral impulses of men.' [31]

To consider the response of the humanist to the issues under discussion is to risk the ambiguities inherent in that protean term. The word 'humanism' is not used here to mean an education in the humanities, nor, as Burtt uses it, to define a secularized religious movement. As a name for a moral and philosophical attitude, humanism implies a respect for our total cultural heritage and a pragmatically selective application of it, including its Christian elements, to the present; a belief in liberalism, individualism, and tolerance as the hall marks of civilization, with the addition today of intelligent social planning; and a set of values operating at the human level and within the limits of nature and history.

This very breadth makes the humanist suspect to the dogmatic Christian, who regards him as a potential, if not actual, atheist; to the narrower practitioner of physical or psychological science, who sees him as an ineffectual trifler; and to the doctrinaire socialist, to whom such well-meaning woolly-mindedness is little better than a betrayal of the revolution. Part of this irritation is the answer of the specialist to the trespassing dilettante; part of it is the reluctant admission that religion, science, and politics are after all human activities, with elevation of the human being as their end and justification. The humanist recognizes no sharp divisions, and he is just as apt to rebuke the sceptic and materialist as he is the rigidly orthodox for a lack of sweetness and light. It is true that when he speaks as a student of the humanities pronouncing on the limitations of science, or as a humanist using the language of the Christian faith, he is too often the ill-informed or illegitimate trespasser. But his persistence in trying to relate all knowledge and all visions to human needs and aspirations is a continual reminder to the man of science and the man of religion that old divisions must be healed to give the life of humanity a healthy wholeness, and that they too are humanists. Indeed, some of the most effective contributions to a philosophy of humanism are made by men speaking from the point of view of religion or science, offering a scientific or a religious humanism as a solution to the conflicts that puzzle and divide us.

Jacques Barzun speaks for a pure humanism when he declares that there always was a plight and a problem, man-made and man-remediable. Before the chaos of misery and injustice

(Newman's 'heart-piercing, reason-bewildering fact') one response is the act of faith in a Divine Omnipotent Mind, with the chaos attributed to man's disobedience. But the other response, the humanistic one, also involves the leap to an act of faith, though not faith in an Absolute Benevolent Power. Such men 'give up any shadow of ultimate guarantee that all will come out right, and at the same time they involve themselves in the responsibility for any and every outcome'. Finding the divine in nature and man can make for humility, not arrogance; regarding the universe as in process of evolution can inspire effort and hope, not despair. There has been a change in the basis of human evaluative judgments over the centuries, and the humanistic view of life is the one which incorporates and gives expression to that change. 'Our modern aesthetic sense, unlike that of the past, is offended by human ugliness and degradation. As for our living philosophy, it is not the metaphysics of sorrow and tragedy but the ethics of equality.' [32]

To Jacques Maritain this liberal humanism makes 'great play with morality and a spiritual point of view', and can even be sincerely devoted to truths of a natural order, but it is utterly incapable of a true, a 'heroic humanism'. Christian impulses, though gone astray, are still 'existentially' what move the hearts of men to action, and the 'materialized spirituality' of this 'bourgeois' humanism cannot stand up to the active materialism of atheistic paganism: 'The time is ripe for Christians to bring things back to the fount of truth, reintegrating in the plenitude of their first origins those desires for justice and that nostalgia for communion (now so misdirected) in which the world finds comfort for its sorrow.' [33] We have had an age of humanism divorced from a belief in the Incarnation, anthropocentric humanism, which sees its ideal in the Renascence hero or the *honnête homme*, rather than in the saint. The notion of personality was evolved by mediæval theology: 'A person is a unity of a spiritual nature endowed with freedom of choice and so forming a whole which is independent of the world . . . man is at once a natural and a supernatural being.' The new humanism will be Thomistic, for Thomism can discern the 'vital energies' at the core of the 'firmest order' (including, presumably, Roman Catholic order), and detect the impulses to revolution and renewal. It will be new, for though the mediæval ideal of a consecrated Christian society was good, and is still a logical entity and a metaphysical essence, 'existentially it corresponds to something come to an end'. St Thomas Aquinas, we gather from Maritain, was a philosophical progressive. Just as he would have taught Christian philosophy in the time of Galileo and Descartes to free itself from the astronomy and mechanics of Aristotle, so now and in the future his principles will be effective against the two opposite inclinations to error—'accumulative inertia' and 'spendthrift disassociation'.

There are many spokesmen today for a scientific humanism, which labours 'to invent and put into practice better truth tests' in areas that include social idealism and morals and religion, and which would extend 'scientific thinking to every kind of individual and social problem', to values as well as to facts.[34] H. J. Muller is the most vigorous and effective of these. He scorns the seekers for the Truth, who always find it by preferring believing to seeing, the fixed to the hypothetical, Aquinas or Marx to Einstein. Any philosophy which still tries to answer the what and the why 'offers only a shambles of irresistible arguments colliding with immovable thinkers'. Faced with the approximations that are the findings of 'exact science' any dogmatic humanist merely looks silly—he should ignore the unanswerable and test his assumptions and pre-conceptions (which he is bound to have) by 'correlating and evaluating the actual experiences of man on this earth', with the help of biology and physiology and psychology.

Muller is, however, quite clear that it takes two to make a conflict, and that the narrower sort of scientist has been partly to blame for the 'flight from reason' that has worried many of our modern thinkers:

> The promiscuous use of the methods and materials of science in an effort to be 'authentic', the substitution of its logic for the logic of imaginative creation, the fear of rhetoric or formal contrivance, the naïve worship of 'facts' . . . the confusion of an inquiry into origins with an evaluation of end-products— . . . they are opposed by the scorn or fear of the 'naturalistic', the retreat to some elegant tradition, the exclusive cultivation of private sensibility, the worship of the blood or the unconscious, ultimately the whole crusade against intellect and the glorification of unreason.[35]

The philosophy of modern physics 'is no specific form of idealism or system of values but an organic, dynamic, functional, pragmatic view, in which values and ideals may be shaped more

o

realistically'. Such principles 'buttress the humanistic ideals of tolerance, flexibility, and catholicity'. Indeed, your true scientist today is your true humanist. No mere fact worshipper, he is aware of truth as something other than exact statement, and recognizes the claims of philosophy and literature to represent a human experience, real and true if not measurable, or statable in terms of abstract laws. He rejects absolutes, but 'the admission of relativity and multivalence does not make value illusory or judgment futile'.[36]

The scientist's disarming pleasure in the discovery that he is the true humanist after all, perhaps overlooks the fact that the true humanist, as Ruth Benedict reminds us, always did have the scientific outlook. The Christian dogmatist, of course, finds the humanist lacking in any firm foundation for his ethical principles. Indeed, the humanist may not find it easy to reconcile Newman's fervent relief at Augustine's words, *Securus judicat orbis terrarum*, with the statement by T. S. Eliot that 'as by Athanasius, orthodoxy may be upheld by one man against the world'.[37] The scientist, on the other hand, sometimes accuses the humanist of treating nature, or human nature, in vague and 'literary' generalities. In reply the humanist may point to Arnold's attempt, following the method of Sainte-Beuve, 'to see things as in themselves they really are', to speak from experience and observation, as in describing the middle-class Nonconformist life of England. Frequently the findings of the psychologist or sociologist, after exhaustive analysis and research, merely confirm the insight of poet or prophet. G. E. Catlin rejects 'organic and rich, but impermanent situations', insisting that scientific sociology must stick to 'elementary but more humble ones such as must be the first objects of scientific study'.[38] Among these, however, 'we may properly assert some absolute permanencies, . . . some elemental social facts'. One such fact, we are grateful to hear, is 'the psychological demand for freedom', which 'must destroy in time, by a certain law of human seismology, every tyranny that does violence to our substantial natures'. Yet what is this but Arnold's 'instinct for expansion in humanity', so often abused as vague or inexact?

Muller is quite right in saying that tolerance, flexibility, and catholicity are the principles of humanism. As discussed in the previous chapter, flexibility is the essence of Arnold's main critical principle. And catholicity as a theme has perennial appeal, though the frame of reference may change from the rigid to the tenuous. Thomas Arnold longed, with the passion if not with the dogmas of Newman, for a universal Christian Church; Matthew Arnold hopefully prophesied an unromanized Catholic Church; E. M. Forster calls only for a spirit of universal tolerance: 'Tolerance is a very dull virtue. It is boring. Unlike love, it has always had a bad press. It is negative. It merely means putting up with people, being able to stand things. No one has ever written an ode to tolerance, or raised a statue to her. Yet this is the quality which will be most needed. . . . This is the sound state of mind we are looking for.' [39] This is the 'right psychology', the 'sound attitude of mind' that must, as a 'hard, scientific truth', underlie any attempts to build a new world or to reform the old.

This is not the whole truth, nor itself a truth without any exception. But it is an important truth, and a basic one. When an atheistic freethinker says he is 'working towards a time when there would not be any Christians to live with on any terms whatsoever', [40] and when a metaphysical idealist permits discussion of other goods than the Ultimate only on the understanding that everything said 'has nothing to do with the real subject [the nature of good]', [41] then the humanist, even allowing for the exaggeration natural to dialogue and debate, may offer up his private prayer to Socrates. His plea for tolerance need not be without dignity or vision, nor does it lack strength. 'There is for me a splendour in common sense', says Ivor Brown, and a reviewer of his *The Way of the World* adds: 'The moral pressures of mid-twentieth century life are driving more and more of the weaker brethren to one extreme or another. There is a lust to lie in almost anybody's bosom rather than continue the struggle to stand upright.' [42]

The humanist knows too that intolerant disagreements are sometimes based on a merely semantic confusion: 'Sometimes thinkers are at loggerheads with one another, not because their propositions do conflict, but because their authors fancy that they conflict.' [43] This reminder is pertinent at a time when the distinction between the capital and the lower case letter has become too subtle for our popular orators, and when the descriptive or defining content of a word is lost in the pejorative label and the partisan name. As an example of a humanist writing with his eye on the object, in this case the biblical text, and balancing his humanistic judgment with a scientific objectivity, this passage from Arnold has point:

> Exception is taken to its being said that there is communism in the Bible, because we see that communists are fierce, violent, insurrectionary people, with temper and actions abhorrent to the spirit of the Bible. But if we say, on the one hand, that the Bible utterly condemns all violence, revolt, fierceness, and self-assertion, than we may safely say, on the other hand, that there is certainly communism in the Bible. The truth is, the Bible enjoins endless self-sacrifice all round; and to any one who has grasped this idea, the superstitious worship of property, the reverent devotedness to the propertied and satisfied classes, is impossible.[44]

Fluid as our contemporary sense of reality is, and varied as the responses are to the questions of fresh or continuing urgency, three factors strike an uncommitted observer as offering a kind of lowest common denominator of formulable experience, which may at least serve as a basis for human communication and collaboration. These are the primary importance of ethics, the catholicity of humanism, and the universal need for belief (the intensity of the need and the object of belief are, of course, as various as human nature itself). A suggestive figure is that of overlapping circles, with a common central area of ethical evaluations and moral principles that make life in a human society possible. In effect, this is how we get along as it is, but without a conscious formulation of a *modus vivendi*. This could be achieved on an 'as if' basis, as the line of thought from William James to Needham and Muller shows; that its philosophical expression is not impossible is evident from Hans Vaihinger's *Philosophie der Als Ob*. An approach to ethics that would treat moral principles as pragmatically true because of their survival value is a dusty answer to those hot for certainty, but it has its merits. At least it deals neither in the gritty abstractions sometimes offered by a social science that would discredit 'value judgments' nor in the Mosaic rigidities of a dogmatism that would deny science any experimental rights in man. Its experiential basis is the theme of a passage in Agnes Newton Keith's book, *Three Came Home*. Existence in a Japanese camp for prisoners of war left her with few illusions about human nature, but it did leave her with a clear-cut ethical judgment of a practical kind: 'In camp we had all of the sins [e.g. gluttony and selfishness]. . . . A common enemy did not bind us together, hunger and danger did not do so, persecution did not, our sex did not. One thing only bound us to comparative peace: the lesson that life was hideous if we surrendered to our hatreds; more liveable only when we tried to be decent.'

There is unanimity about what is to be preserved, even if there is no unanimity about how to preserve it. We can listen to the religious philosopher: 'It is moral aspiration which has humanized the human animal, and we dare not believe that the humanization of man is an illusion, or a bad joke.' [45] Or to the natural scientist: 'Man is above all a leader charged with survival of the "values" which are in his keeping.' [46] Chief among these values is altruism, as the ethical philosopher will agree in arguing against an egoistic hedonism: 'For two things are quite certain: (a) that men do in fact often act altruistically, and (b) that moral codes universally advocate altruism and condemn selfishness.' [47] With all his emphasis upon new social techniques for the task of 'democratic value guidance', and upon education for change, the sociologist can be quite clear that we must have 'courage to agree on some basic values which are acceptable to everybody who shares the traditions of Western civilization'.[48] And Popper, like Sherrington, states that, though we are products and facts of nature, 'yet responsibility, decisions, enter the world of nature only with us', and adds that the world of moral demands is more urgent, more important than the other man-made worlds of language, art, and science.

Humanistic catholicity is evident in the common ground of these utterances. The extent of agreement possible on the values to be preserved, along with a complete disagreement on how best to preserve them, is summed up for us by Margaret Knight: 'To the humanist, moral behaviour is primarily kind, disinterested, self-transcending behaviour—to use Koestler's word. Whereas to the Christian, moral behaviour is behaviour in accordance with God's will. In nine cases out of ten it comes to the same thing in practice, but the sanctions are different.' [49] One sees in the word 'self-transcending' the inevitable dualism that marks all realistic treatment of the ethical problem, as in Arnold's talk of the true or best or higher self. To the ethical idealist or the scientific humanist this higher level of being is 'natural'; to the Christian it reflects a level of being above nature and outside time.

Disagreement is found on the question of whether moral progress is possible. To C. S. Lewis nothing new is to be found

in the realm of values. The 'ultimate platitudes' or 'first prin-
ciples' are premisses, not conclusions: 'What purport to be new
systems . . . all consist of fragments from the *Tao* itself, arbi-
trarily wrenched from their context in the whole and then
swollen to madness in their isolation.' [50] And the attempt to
conquer Nature, extended to the analysis and conditioning of
man as a piece of nature, offers the ironic spectacle of Nature
conquering man through the rule of the Conditioners, un-
trammelled by values. Morris Ginsberg, however, points to the
universalizing of the brotherhood ideal and the internalizing of
conscience as advances over the primitive. Moral progress is
'the clarification of ideals, in obtaining a firmer grasp of the
conditions of their realization and in the widening of human
sympathies through an extension of the power of imaginative
identification'. [51] It is only realistic to admit reversion and retro-
gression, but a long view of human moral development through
the ritualistic to the analytical to the empirical suggests grounds
for hope in this third stage, 'in which ethical theory is combined
with a factual study of human needs and motives and of the
consequences of action'.

If the catholicity of humanism is to be effectively expressed
in a pooling of moral resources, then not only these disagreements
but the different sanctions must be regarded with tolerance. A
may relieve B's suffering because it is the will of God that he do
so, C because it is the reasonable, humane thing to do. But what
really operates is Ginsberg's 'power of imaginative identification',
for A's conscience might as easily tell him that B is destined to
suffer by the will of God, and C's conscience could be persuaded
to present B as an idle fellow to assist whom would be folly. It is
this power which carries us from the necessary basis of tolerance,
essentially passive, to the plane of active altruistic impulse. This
power is the half-way house to love, that strongest of motivations
and profoundest human force that is yet so often vaguely or
sentimentally idealistic, and so dangerously prone to engender
hatred through a tyrannic or fanatical benevolence. As Forster
says, it is nonsense to talk of one marketing-board loving another
marketing-board, or a man in Portugal loving a man in Peru
whom he has never seen. Yet tolerance is no more than the
starting-point. To clarify and to apply ethical ideals and moral
values requires a 'power of imaginative identification', a 'widening
of human sympathies'. The pooling of resources should be

possible to a humanist who can say of his humanistic faith, 'It can retain the poetry and wisdom of Christianity', and to a Christian metaphysician who can say, 'Suppose, what is quite arguable, that the parable of the good Samaritan is not the utterance of Christ. What does it matter so long as it is a part of Christianity?' [52]

There are two persisting points of view from which this humanistic collaboration within an ethical centre of agreement, as a conscious 'philosophy' of moral living, would be suspect. On the one hand is the dogmatic certainty that morals are impossible except as the expression of religious faith. Referring to the 'new Christians' who would make this assertion by a return to the 'unbroken harmony and unity' of the Middle Ages, Popper says bluntly, 'It is a Christianity that refuses to carry the cross of being human.' On the other hand is the limitation of significant statements, including those about man and society, to the findings of a strictly scientific methodology. Perhaps a third such view is that of a doctrinaire secular authority imposing uniformity of belief, but the inevitable confusion here, the lack of even a working semantic agreement on such words as justice, freedom, or tolerance, makes consideration profitless.

The argument of the dogmatist is that he cannot afford to be tolerant of error and sin, for these undermine that authority which alone can establish and preserve moral codes and principles. Error and sin are defined, by authority, in terms of a doctrinal orthodoxy that is ultimately the 'inspired' interpretation by human reason of a supernatural wisdom. To the humanist it is not truth which speaks thus, but power. By confusing truth with power, the dogmatist intellectually absolves himself from guilt, and may even clothe himself with humility. This confusion is from one point of view a supreme historic irony. From Augustine to Newman the great theologians have rebuked intellectual arrogance, have warned against private judgment and the liberal inquiring spirit as opening the way to the deadly sin of pride. Yet to the humanist the dogmatic formulations of the Church, culminating in the claim of papal infallibility, are but the elevation of erring humanity into the judgment seat. Against such pretensions a Socrates, a Christ, or a Joan must inevitably speak in their different ways, and perish. 'Human eyes', as Shaw tells us, 'cannot tell the saint from the sinner.' Human reason, finding its own intellectual sustenance and emotional satisfaction in a disciplined orthodoxy, is at fault if it cannot tolerate the humane flexibility of a rationalism seeking some of the same ends and preserving some of the same inheritance. Dostoevsky's brilliant Ivan, of 'earthly, Euclidean understanding', is outraged in his sense of justice by the sufferings of innocent children; Alyosha's love can in its simplicity and integrity embrace all sufferers and absorb even the painful mystery of evil; Father Zossima's triumphant faith can say, 'Believe to the end, even if all men went astray and you were left the only one faithful; bring your offering even then and praise God in your loneliness. And if two of you are gathered together—then there is a whole world, a world of living love.' Different as these levels and values may be, a focal point of relationship can be seen in Zossima's words, 'Equality is to be found only in the spiritual dignity of man.'

If the dogmatic restriction of moral pronouncements to religious authority is one unco-operative extreme, the other is the refusal, in the name of scientific objectivity, to permit moral pronouncements at all, such 'evaluative judgments' being thought of by many social scientists as 'premature generalizations'. Wallas warned forty years ago that a 'society whose intellectual direction consists only of unrelated specialisms must drift',[53] and Durkheim admitted that 'we shall often be bound to take sides on those questions without waiting for our science to be sufficiently advanced to guide us; the necessity for action often forces us to precede science'.[54] These realistic reservations go unheeded by some specialists, whose disinclination to establish points of contact with still-working sanctions and values often amounts to a denial that their tabulations and observations have any relevance to the needs and wishes of humanity. This attitude partly reflects the old quarrel with *a priori* modes of thought, and with what Durkheim calls the 'mind complacent in the face of a reality which has little to teach it, . . . since it is the mind . . . that determines the matter'. But it reflects also a resignation before the multiplicity of observed facts, even at times a despairing resignation, and carries the danger of rejecting positive correlations with human needs and aims until the hypothetical happy day when all imponderables will be eliminated.

The attempt to apply with rigour an attitude and a method, entirely appropriate in the physical world, to the whole range of human nature and social relations, has met with real success. Yet a rigid and exclusive use of the method could bring about a sterility of the moral will, or at least an impoverishment of what I have called the ethical centre of agreement. Catlin says in his introduction to Durkheim's *Rules of Sociological Method* that only philosophy and poetry are concerned with 'the essential stuff and character of real societies', with their 'spiritual characters'. The sociologist and political scientist have as 'their humble business' to understand 'that which is common to human behaviour in frequently recurring social situations', these being 'deliberately abstracted for study so as to yield to treatment by a satisfactory methodological process'. Propounded in the sphere of practical living, this would indeed be a feast of sow thistle and bramble to offer the hungry sheep lured away from discredited poets and prophets. A Thurberian picture comes to mind of a skilled and devoted tracker following with studiously downcast eyes the spoor of a large and mysterious animal to some hypothetical lair, while close behind, with diminishing curiosity and with increasing and salivating impatience, comes the animal itself.

That a flexible and catholic humanism, scientific in approach, can nourish and expand the ethical centre—such a formula would relate the faith of natural scientists like Needham and Sherrington to that of social scientists like Mannheim and Popper. Sherrington gives it expression when he has Nature speak to man, the only recognizer of 'values', who must shoulder his responsibilities and use his own judgment. 'I cannot love,' she tells him, 'neither can I hate. But now that I have brought forth you and your kind, remember that you are a new world unto yourselves, a world which contains in virtue of you, love and hate, and reason and madness, the moral and immoral, and good and evil. It is for you to love where love can be felt. That is, to love one another.' [55] Popper brings out most clearly the comprehensive terms of a humanistic faith when he replies to Toynbee's attack on the humanist for not seeing that only faith in a superhuman whole will save. 'But humanism is, after all, a faith which has proved itself in deeds, and which has proved itself as well, perhaps, as any other creed. And although I think, with most humanists, that Christianity, by teaching the Fatherhood of God, may make a great contribution to establishing the brotherhood of man, I also think that those who undermine man's faith in reason are unlikely to contribute much to this end.' [56]

This faith in human potential, in rationality and altruism— and faith is the word used—brings us to the final point, the need

206 THE ETHICAL IDEALISM OF MATTHEW ARNOLD

for belief. Here again the widest tolerance must operate. The need of the individual is for an object of belief that will give meaning to *his* life. It may be the Moral Law, a loving and personal God, a significant pattern in experience or in history, the certainty of truth, the possibility of human betterment, the keeping of one's own integrity, the honouring of the social or moral code. The extreme of a nihilistic irresponsibility, which in terms of human values expresses no belief, and the extreme of a tyrannically imposed conformity may fairly be thought to fall outside the bounds of tolerance. This is merely to say that the life process can tolerate all forces acting upon or within it except those that would rob it of life. But the diversity of efficient beliefs is bound to reflect the diversity of human temperament and to be diversely expressed. We may, like Whitehead, agree with William James that religion is 'the feelings, acts, and experiences of individual men in their solitude'. Or we may share Dean Inge's view: 'Religion is not, as Professor Whitehead says, what a man does with his solitariness, but rather, as Royce declared, loyalty to a beloved community.'

One cannot, of course, refer to all these motivating beliefs as religious. The pragmatic concession of James that religious experience involves 'union with *something* larger than ourselves' is echoed in the idealistic assertion of Niebuhr that we have a need to believe in 'a reality larger and more inclusive than ourselves'. Such statements usually point the way to orthodox supernaturalism, to the mystical vision and transcendent peace. But they need not be abandoned altogether in turning to the other level of belief, the scientific and humanist faith in the altruistic and rational potential of man. We see this when Bouglé describes Durkheim's work as culminating in 'a theory of the human spirit', in a view of society as 'preparing the conditions of spiritual life'.[57] For idealism is present to some degree in any transcending of limitations, and supplies the element of hope and prophecy in every belief. By idealism here I do not mean a logically reasoned belief in a metaphysical reality; I mean what Maritain calls 'the natural platonism of our minds', the belief, vague as it often is, in the value of the unrealized or the immaterial.

This idealistic evaluation can operate in many ways. Even the 'humanist exaltation or idealization of human nature', says Dawson, 'found a justification in the existence of heroes and poets who transcend the limits of common experience in moments of inspiration and creative imagination'. It can be an illuminating component in the rationalism of the scientific humanist:

> To believe that the natural order is determined by our moral order is presumptuous. . . . But to say that nature sanctions and supports as well as frustrates our lofty aspirations, that there may be 'preëstablished harmonies' between its order and our ideals, is simply to restate the very premises of naturalism. Our values are the fine flowering of our purposes, and our purposes are rooted in natural conditions.[58]

We may indeed feel that we have the extreme of an optimistic idealism, a kind of mass operation of Babbitt's inner check, when Mannheim offers his vision of what voluntary co-operation of all educational agencies could achieve in the way of democratic self-discipline: 'It is very likely that a democratically controlled planned society will be mainly based upon a new kind of self-control, where people stop arguing about differences when it comes to action and decision.'[59] Finally, this 'idealism' can operate as a stabilizing force upon those who, theoretically, reject all value judgments, or the framing of them, as meaningless. The existentialist will no doubt pay you back the money he borrowed; the logical positivist will probably react strongly if you tell him his son is a bad boy. The assertion that ethical statements are merely rhetorical utterance is, Toulmin reminds us, a logical point, not an empirical one: 'One soon discovers in practice that advocates of the doctrine are no less cheerful or "idealistic" (in the everyday sense) than others, and that they will happily support the most rigorous of ethical judgments.'[60]

The common feature in this range of attitudes, of refractions of 'faith', and of the evaluations they make possible, is the quality of interplay, tension, or polarity I attributed to Arnold's critical principle, as it functioned in his ethical idealism. Emil Brunner gives a lyrical description of it: 'As the butterfly is attracted by light, so irresistibly is man drawn by this higher element', which may be the true, the righteous, the good, the beautiful, the holy or just the 'truly human'. As the 'tension of the bowstring makes the bow, so it is this tension between him and this higher element which constitutes the essential human quality in human existence, without which man would be only a particular kind of animal'.[61]

To express the higher or ideal element in this tension or polarity by such a variety of terms, including the 'truly human', is to recognize what I have called the diversity of efficient beliefs, with objects ranging from the eternal transcendent to the temporal mundane. The more the ideal element partakes of the temporal and mundane, the more difficult it will be to maintain the tension as a dynamic force in moral and spiritual life, a fruitful source of creative moral energy. It may slacken and fail; it may break under unbearable strain. Before the stupidity and selfishness of men, the intractability of the human material, the fine mind and the sensitive nature may easily despair. It is understandable that some should find the problem posed by Newman's 'heart-piercing, reason-bewildering fact' insoluble in human terms, or by the unaided individual reason.

Yet there are those who find it impossible to believe in some metaphysical reality, or in the Christian God as defined by traditional orthodoxy, and who cannot surrender their free minds to the substitute metaphysics and orthodoxy of a class ideology or *Führer-Prinzip*. They hold against odds to a faith in rationality and altruism, knowing that these attitudes of mind are as much facts of human nature as the attitudes of worship and surrender, and believing that they are the attitudes which have been and will be productive of any amelioration of the human condition. To hold this faith is anything but easy; it is, as Popper says, to bear the cross of being human. The humanism of Sherrington or Mannheim is no mere sentimental humanitarianism, and when any of our 'new Christians' rebuke such a working belief as vaporous or futile or degenerate, they invite and deserve the retort that perhaps the joy of being men of distinction lends added though unchristian charm to the restored beatific vision.

It is because Arnold's ethical idealism expressed itself at both the actual and ideal levels that his ideas are still relevant, as useful ingredients in the intellectual activity that affirms, even while modifying, the relationships between ethics and the special studies of man as a political or social or scientific or other kind of being. He asserted, without seeing or admitting the assertion as an act of faith, the certainty of moral order in the universe, calling it the 'Eternal not ourselves that makes for righteousness'. Had he succeeded in constructing a logical proof for the necessity of his metaphysical reality, as Bradley and Bosanquet did for theirs, he would be of as little general interest today as they are.

But he did not think of his 'Eternal not ourselves' as a transcendent reality, rather as a real and verifiable operating principle that finds expression in our own higher (but still human) natures. His idealism was always expressing itself on an oblique rather than a vertical axis, with the higher element in the tension or polarity a vision described in human and temporal terms. The kingdom of God is to be a better life on earth; the resurrection is spiritualized as the rising to a higher level of (human) life; on this level Jesus, unique in his goodness to the point of being an absolute in the eyes of erring humanity, exhibits a perfection that we can apprehend only by the word 'divine'. Such an idealism tends to confuse two kinds of fact or reality when 'verification' of its truth is claimed, and to use loosely words used with precision by systematic philosophy or theology. But the attacks on Arnold on logical or semantic grounds lose their effect in a humanistic setting, where the residual force of 'idealistic' value judgments has both psychological impact and ethical meaning. These serve as reminders to the positivist scientific mind and to the systematic philosophic mind that, as Gates remarks, diverse readers are 'open to countless other appeals than that of sheer logic'. For the logical and metaphysical thinker, the shifting plane of Arnold's polarity was a fatal weakness; for the social and ethical thinker, it makes his idealism viable in the context of a humanistic and scientific culture.

Understanding of what Arnold was attempting, and approval of the practical import of this Ritschlian type of ethical idealism, was expressed by the Jesuit George Tyrrell: 'Far from abandoning metaphysics, to deduce it from life and conduct rather than from notions and concepts is to place it for the first time on a firm basis, and to give it that interest which attaches to every study that bears, however remotely, on life and action.' [62] This sincere convert to Roman Catholicism, excommunicated for his rebellious modernism, is an interesting example of how far the genuinely religious temperament can go with Arnold, and where it must draw the line. When Tyrrell rebukes obscurantists for forgetting 'that Christ meant that which "saves" a man and makes him a Christian is not science and theology and history, but a spirit and a temper'; when he says that a man can have faith in the Church and her tendencies but regard her 'consciously formulated ideas and intentions about herself as more or less untrue to her deepest nature'; when he says that 'the miraculous theory' must go the way of all 'fond illusions', and 'Catholicism like Judaism have to die in order to live again in a greater and grander form', for

'Rome will never reform herself'; when he says that 'experiment-
ally man gropes his way to the sort of conduct that best furthers
the expansion and elevation of his spiritual nature', and that by
dogmatic excesses 'one is driven back always to the religion *of*
Jesus and away from that *about* Jesus'; when he says that schism is
bad 'because there were vigorous vital elements of goodness and
truth in nearly every schism, which were thus dissipated and lost
to the Church'—in all this he is 'very Catholic in the non-
sectarian sense, which is more or less the Matthew-Arnoldian, but
not at all the Wilfrid-Wardian sense'.[63]

There are two ways in which Arnold is, however, inadequate
to such a man, inadequate in his religious psychology. Arnold
found the higher or moral self 'natural' to man; Tyrrell goes
further and finds the supernatural, the super-rational, 'natural'
to man. What Arnold was so anxious to explain away, under the
influence of a rigorously positivist science, Tyrrell sees as an
essential part of man's religious experience, and he has the support
of Jamesian psychology in regarding the mystical and trans-
cendental states of mind as at least important *facts* of the religious
life.

The other inadequacy to Tyrrell was in the concept of God,
which could not satisfy the need for love. He found something
'frigidly Anglican and respectable in Matthew Arnold's "righteous-
ness" as the characteristic of the Divinity'. It is a 'sort of uni-
versity God, a personification of the Nicomachean ethics'. It is
true that he could later, and in more serious mood, tell a corre-
spondent that faith is at its best in certain moments of experience
of God, adding, 'And the object of this faith, the reality thus
apprehended, what is it but what Matthew Arnold calls the
"Power that makes for Righteousness"?'[64] Yet the deficiency is
there for him and for others, and is not compensated by an appeal
either to poetry or to the imaginative reason. That Arnold saw
the power of love in religion is clear from his exalting of St
Theresa over John Knox, and his finding in Jesus as guide to the
good life an emotional compulsion of love missing in Marcus
Aurelius and Spinoza. In spite of the fact that he stressed the
need for 'warmth' in religious ideas, however, and brought the
gospel teaching into his social prophecies, he has in the main
addressed himself to the reason rather than to the emotions.

Another polarity in Arnold's ethical idealism, by which it
moves towards social ethics but always returns to the ethics of

self-perfecting, perhaps requires for motive power an emotional synthesis. Such a thought occurs on reading Albert Schweitzer, whose ethic of 'reverence for life' embraces science, religion, and humanitarianism to produce an active spirituality. Like Arnold, he accepts the Spinozist idea that our will to live 'carries within itself the impulse to realize itself in the highest possible perfection'. Indeed, 'the basic principle of the moral must be recognized as a necessity of thought'. But such rationalism is not enough, for 'if rational thought thinks itself out to a conclusion, it arrives at something non-rational which, nevertheless, is a necessity of thought'. In other words, rational thought is the way to a true mysticism, and we must accept the paradox that without a non-natural element, our views of the world and of life will have neither value nor vitality. Our post-Renascence 'world-and-life-affirmation' has increasingly been merely 'a confidence in discovery and invention and not in any profounder view of life'.

To synthesize the ethics of self-perfecting developed in the Spinoza-Kant-Fichte line, and the ethics of social utilitarianism, or altruism, a principle is needed that is both active and reflective while free of the limitations of the natural and rational. Only the ethic of 'reverence for life' will supply this today. 'Ethics are responsibility without limit towards all that lives.' Legality, expediency, and compromise mark the course of ordinary ethics, and we can accept forgiveness for guilt by being sincere with ourselves. But the ethical principle is absolute: 'It is good to maintain and to encourage life; it is bad to destroy life or to obstruct it.' Only by such a principle will belief in moral and spiritual progress be possible, and the religious impulse return: 'Ethical mysticism reveals to [men] the necessity to thought of the religion of love, and thus leads them back to paths which they believed they had abandoned forever.' [65]

What Schweitzer offers us in his ethical principle is the inspiring and noble affirmation that is impossible fully to apply. He knows this. He would have to agree with Sherrington that man 'has set himself deliberately to exterminate those lives which invade and incapacitate and destroy his own', like *plasmodium malariæ*, and that in answer to the question, 'Is life a sacred thing?' man's reply is that there is 'life' from which the planet has to be rescued. But he believes strongly that unless we set up his principle as an absolute, and in our sincerity recognize deviation from it, no matter how unavoidable, as guilt, we run the risk of confusing expediency or legality or mere survival with principle. In that case our ethical position is hopeless. Hence his emphasis on the paradox of his ethical mysticism, which like the great Christian paradoxes that we must lose our lives in order to save them, and that we must love our enemies, supplies the idealism without which men cannot hope to rise even as far as the 'truly human'. And the paradox can be morally and spiritually effective only when a large and idealized abstraction can be apprehended by the imagination in personal and concrete terms. So certain eminent scientists have told us in their grim warning that thermonuclear weapons have put upon mankind the choice of abolishing war or risking race suicide: 'What perhaps impedes understanding of the situation more than anything else', the statement reads, 'is that the term "mankind" feels vague and abstract. People scarcely realize in imagination that the danger is to themselves and their children and their grandchildren, and not only to a dimly apprehended humanity.' [66]

These words recall Arnold's final claim for the power of Christianity, that it engages 'for the government of man's conduct, the mighty forces of love, reverence, gratitude, hope, pity and awe', and the lines he quotes from Wordsworth have an added significance:

> Survives *imagination* to the change
> Superior? Help to virtue does she give?
> If not, O mortals, better cease to live!

He knew that men will not rise as far as they are capable of rising unless challenged up to and beyond their limits by such an 'absolute' as that offered in the 'lovely perfection' of Jesus. But in his own ethical idealism he tried to avoid the mystical as well as the metaphysical, believing that the highest moral or religious power will be effective only as it is felt to have practical import in the lives of men. It must be capable of apprehension by the reason, however dimly, and even the highest flights of the 'imaginative reason' must not carry us beyond the bounds of our total experience. The interplay of inward self-perfecting and social solidarity, the reiterated plea for the harmonious expansion of all our powers, the frequency of tribute to the 'sweet reasonableness' of Jesus, all point to the essentially humanistic quality of Arnold's 'philosophy of middle principles'. His reason blends too easily with intuition or imagination to satisfy the demands of logic or system; his rationalism cannot meet the needs of those who find no faith except in an *O altitudo!* Yet in an age which can solve the problem of survival only by more than mere physical co-operation, by a pooling of moral and spiritual resources, the sanity and catholicity of attitudes like his are desperately needed. The practical idealism of his values can give meaning and purpose to education, which too often has neither, and it can be a means of reconciling the persisting differences of Christian, scientist, and humanist.

P

Acknowledgements

The publishers wish to thank the following for their permission to quote passages from copyright material in this book: the Syndics of the University Press, Cambridge, for the passage from Sir Charles Sherrington's *Man on His Nature* quoted on page 191; the Louisiana State University Press for the passage from H. J. Muller's article 'Humanism in the World of Einstein' published in the *Southern Review*, Volume 5, 1939, quoted on page 197; the editor of *Mind* for the passage from J. H. Muirhead's article 'How Hegel Came to England' quoted on page 27; *The New Yorker* for the passage from Edmund Wilson's article 'On First Reading Genesis' quoted on page 76; the Editor of *Theology* and the Society for Promoting Christian Knowledge for the passage quoted on page 186; and Yale University Press for the passage from E. Gilson's *God and Philosophy* quoted on page 168, and the passage from H. J. Muller's *Science and Criticism* quoted on page 207.

Notes

CHAPTER I

(Throughout this book all references to the works of Arnold are to the 15-volume Macmillan edition [London, 1903], except where otherwise specified.)

1. *Letters*, 15:93. Manipulators of statistics might make much of the fact that the percentage of articles in the *Contemporary Review* on religious subjects (reviews excluded) shows the following decline: Vol. 1, 1866, 17 out of 30, or 57 per cent; Vol. 14, 1870, 15 out of 34, or 44 per cent; Vol. 21, 1872-3, 16 out of 50, or 32 per cent; Vol. 30, 1877, 15 out of 52, or 29 per cent; Vol. 45, 1884, 11 out of 54, or 20 per cent.

2. Quoted in *God and the Bible*, 8:xv.

3. Quoted by J. M. Robertson, *History of Freethought in the Nineteenth Century*, 2:404.

4. *Ibid.*, p. 395.

5. *Ibid.*, p. 396.

6. E. Abbott and L. Campbell, *The Life and Letters of Benjamin Jowett*, 2:88. In another letter of 1864 (1:369), Jowett had declared that the Bishops were fighting, not a few clergymen, but Truth, Science, Criticism, and the 'moral perceptions of mankind'. On the other hand, both Utilitarianism and German theology fell down through having no substitute for what they displaced: 'The attempt to show the true character of the Pentateuch and the Gospel History is very important negatively. But it does nothing towards reconstructing the religious life of the people.' This was precisely Arnold's position in his attack on Colenso.

7. Robertson, *History of Freethought in the Nineteenth Century*, 2:398.

8. Otto Pfleiderer, *The Development of Theology in Germany since Kant, and its Progress in Britain since 1825*, p. 371.

9. A. D. White, *A History of the Warfare of Science with Theology*, 2:334.

10. R. E. Prothero and G. G. Bradley, *Life and Correspondence of Arthur Penrhyn Stanley*, 2:40.

11. Quoted by V. F. Storr, *The Development of English Theology in the Nineteenth Century*, p. 423. Writing in *Fraser's Magazine* in October, 1870, Leslie Stephen remarked drily that the trend was hardly hospitable to Matthew Arnold's liberal views of the Bible and the Church, what with the new dogma from Rome and with 11,000 Protestant clergymen publicly affirming their belief in literal inspiration and everlasting punishment (82:414).

12. *Life and Letters*, 1:345 (italics mine). H. B. Wilson and Rowland Williams, two of Jowett's collaborators on *Essays and Reviews*, were in 1862 given a year's suspension for heresy by the Court of Arches, a decision reversed in 1863 by a judicial committee of the Privy Council. This action pointed up the comment made by Jowett, 'It would be a strange and almost incredible thing that the Gospel, which at first made war only on the vices of mankind, should now be opposed to one of the highest and rarest of human virtues— the love of truth' ('On the Interpretation of Scripture', *Essays and Reviews* [London; Parker, 1860], p. 374).

13. *Life and Letters*, 1:444.

14. A. P. Stanley, *Life and Correspondence of Thomas Arnold, D.D.*, p. 232. In *The Dissidence of Dissent* (Chapel Hill: University of North Carolina Press, 1944), F. E. Mineka offers an analytical study of the *Monthly Repository*, and points out that this radical Unitarian periodical anticipated by 40 years, though to a limited reading public, the positions in *Essays and Reviews*.

15. Quoted in H. L. Stewart, *A Century of Anglo-Catholicism*, p. 184. The term Lower Criticism has sometimes been used to distinguish historical and rational research into the probable accuracy of factual and mechanical detail, from the subtler Higher Criticism which dealt with questions of style and tone, and with the presence or absence of a doctrinal or metaphysical turn of phrase or bent of mind. Most of Colenso's work lay in the former area. His larger conclusions were that Moses may never have lived, that Joshua was a myth, that the Chronicles were fictitious, and that Christ was as apt to err as any other Jew in speaking of Moses and the *historical* past.

16. Prothero and Bradley, *Life and Correspondence of Arthur Penrhyn Stanley*, 2:170. Though Stanley defended Colenso's right of research and inquiry, he deplored, like Arnold, giving prominence to negative findings. A positive attitude was needed, to preserve 'the eternal verities'. How soon a more robust spirit was to emerge is seen in J. E. Carpenter, *The Bible in the Nineteenth Century*. He praises Colenso, but finds in Stanley's lectures on the Jewish Church an 'unwillingness to place his subject in the sharp focus of historical fact. . . . The method of enveloping persons and events in a golden haze in which all definite outline disappears in poetic radiance, may be not inapt for piety and edification, but it is useless to the searcher after truth.' (P. 127.)

17. Quoted in F. D. Maurice, *The Claims of the Bible and Science*, p. 138.

18. Pfleiderer, *The Development of Theology in Germany*, p. 354. Speaking of the ignorance about Strauss, and the ignoring of Charles Hennell, J. E. Carpenter tells us, 'The truth was that English thought was not yet ripe for a Christianity without miracle, for it had then no philosophy, whether of religious belief or religious experience on which to rest' (*The Bible in the Nineteenth Century*, p. 286).

19. 'Browning and the Higher Criticism', *Publications of the Modern Language Association*, 44:590. See also J. H. Muirhead, 'How Hegel Came to England', *Mind*, 36:434. 'The curse of British philosophy in the first half of the century was the survival within the Universities of the theological bias, outside of them of the positivist Humean tradition inherited, notwithstanding all that had been done in the direction of naturalizing Kant's work in England, from the pre-critical stage of thought.' Compare J. S. Mill's comment: 'The whole of the prevalent metaphysics of the present century is one tissue of suborned evidence in favour of religion' (*Three Essays on Religion*, p. 72).

20. Stanley, *Life and Correspondence of Thomas Arnold, D.D.*, p. 322.

21. Stewart, *A Century of Anglo-Catholicism*, p. 122.

22. In the famous concluding *Tract XC* in 1841, Newman 'adjusted' the meaning of the Thirty-nine Articles to allow for other sacraments than baptism and the Lord's Supper, for belief in the Real Presence, purgatory, and the Invocation of the Saints, for justification other than by faith alone. At the same time he insisted that he and his fellows had never condemned Roman teaching in itself, but only certain abuses. To most English readers, this was

a casuistical juggling with what they had been taught to regard as a denial of Romish error and superstition.

23. Quoted in *Quarterly Review* (July–Oct., 1874), 137:547. The Rev. Dr Littledale was a formidable scholar and controversialist, who though a Ritualist wrote much against Rome.

24. Henry Alford, 'The Union of Christendom in its Home Aspect', *Contemporary Review* (1868), 7:173.

25. The Earl of Oxford and Asquith, *Memories and Reflections* (London: Cassell, 1928), 1:36.

26. John Keble, *Letters of Spiritual Counsel and Guidance*, p. 236.

27. Quoted in J. Y. Simpson, *Landmarks in the Struggle between Science and Religion*, p. 175.

28. E. L. Woodward, *The Age of Reform*, p. 557.

29. Maurice, *The Claims of the Bible and Science*, p. 155.

30. F. W. Newman, *The Bigot and the Sceptic*, p. 14. The confidence here shown in 'ethical proof', common to the most agnostic of Victorians, reminds us of Arnold's 'verification', and of the attack such a concept invited from the logician and philosopher. That the divergent careers of the brothers Newman offer an illuminating line of approach to a study of the nineteenth century has recently been emphasized by Professor Basil Willey (*More Nineteenth Century Studies*).

31. Woodward, *The Age of Reform*, p. 557.

32. *Quarterly Review* (July–Oct., 1874), 137:43.

33. John Tyndall, *Fragments of Science*, 2:191.

34. *Christian Observer*, Oct., 1874.

35. Tyndall, *Fragments of Science*, 2:196.

36. James Martineau, *Modern Materialism: Its Attitude towards Theology*, p. 2.

37. James Martineau, *Essays, Reviews and Addresses*, 1:272.

38. Tyndall, *Fragments of Science*, 2:230.

39. Martineau, *Modern Materialism*, p. 59.

40. *Ibid.*, p. 71.

41. W. R. Greg, *Enigmas of Life*, p. 38.

42. *Ibid.*, p. 40.

43. G. M. Young, *Victorian England*, p. 75. Noel Annan has noted this quality in Leslie Stephen: 'Stephen wanted, not only comfort, but also certitude in the realm of the uncertain. And this he had asserted was unobtainable. He breaks faith with himself when he seeks to answer scientifically the very questions which he as an agnostic proclaimed to be unanswerable; unanswerable, that is, in a uniform manner which is to hold good for the whole world.' (*Leslie Stephen*, p. 220.)

44. Mrs Humphrey Ward, *A Writer's Recollections*, p. 299. In 'The Background of Arnold's *Literature and Dogma*', *Modern Philology*, 43:130–9, W. Blackburn explores the controversies of 1870. These included the quarrel over the Education Bill and religious instruction; the scandal of Stanley's invitation to the Prayer Book revision committee, the Unitarian Vance Smith among them, to attend Communion at Westminster Abbey, and the storm that followed Stanley's election as Select Preacher at Oxford; and the fight over the Athanasian Creed, with Pusey's High Church party winning. The Education Bill of 1870, largely shaped by Arnold's brother-in-law Forster, gave local authority

to school boards, founded a national though not yet compulsory system of education, and proposed 'to exclude from all rate-aided schools every catechism and formulary distinctive of denominational creed, and to sever altogether the connection between the local school boards and the denominational schools, leaving the latter to look wholly to the central grant for help' (quoted from the biography of W. E. Forster, *Dictionary of National Biography*, Vol. 7, 1908). The alarm over this move to secularize education, among both Churchmen and Dissenters, was such that three months were needed to defeat an amendment which refused to leave the question of religious instruction to the choice of the local authorities. G. K. Clark tells us that the more far-sighted Nonconformists gave up the long struggle against government control and state aid, seeing that democratic education could be had in no other way: 'In 1869 a group which contained such eminent Dissenters as Joseph Chamberlain the Unitarian and R. W. Dale the Congregationalist founded the Educational League which demanded that the government should provide a system of education for the whole country which should be compulsory, unsectarian and free' (*The English Inheritance* [London: SCM Press, 1950], p. 136). Another fight, that over the Irish Disestablishment Bill of 1869, a long overdue concession to simple justice, was in large part the expression of a fear that disestablishment for the Church of England would follow. Yet the decades passed without such action, and with decreasing likelihood of it. H. L. Stewart suggests that the combination of fierce Protestantism, fierce rationalism, and fierce Catholicism seeking disestablishment is just what the average Englishman most dislikes. At heart he wants (even if he does not attend) a Church that is a national acknowledgement of Christianity, that keeps certain communal ideals alive, that shows a tolerant breadth, and that contrives to offer a religion for all yet to preserve an aristocratic bearing.

45. Muirhead, 'How Hegel Came to England', p. 423. J. M. Robertson, after damning Arnold with consistent ferocity, closes with a modicum of faint praise which is perhaps more of a concession than he realized. It expresses, in polemical negatives, what Arnold was admittedly trying to do, and offers a variation in a minor key on Muirhead's statement. Arnold's main service, says Robertson, was in leading 'the largest number of conventionally-trained people of moderate thinking powers to give up their more irrational traditional opinions' (*Modern Humanists* [London: Swan Sonnenschein, 1901], p. 183).

CHAPTER II

1. *Letters*, 15:107.
2. *Literature and Dogma*, 7:313.
3. *Ibid.*, p. 108.
4. *Essays in Criticism, First Series*, 3:174.
5. *God and the Bible*, 8:xi.
6. *Ibid.*, p. 50.
7. *Ibid.*, p. xlv.
8. *Mixed Essays*, 10:116. In a review of *God and the Bible* (*Academy*, Dec. 18, 1875), Albert Réville effectively summarized the radical-conservative opposition in Arnold's ideas, an opposition that puzzled and irritated many critical readers: 'We have here to deal with a thinker who has broken theoretically

with all the theologies and metaphysics of the past, who has saturated himself with the results of independent criticism, who absolutely rejects the supernatural, who has adopted the idea that God may be nothing but an impersonal force, an unconscious influence, in a word a thing rather than a person; and who at the same time is an ardent supporter of the Christian tradition, who shows himself every moment more severe towards its assailants than its defenders, who feels all the enthusiasm of a mystic for the Jahveh of the Jews and the Saviour of the Christians, and who above all professes a reverence for the Bible which scarcely yields to that of the most devoted partisans of verbal inspiration.'

9. *Irish Essays*, 11:323.

10. *St Paul and Protestantism*, 9:48.

11. *Literature and Dogma*, 7:366.

12. *Last Essays on Church and Religion*, 9:182.

13. *St Paul and Protestantism*, 9:48.

14. *Ibid.*, p. 23.

15. *Ibid.*, p. 65.

16. This mystical conception of *dying to sin*, with all its implications, is described by Arnold as *necrosis*, a doctrine which he esteems as original with Paul and central to his teaching.

17. *St Paul and Protestantism*, 9:79.

18. *Essays in Criticism, First Series*, 3:282–3.

19. *Literature and Dogma*, 7:291.

20. *Essays in Criticism, Second Series*, 4:241.

21. *Ibid.*, pp. 209–10.

22. *Literature and Dogma*, 7:11.

23. *Ibid.*, pp. 22–3.

24. *Ibid.*, p. 57.

25. *Culture and Anarchy*, 6:xl.

26. *God and the Bible*, 8:xli.

27. *Literature and Dogma*, 7:387.

28. *Essays in Criticism, First Series*, 3:313.

29. *The Study of Celtic Literature, and Other Essays*, p. 158.

30. *Ibid.*, p. 160.

31. Arnold, 'The Bishop and the Philosopher', *Macmillan's* (Jan., 1863), 7:256. W. R. Greg gave expression to the widespread surprise at the author of *Literature and Dogma* for assuming the same liberties he attacked in Colenso a decade earlier, and treating orthodox creeds with a scorn 'admirably calculated to give spirit and confidence to less audacious free thinkers' (*The Creed of Christendom*, 1:xxiv).

32. *God and the Bible*, 8:vi.

33. *Last Essays on Church and Religion*, 9:181.

34. *Literature and Dogma*, 7:129 (see *King John*, III, iv, 153). This point of view was a commonplace of biblical criticism by 1912, in the work of orthodox scholars. We are told that Christ may have 'transcended' the conditions of his time and place, but he spoke and taught in Aramaic and used 'the terminology of the time in regard to physical phenomena' and 'the Old Testament'. The apostles endorsed the 'general spirit and drift of the teaching' of the Old Testament, and 'not every fact or statement' (S. R.

Driver and A. F. Kirkpatrick, *The Higher Criticism*). There was not agreement, however, that the critical 'tact' of a man of culture was the best instrument, for getting at the 'scientific' truth, and F. W. Newman sourly remarked that Arnold's prescription for saving the Bible for the 'lapsed masses' seemed rather to pass 'a sentence of moral death on the vast majority of mankind' ('Literature and Dogma', *Fraser's*, 88:114).

35. *God and the Bible*, 8:299. In the radical criticism of the New Testament developed during the nineteenth century, three major interpretations may be seen: the mythical (Strauss), the legendary (Renan), and the logical-historical (Baur). In the first the Gospels are thought to exhibit a naturally expanding mythus, in the second, a great number of accretions gathering about a basis of fact, in the third, a number of existing theological and metaphysical tendencies logically and consciously developing. To this last school the Fourth Gospel is, of course, of prime importance.

36. *Last Essays on Church and Religion*, 9:379.

37. *Ibid.*, p. 417.

38. *Ibid.*, pp. 183–4.

CHAPTER III

1. *Unpublished Letters*, ed. A. Whitridge (1923), p. 65.

2. *Ibid.*, p. 56 (italics mine). We may at this point recall Arnold's analysis, in the essay 'Literature and Science', of human nature as made up of four powers. His discussion of three of them (beauty, intellect, social life and manners) closely parallels the point of view of Newman in the latter's discourses in the *Idea of a University*. The unbridgeable gulf between the two men is apparent, however, in Arnold's including of the fourth power, conduct, in his broadly cultural approach. However Newman influenced Arnold, it was not as a Catholic theologian.

3. *Essays in Criticism, Third Series*, ed. E. J. O'Brien (1910), p. 148.

4. *God and the Bible*, 8:xxxv.

5. Harold Nicolson, 'Swinburne and Baudelaire', *Transactions of the Royal Society of Literature*, n.s. (1926), 6:122.

6. *Essays in Criticism, First Series*, 3:175. Arnold came to Goethe and to other German writers through Carlyle, whose calls to duty and to idealistic self-transcendence he, like other young men of his day, found stimulating, though not for long. According to J. B. Orrick, this introduction aggravated the natural tendency of a son of Dr Thomas Arnold to find in Goethe the artist merely a moral help. Arnold's ideas can all be paralleled in Goethe, but he 'has learnt no habits and methods from Goethe', whose influence was fundamental 'only where it corresponded with certain preconceived attitudes in Matthew Arnold' ('Matthew Arnold and Goethe', *Publications of the English Goethe Society*, n.s. [1928], 4:52). It is hard to see how Arnold's definitions of cultural totality could reflect merely 'preconceived attitudes', and it can safely be asserted that the modern and naturalistic Goethe was largely responsible for the attitude or 'ruling idea' in Arnold which came closest to being 'scientific' —namely, his insistence that established customs, beliefs, creeds and intellectual patterns must come before the joint tribunal of general culture and cumulative human experience. Yet we can agree that Arnold was inclined to over-

emphasize the moral element in Goethe at the expense of the æsthetic and the sensuous. In L. P. Jacks, *Life and Letters of Stopford Brooke*, 2:548, there is an entertaining comment on this tendency from Stopford Brooke's diary for July, 1901: 'I sat by the lake and read Goethe. I came across M. Arnold's favourite passage,

> "Uns vom Halben zu entwöhnen
> Und im Ganzen, Guten Schönen
> Resolut zu leben;"

and much amused was I to find (because M. Arnold uses it only as an invitation to a high moral life) that life "im Ganzen", etc., includes not only strenuous action towards the good and the whole, but also these things

> "Den Philistern allzumal
> Wohlgemuth zu schnippen,
> Jenen Perlenschaum des Weins
> Nicht nur flasch zu nippen,
> Nicht zu hiben leis mit Augen
> Sondern fest uns anzusaugen
> An geliebte Lippen."

I wonder if Matt included the last two. He certainly did the first.'

7. *Life and Correspondence*, p. 420.

8. *God and the Bible*, 8:154.

9. S. T. Coleridge, *Miscellanies, Aesthetic and Literary*, ed. Ashe p. 324.

10. S. T. Coleridge, *Confessions of an Inquiring Spirit*, p. 58. Coleridge may be regarded as the virtual founder of the Broad Church movement. John Tulloch credits him with three influences: '*1st*, by a renovation of current Christian ideas; *2dly*, by an advance in Biblical study; *3rdly*, by an enlarged conception of the Church' (*Movements of Religious Thought in Britain during the Nineteenth Century*, p. 11).

11. *Essays in Criticism, First Series*, 3:300.

12. *Irish Essays and Others*, 11:311 (italics mine).

13. *Last Essays on Church and Religion*, 9:221. Coleridge's tributes to Smith occur in *Aids to Reflection*, p. 221n., and in *Literary Remains*, 3:415–16.

14. *Essays in Criticism, First Series*, 3:34.

15. *Letters*, 13:147. Arnold no doubt approved Renan's view of Paul as misunderstood by later generations, as a man of ideas who was at the same time a man of action, as a man of psychological insight, as a teacher who stressed the positive and moral and edifying side of religion, as one to whom, although a man of his age, 'the religion of the Christian is a religion of reason, without any other sacrifice than that of one's self' (*Saint Paul*, p. 280). But he could hardly accept Renan's view of Paul as a jealous wrangler, a man with a frantic and Luther-like attachment to 'a thesis embraced as the absolute truth', a man whose reign is ending because 'what makes Christianity live is the little we know of the word and person of Jesus'. L. F. Mott suggests that in this work of Renan Arnold found ideas kindred to his own, richly and happily expressed: 'In religion there was the sense of that stream of tendency by which all things strive to fulfill the law of their being; there was faith in the divine and denial of the supernatural; infallible doctrine was rejected, sacred history was treated as in no respect different from profane history, yet

religion itself, let the doctrine and symbol be what they may, was glorified as the highest manifestation of the human spirit.' He points to the parallel courses of Renan and Arnold, with the latter, in point of time, always a bit behind, and concludes that there was influence, if not actual debt. Yet he has to admit that there is insufficient evidence that *Culture and Anarchy* and *St Paul and Protestantism* were influenced by 'analogous works of Renan'. In the latter book (as is obvious from Arnold's own remarks on the first page), the 'whole tenour is in opposition to Renan's judgment that the normal outgrowth of St Paul's doctrines is protestant dissent' ('Renan and Matthew Arnold', *Modern Language Notes* [1918], 33:67).

16. *Mixed Essays* (London: Smith, Elder, 1880), p. 320.

17. *The George Sand–Gustave Flaubert Letters*, p. 351.

18. *Letters of Matthew Arnold to Arthur Hugh Clough*, ed. H. F. Lowry (1932), p. 51.

19. *Ibid.*, p. 116.

20. *Ibid.*, p. 143.

21. *Essays in Criticism, First Series*, 3:365. R. H. M. Elwes speaks of Arnold's 'brilliant essay' on Spinoza as, prior to Pollock's study in 1880, one of the few 'authorities to which the English reader could be referred' (*Chief Works of Benedict Spinoza*, p. vi).

22. *The Autobiography of Goethe: Truth and Poetry*, trans. J. Oxenford, 2:65.

23. *Works*, 1:91.

24. *Ibid.*, p. 80.

25. *Ibid.*, p. 197.

26. *Ibid.*, p. 175.

27. *Ibid.*, p. 199.

28. *Ibid.*, p. 162 (italics mine).

29. R. A. Duff, *Spinoza's Political and Ethical Philosophy*, p. 242. Arnold uses the phrase, 'an extension of oneself'.

30. *Last Essays on Church and Religion*, 9:309. A characteristic use by Arnold of Spinozist idiom occurs in the essay 'Literature and Science' (*Discourses in America*, 4:347), the whole point of which is to show the necessity of letters for human nature: 'And so at last we find flowing in favour of the humanities the *natural and necessary stream of things*' (italics mine). E. C. Mossner analyses Butler's reputation in terms which prove the justice of Arnold's criticism. He also points out that one factor in damaging Butler in the nineteenth century was the use of the argument from probability by Newman and his followers. (*Bishop Butler and the Age of Reason* [New York: Macmillan, 1936].)

CHAPTER IV

1. *God and the Bible* (1906), p. 21.

2. Introduction to *The Hundred Greatest Men*.

3. *God and the Bible* (1906), p. 67.

4. *Letters*, ed. G. W. Russell (London, 1895), 2:120.

5. *Fortnightly Review* (1888), 43:724.

6. Quoted in J. Huizinga, *Erasmus of Rotterdam*, p. 110.

7. *Ibid.*, p. 230.

8. Edmund Wilson, 'On First Reading Genesis', *New Yorker*, May 15, 1954, p. 128. The amateur philosopher Henry St John Bolingbroke, whose cool and astringent comments on matters theological reflect the temper of his times, anticipates Arnold in remarking that the Jews received the doctrine of the long-awaited Messiah 'agreeably to their prejudices and habitudes', and also were used to 'type and figure' the simple into the marvellous. 'This ignorance and learning conspired to turn the plainest religion that ever was into a chaos of theology, from which it has never been reduced again to an uniform consistent and intelligible system' (*Philosophical Works*, 3:106).

9. *God and the Bible* (1906), p. 10.

10. *Isaiah of Jerusalem* (1883), p. 44. Arnold had arranged and edited chapters 40–66 of Isaiah in 1872 as *A Bible Reading for Schools*. It was this earlier effort that was the subject of these reviews, which praised both the aim and, with some reservations, the scholarship and 'tact'. That Arnold was justified in thinking of himself as inheriting his father's critical 'line' is suggested by the following passage from Thomas Arnold: 'Questions of words . . . that provoke the intellect to reason rather than the heart to love, may indeed have to do with the same subjects with which God's word has to do, but they are not themselves God's word, inasmuch as they do not minister to the edification of God's people' (*Sermons, Chiefly on the Interpretation of Scripture*, p. 293).

11. *God and the Bible* (1906), p. 59. Cf. Coleridge's statement: 'Armed with the two-fold knowledge of history and the human mind, a man will scarcely err in his judgment concerning the sum total of any future national event, if he have been able to procure the original documents of the past . . . and if he have *a philosophic tact* for what is truly important in facts' (*Biographia Literaria*, 1:147, quoted in C. R. Sanders, *Coleridge and the Broad Church Movement* [Durham N.C.: Duke University Press, 1942], p. 55).

12. *Letters*, ed. Russell, 2:88.

13. F. H. Bradley, *Ethical Studies*, p. 283.

14. J. E. Carpenter, *The Bible in the Nineteenth Century*, p. 397.

15. D. S. Miller, 'Matthew Arnold on the "Powers" of Life', *International Journal of Ethics* (April, 1906), 16:354.

16. Lionel Trilling, *Matthew Arnold*, p. 364.

17. *Last Essays on Church and Religion*, 9:221.

18. *Essays in Criticism, First Series*, 3:283.

19. A. Vinet, *Vital Christianity*, p. 197.

20. J. H. Newman, *Discourses to Mixed Congregations*, p. 156.

21. *Vital Christianity*, p. xix. This distinction is seen in one of Arnold's favourite moralists: 'It is supposed that those who stick to virtue as a result of reasoning would abandon it in favour of a profitable vice. Yes, if vice could be such, in the view of a reasonable mind.' (Vauvenargues, *Reflections and Maxims* [London: O.U.P., 1940], Item 293, p. 105.) Edmond Scherer points out that Vinet, while a believer in supernatural Christianity, was a dissolvent of dogma: 'Vinet, par l'indifférence respectueuse qu'il a observée à l'égard des dogmes purement spéculatifs et des parties purements miraculeuses du christianisme, est devenu, à son insu, l'auteur d'une révolution au sein du protestantisme' (*Études sur la Littérature Contemporaine* [Paris: Lévy, 1885], 1:291).

22. S. T. Coleridge, *Aids to Reflection*, p. 173.

23. J. Butler, *Fifteen Sermons Preached at the Rolls Chapel*, p. 180. There is no theoretic assessment in Arnold of *reason* at different levels, as there might have been had he followed a Platonic or Kantian pattern. Hence there is ambiguity in his use of the term. In the introduction to *Literature and Dogma* the masses are 'rude and hard reasoners'; later on we are told that they go straight to the heart of the matter by a 'rude practical instinct'.

24. *Literature and Dogma*, 7:xix. 'Our natural capacity and judgment', says Hooker, 'must serve us only for the right understanding of that which the sacred Scripture teacheth' (*Works*, ed. Keble, 1:299). And this use of 'reason' is in harmony with the Divine purpose: 'For to the author and God of our nature, how shall any operation proceeding in natural sort be in that respect unacceptable?'

25. John Smith, *Select Discourses*, p. 397.

26. E. T. Campagnac, *The Cambridge Platonists*, p. x. In this Platonist-Spinozist view of man's religious striving towards perfection as a necessary form of self-realization, as the key to his *nature*, there is of course the fundamental optimism that is the soul of ethical idealism. The practical conclusion is essentially the same as that of Dean W. R. Inge in his study of the religious experience of mystics, although the context is different: 'Christianity agrees with Aristotelianism in teaching that the nature of a thing is its ultimate potentiality of development' (*Studies of English Mystics* [London: Murray, 1906], p. 24).

27. Smith, quoted in F. J. Powicke, *The Cambridge Platonists*, p. 19.

28. *Aids to Reflection*, p. 168.

29. *Table Talk*, ed. Ashe, p. 77. On page 175 Coleridge makes a sharp distinction: 'Faith is subjective. I throw myself in adoration before God . . .: but when I rise from my knees, I discuss the doctrine of the Trinity as I would a problem in geometry; in the same temper of mind, I mean, not by the same process of reasoning.'

30. J. H. Muirhead, *Coleridge as Philosopher*, p. 248.

31. *Ibid.*, p. 252.

32. John Tauler, *The Inner Way*, p. 128. The mystical attitude to truth is apparent, according to A. W. Hutton, in Arnold's sonnet, 'Lines Written in Butler's Sermons'.

33. *Essays in Criticism, Third Series* (1910), p. 243.

34. *St Paul and Protestantism*, 9:70.

35. *God and the Bible*, 8:86.

36. *Vital Christianity*, p. 51.

37. W. James, *The Will to Believe*, p. 61.

38. W. James, *The Varieties of Religious Experience*, p. 53.

39. The case against the more aggressive scientist was strongly put by Connop Thirlwall, a theologian regarded by Tyndall as 'tolerant and reasonable', in an address presenting the case for literature as against science. He rebels against the scientist who would go beyond positive teaching and aim to furnish him 'with a key to the mystery of my whole being', to say 'that there is nothing of a different and higher order which . . . may not be accounted for by his theory. I know, with the most intimate conviction with regard to myself, that his assertion is untrue; that he has not in fact brought me a single step nearer to the understanding of what I have been used to call

my moral and spiritual nature; . . . He is not now demanding my assent to the well-ascertained results of observation and experiment, but to a more private metaphysical speculation.' (*Essays, Speeches, and Letters* [London: Bentley, 1880], p. 300.)

40. J. Joubert, *Pensées and Letters*, p. 86.
41. E. Renan, *Vie de Jésus*, p. xxxi.
42. *Ibid.*, p. 78.
43. *Irish Essays*, 11:319.
44. E. Renan, *Essais de Morale et de Critique*, pp. ii–iii.
45. H. Spencer, *First Principles*, p. 15.
46. J. S. Mill, *Three Essays on Religion*, p. 74.
47. L. Huxley, *Life and Letters of Thomas Henry Huxley*, 2:11.
48. T. H. Huxley, *Science and Christian Tradition*, p. 310 (italics mine).
49. T. H. Huxley, *Evolution and Ethics*, p. 8.
50. *Science and Christian Tradition*, p. 268. Dr Arnold observed that a work like *Pilgrim's Progress* 'seems to be a complete reflection of Scripture, with none of the rubbish of the theologians mixed up with it' (A. P. Stanley, *The Life and Correspondence of Thomas Arnold, D.D.*, p. 295).
51. *Life and Letters*, 3:272.
52. A. S. Pringle-Pattison, *The Idea of God in the Light of Recent Philosophy*, p. 252.

CHAPTER V

1. *Unpublished Letters* (1923), p. 18.
2. *Essays in Criticism, First Series*, 3:368.
3. *The Chief Works of Benedict Spinoza*, 1:65.
4. *Ibid.*, pp. 179–81.
5. R. A. Duff, *Spinoza's Political and Ethical Philosophy*, quoting from Letter 43, *Correspondence*.
6. *Works*, 2:299. Here is the parallel to Arnold's emphasis on the spiritual side of the resurrection, and the real miracle of the Christian's continuing spiritual resurrection as against the illusory one of Christ's physical resurrection.
7. In Duff, *Spinoza's Philosophy*, p. 236.
8. *Works*, 2:365.
9. *Ibid.*, p. xxviii.
10. T. H. Huxley, *Science and Christian Tradition*, p. 140.
11. E. Abbott and L. Campbell, *The Life and Letters of Benjamin Jowett*, 2:78.
12. S. A. Brooke, *Life, Letters, Lectures and Addresses of Frederick W. Robertson*, p. 251.
13. *The Idea of God in the Light of Recent Philosophy*, p. 222.
14. D. F. Strauss, *The Life of Jesus*, p. 773. Strauss's description of the 'resurrection' involved in achieving the higher life closely parallels in psychological terms Arnold's detailed account of the 'necrosis' operative in the Pauline version of Christianity, as explained in chapter II. Strauss says, 'The believer, finding himself environed with the conditions of nature, must, like Christ, die to nature—but only inwardly, as Christ did outwardly—must spiritually crucify himself and be buried with Christ, that by the virtual

suppression of his own sensible existence, he may become, in so far as he is a spirit, identical with himself, and participate in the bliss and glory of Christ' (p. 778).

15. Wolfgang von Goethe, *Conversations with Eckermann and Soret*, 2:357. The strain of Spinozist stoicism and Goethean naturalism seems to me to be perfectly blended at the end of Arnold's poem 'A Wish'. Concerning this poem there is a poignant comment in a letter of 1873 from Arnold to his sister Fan. He mentions having had a letter 'from the State of Maine in America, from a young man who wished to tell me that a friend of his, lately dead, had been especially fond of my poem, "A Wish", and often had it read to him in his last illness. They were both—the writer and his friend—of a class too poor to buy books, and had met with the poem in a newspaper.' (*Letters*, ed. G. W. Russell [1895], 2:110.)

16. S. T. Coleridge, *Table Talk*, p. 313.

17. *Aids to Reflection*, p. 161. A prayer to the All-Highest curiously super-imposes Christian faith upon an idiom derived from Spinoza and Kant: 'To God, as the reality of the conscience and the Source of all obligation; to free-will as the power of the human being to maintain the obedience, which God through the conscience has commanded, against all the might of Nature; and to the immortality of the soul, as a state in which the weal and woe of man shall be proportioned to his moral worth. With this faith all nature,

—all the mighty world
of eye and ear—

presents itself to us, now as the aggregated material of duty, and now as a vision of the Most High revealing to us the mode, and time, and particular instance of applying and realizing that universal rule, pre-established in the heart of our reason.' (*The Friend*, p. 67.)

18. J. H. Newman, *Discourses Addressed to Mixed Congregations*, p. 262. J. M. Robertson links the names of Coleridge and Newman in this way, though the contempt of the 'rationalist' mind for both men is apparent: 'It is very probable that had he [Coleridge] been in the society of cultured Catholics who showed him the same protecting affection [i.e. as the Gilmans] he could have come round to the Catholicism of which he spoke in such terms of aversion. All his solutions being in terms of surrender to feeling—despite his express repudiation of the principle—he could have taken the way of Newman with little difficulty.' (*History of Free-thought in the Nineteenth Century*, 1:98.)

19. John Smith, *Select Discourses*, p. 45. In Cudworth the ontological proof of God is offered: 'A Being absolutely perfect . . . is that alone to which necessary existence is essential, and of which it is demonstrable' (quoted by G. P. H. Pawson, *The Cambridge Platonists and Their Place in Religious Thought*, p. 76). In Smith, neo-Platonic emanationism is the process informing the thought. The immanent God is pure and perfect Reason, infinite Power, almighty Love: 'He cannot act against those laws which are rooted in His very Nature. Nor can He will himself to be other than He is.' (*Ibid.*, p. 42.) By our own wills, stronger than our reason, we have a restless appetite to achieve the serenity possible only by resting in the changeless One.

20. *Select Discourses*, p. 141. One may think of Arnold's 'wisdom and goodness' formula as resting upon a joint foundation of Spinoza and the

Cambridge Platonists: 'wisdom' reflects Spinoza who finds self-realization in a knowledge, however fragmentary, of God; 'goodness' reflects the practical emphasis of the Cambridge group, especially Smith and Whichcote. This is not to suggest a division but merely a distribution of emphasis.

21. *Literature and Dogma*, 7:28.

22. *Ibid.*, p. 319.

23. *Life of Jesus*, p. xviii.

24. Quoted by Arnold in *Essays in Criticism, First Series*, 3:313. In a letter of January 14, 1864, Arnold told his mother to make Arthur Stanley read Joubert, saying, 'if he has ever read better religious philosophy than Joubert's I have not' (*Letters*, 13:285).

25. H. Spencer, *First Principles*, p. 118.

26. *Idea of God*, p. 214. Arnold, says T. S. Eliot, 'girds at (apparently) Herbert Spencer for substituting *Unknowable* for *God*; quite unaware that his own Eternal not ourselves comes to exactly the same thing as the Unknowable' (*Selected Essays*, p. 397). William James is again in agreement with Arnold, however: 'God is the natural appellation, for us Christians at least, for the supreme reality' (*The Varieties of Religious Experience*, p. 515).

27. *Literature and Dogma*, 7:122.

28. F. H. Bradley, *Ethical Studies*, p. 285.

29. *Idea of God*, p. 231.

30. R. H. Hutton, *Criticisms on Contemporary Thought and Thinkers*, 1:220.

31. James Martineau, *Essays, Reviews and Addresses*, 4:289.

32. *Idea of God*, p. 246.

33. *Ibid.*, p. 254.

34. *Man's Place in the Cosmos, and Other Essays*, p. 154.

35. *The Victorian Transformation of Theology*, p. 39.

36. J. R. Seeley, *Natural Religion*, p. 184.

37. J. S. Mill, *Three Essays on Religion*, p. 165.

38. *The Non-Religion of the Future*, p. 135.

39. *Ibid.*, p. 180.

40. *Literature and Dogma*, 7:389. The 'hardly yet ripe' is an interesting piece of evidence on the distance that Arnold has travelled from the position of his father, to whom an education not distinctively Christian was a contradiction in terms. F. W. Robertson, however, writes in a similar vein: 'I say that though in the long run, perhaps after centuries of anarchy and blood, mental cultivation alone will result in moral good, . . . for the present, the harvest will be bitter fruit and ranker villainy' (*Life, Letters*, p. 221). It is surprising to find the same thought expressed by Newman. In 1829 he wrote, 'It is no reply to say that the majesty of truth will triumph, for man's nature is corrupt; also, even should it triumph, still this will only be ultimately, and the meanwhile may last for centuries' (*Life and Correspondence*, 1:204, as quoted in C. F. Harrold, *John Henry Newman* [New York: Longmans Green, 1945], p. 26).

CHAPTER VI

1. *Letters of Matthew Arnold to Arthur Hugh Clough*, p. 110. G. K. Chesterton was to remark that under his surface raillery Arnold was, 'even in the age of

Carlyle and Ruskin, perhaps the most serious man alive'. That Clough, in spite of occasional reproaches, held this opinion at the time, is evident from a mention of Arnold in a letter of 1849: 'Do we not work best by digging deepest? by avoiding polemics, and searching to display the real thing? If only one could do the latter!—Emerson is an example, and also Carlyle, and, in his kind, Matthew Arnold.' (*Poems and Prose Remains*, 1:165.) It is Clough, however, whose remark on the insecurities and anxieties of the age, so constant a theme in Arnold's verse, lent colour to the Stracheyan portrait of Thomas Arnold: 'Is it, perhaps, that in our time the conscience has been over-irritated?' (*Ibid.*, p. 297.)

  2. *Essays in Criticism, Second Series*, 4:368.

  3. E. P. de Senancour, *Obermann*, p. 125. Arnold must have frequently heard his father put the same thought in Christian terms: 'We cannot be in a state of salvation ourselves, if we are wholly without zeal for the salvation of others' (Thomas Arnold, *Sermons, Chiefly on the Interpretation of Scripture*, p. 74).

  4. *The Chief Works of Benedict Spinoza*, 2:201.

  5. R. A. Duff, *Spinoza's Political and Ethical Philosophy*, p. 127.

  6. *Works*, 2:210.

  7. R. A. Duff, *Spinoza's Philosophy*, p. 179.

  8. *St Paul and Protestantism*, 9:43.

  9. B. Whichcote, *Mora land Religious Aphorisms*, ed. W. R. Inge, p. 69. Pringle-Pattison puts the problem in terms of the actual and the potential: 'The essence of human nature is just . . . the contrast between the actual present and the unrealized future, passing into the deeper contrast between the "is" and the "ought-to-be", and the duality of what is commonly called the lower and the higher self, with the discord and the struggle hence resulting' (*The Idea of God in the Light of Recent Philosophy*, p. 254).

  10. *Discourses*, ed. Long, p. 21.

  11. *Literature and Dogma*, 7:89. ·

  12. Wolfgang von Goethe, *Conversations of Goethe with Eckermann and Soret*, 1:382. Georg Brandes too points out that Goethe, like Spinoza, passes from a passive stoicism to an active, adding to self-restraint and self-conquest the positive sanction of joy: 'The greater the joy, the nearer perfection and the deity' (*Wolfgang Goethe* [New York, Frank-Maurice, 1925], 1:436).

  13. *Literature and Dogma*, 7:98. The utilitarian Herbert Spencer is not far from Arnold's position when he says, 'conduciveness to happiness is the ultimate test of perfection in a man's nature', and goes on to say that this ultimate moral aim is 'as much a necessary form of moral intuition as space is a necessary form of intellectual intuition' (*Data of Ethics*, pp. 37, 51).

  14. *Principia Ethica* (Cambridge, 1903), p. 114.

  15. T. H. Huxley, *Evolution and Ethics*, p. 44.

  16. S. T. Coleridge, *Aids to Reflection*, p. 78.

  17. *Select Discourses*, p. 458. These comments on the limits of stoicism, and the positive superiority of the Christian religion, recall Spinoza's addition to stoicism of a rational emotion (love) as superior to the rational intellect for the exorcising of evil, an addition which, Arnold finds, appeals to both Goethe and himself as representing the substitution of a joyful activity for a mere passive restraint.

18. *Essays in Criticism, First Series*, 3:381. Similarly Arnold finds Epictetus, Augustine, and Emerson superior to Carlyle, even to Wordsworth at times, in their stress upon happiness as the root desire in humanity, as opposed to a mere call to duty: 'In the life of the spirit is happiness, this is Emerson's contribution' (*Discourses in America*, 4:380). Renan perhaps uses more realistic language in writing of Paul's success in preaching the Kingdom of God: 'A few sages . . . Marcus Aurelius and Spinoza . . . have practised the highest virtue without hope of remuneration. But the multitude is never heroic.' (*Saint Paul*, p. 250.)

19. *Thoughts of the Emperor M. Aurelius Antoninus*, ed. Long, p. 91.

20. *Essays in Criticism, First Series*, 3:333. The knowledge of the profound meaning of Christian teaching, of the humanizing and purifying result possible to grief and suffering, Arnold came at by experience, as much as he did his knowledge of the virtues and shortcomings of middle-class Puritan nonconformity during his travels as school inspector. Losing two sons in 1868, and a third in 1872, he was indeed tempered by sorrow. The story of George Russell's calling on the bereaved father and finding him consoling himself with Marcus Aurelius suggests an iron control; how much went on under that control may be guessed from the one revealing sentence in a letter to his mother in February, 1872: 'I cannot write his name without stopping to look at it in stupefaction at his not being alive.'

21. *Irish Essays*, 11:327. The feeling for solidarity, in the form of a condemnation of suffering and flagrant inequality, may be seen in the early sonnet 'To a Republican Friend', where Arnold assures Clough of his contempt for 'the barren optimistic sophistries of comfortable moles', and his awareness of 'the armies of the homeless and unfed'.

22. *Culture and Anarchy*, 6:207.

23. *Essays in Criticism, Second Series*, 4:312.

24. *The Journals of André Gide*, 4:39. That erotic libertinism may be connected with the downfall of states is not merely a Victorian notion—as Trilling points out, Aldous Huxley follows his grand-uncle Matthew Arnold in postulating a connection. A French writer whose analysis interested Arnold, and perhaps helped to convince him that he was on the right track, was Émile de Laveleye. Pointing to the greater development in prosperity and civilization in the Protestant nations as a group, de Laveleye attributed the advantage to Protestant morality, a sturdy growth from the championing of liberty by moral and religious men. In France the overthrow of a churchly absolutism, already weakened by Voltairian mockery, had discredited the moral absolutism that it had taught. Nor could devotion to a state, in the face of its corrupt and fluctuating fortunes, replace belief in a divine law. All that was left in France to restrain the soldier, citizen, statesman, was a concept of 'honour', which as often as not was an appeal to vanity, and in any case was a feebler spring of action than a concept of duty. The Roman Catholic religion, de Laveleye gloomily maintained, had not 'fitted the French to live in freedom, to tolerate each other, and to govern themselves' (*Protestantism and Catholicism in Their Bearing upon the Liberty and Prosperity of Nations*, p. 46).

25. *Essays in Criticism, Second Series*, 4:340.

26. *Literature and Dogma*, 7:20. See chap. ii, n. 23, for pagan-Christian parallels.

27. F. H. Bradley, *Ethical Studies*, p. 281.

28. *Essays in Criticism, First Series*, 3:379. For a full analysis of the process culminating in faith, see chapter II.

29. *God and the Bible*, 8:x.

30. T. H. Huxley, *Science and Christian Tradition*, p. 316.

31. *Mélanges d'Histoire Religieuse*, p. 64. Renan finds in his 'naturalistic' Jesus a uniqueness of moral superiority and challenge which guarantees a continuing force for the future: 'Des hommes d'une médiocre moralité ont écrit de fort bonnes maximes. Des hommes très-vertueux, d'un autre côté, n'ont rien fait pour continuer dans le monde la tradition de la vertu. La palme est à celui qui a été puissant en paroles et en œuvres, qui a senti le bien, et au prix de son sang l'a fait triompher. Jésus, à ce double point de vue, est sans égal; sa gloire reste entière et sera toujours renouvelée' (*Vie de Jésus*, p. 97).

32. *Literature and Dogma* (Nelson), p. 22.

33. *Literature and Dogma*, 7:142.

34. *The Victorian Sage*, p. 215.

35. F. C. S. Schiller, 'The Ethical Basis of Metaphysics', *International Journal of Ethics* (July, 1903), 13:434. According to A. W. Moore: 'Philologically a pragmatist might be expected to agree with Matthew Arnold that life is three-fourths conduct, and perhaps to add that the remaining fourth is very like the other three' (*Pragmatism and Its Critics* [University of Chicago Press, 1910], p. 3).

36. 'The Christian Doctrine of God', in *Lux Mundi*, ed. C. Gore, p. 68.

37. C. S. Pierce, 'Illustrations of the Logic of Science', *Popular Science Monthly* (March, 1878), 12:612.

38. *Last Essays on Church and Religion*, 9:339. The function of religion in aiding and inspiring this necessarily relative and approximative effort is emphasized by Reinhold Niebuhr. Religion, he says, makes the attempt at a better world possible. It gives the courage to achieve the vision which cannot be achieved, in a society compounded of fulfilment and frustration: 'The vision is an impossible one, which can be approximated only by those who do not regard it as impossible' (*Moral Man and Immoral Society* [New York: Scribner's, 1934], p. 81).

39. *Last Essays on Church and Religion*, 9:197. This is Arnold's last word, at the end of his preface. The substitution of 'Christianity' for the 'conduct' of *Literature and Dogma* reveals perfectly the paramount concern and unifying force in Arnold's life, namely, the moral seriousness which was his from the beginning, and the imaginative need for religious truth which deepened steadily throughout his life. His definition of religion was no catch-phrase; the emotional heightening which fed the imagination was as necessary, in the search for 'joy whose grounds are true', as the sense of security obtained for the will and the reason in equating religion with morality.

CHAPTER VII

1. 'Puritanism and the Church of England' in *St Paul and Protestantism* (1870), p. xxxi.

2. S. T. Coleridge, *On the Constitution of the Church and State*, p. 71.

3. A. P. Stanley, *The Life and Correspondence of Thomas Arnold, D.D.*, p. 232.

NOTES 233

4. *Life and Correspondence*, p. 219. This view of the relationship of Church and State derives from the theologian Hooker and the statesman Burke, from a conservative and Anglican tradition. In Lionel Trilling's view it also is part of a larger modern movement of thought: 'Arnold's ecclesiastical theory is the perfect exemplification of that post-Reformation movement which Hegel has described, the "recognition of the Secular as capable of being an embodiment of Truth"; "State and Laws", Hegel declared, "are nothing else than Religion manifesting itself in the relations of the actual world" ' (*Matthew Arnold*, p. 56).

5. J. H. Overton and A. K. C. Relton, *The English Church from the Accession of George I to the End of the Eighteenth Century* (London: Macmillan, 1906), p. 1.

6. N. Sykes, *Church and State in England in the Eighteenth Century*, p. 130.

7. 'Mr Matthew Arnold and the Dissenters', *Congregationalist* (1873), 2:427–34.

8. 'Mr Matthew Arnold and Puritanism', *British Quarterly Review* (July–Oct., 1873), 52:417. It is this review which Mr R. V. Osbourn considers a fair and temperate answer to Arnold, showing up the unfairness and injustice of Arnold's manner and method (*Review of English Studies*, n.s. [April, 1950], 1–2:147–52).

9. Gladstone Papers, British Museum Add. Mss., 342:44427 (June 4 and 11, 1870).

10. John Hales, 'A Tract Concerning Schism and Schismatics' in *Several Tracts*, p. 182.

11. William Chillingworth, *Works*, 1:404.

12. T. Lyon, *The Theory of Religious Toleration in England*, p. 180.

13. Quoted in P. E. More and F. L. Cross, eds., *Anglicanism* (London: SPCK, 1935), p. 12.

14. Chillingworth, *Works*, 1:v.

15. Edward Stillingfleet, Prefatory Letter in *The Mischief of Separation*.

16. Quoted in W. H. Hutton, *The English Church from the Accession of Charles I to the Death of Anne*, p. 250.

17. John Stoughton, *History of Religion in England from the Opening of the Long Parliament to 1850*, 3:112. Stoughton points out that the Bill of Uniformity (containing in germ the Test Act and the Conventicle Act) passed the House of Commons two weeks before the Savoy Conference broke up: 'The proceedings of a Royal Commission to review the Prayer Book, and make alterations for the satisfactions of tender consciences [the words of Charles's promise when invited to return to England] were, by this premature act, really treated with mockery' (*ibid.*, p. 185).

18. *Last Essays on Church and Religion* (1877), p. 155.

19. Leslie Stephen, 'Mr Matthew Arnold and the Church of England', *Fraser's* (Oct., 1870), 82:422. In the privacy of a letter to his mother in 1871, Arnold himself made a comparison unfavourable to churchmen. Leaving his Hackney school district and managers who were Independents, he was curious to see what his experience would be with 'clerical managers'. They would be less interesting, being familiar specimens. 'But I also imagine they will be more inclined to expect to have the law a little strained in their favour, and less content with plain absolute fairness than the Nonconformist managers' (*Letters*, ed. G. W. Russell [1895], 2:53).

20. H. H. Henson, *Retrospect of an Unimportant Life*, 1:158. W. P. Bliss

noted in 1888 that socialism was stronger in the Church of England than among the Dissenters, with their bourgeois membership of laissez-faire commercial classes, and stronger even in High Church than in Broad Church. He gave as reasons the familiarity of the churchman with the State idea and with State action, and the extremes within the Church itself, including many poor and humble clergymen whose intimacy with the poorer classes bred a more democratic feeling. ('Socialism in the Church of England', *Andover Review* [1888], 10:491.)

21. *Matthew Arnold and His Relation to the Thought of Our Time.*

22. R. W. Dale, 'Mr Matthew Arnold and the Nonconformists', *Contemporary Review* (July, 1870), 14:549.

23. J. Drummond and C. B. Upton, *Life and Letters of James Martineau*, 2:6. H. McLachlan remarks on Arnold's ignoring the contributions of Unitarians and his degree of kinship with them. In his study of the Beard family, in which Charles Beard was Arnold's contemporary, he says, 'It is not without interest that whilst Matthew Arnold was writing, June, 1867, that "the greatest thing is to drag the dissenting middle classes into the great public arena of life and discussion, and not let it remain in its isolation, from which all its faults come", Beard was engaged in cultivating relations with liberals at home and abroad, translating foreign theology into English, and describing in popular journals the ecclesiastical and doctrinal developments in England, France and Germany' (*Records of a Family, 1800–1933* [Manchester University Press, 1935], p. 23).

24. R. W. Dale, 'The Disestablishment Movement', *Fortnightly Review* (March 1, 1876), 19:311–39.

25. R. H. Hutton, 'Mr Arnold on St Paul and his Creed', *Contemporary Review* (June, 1870), 14:332.

26. J. H. Newman, *Essays Critical and Historical*, 2:83.

27. E. G. Selwyn, *Essays Catholic and Critical*, p. xiii.

28. *Last Essays* (1877), p. 177.

29. Stewart, *A Century of Anglo-Catholicism*, p. 209.

30. 'Modern Culture', *Quarterly Review* (July–Oct., 1874), 137:389–415. The attitude the reviewer complains of may be seen in Pater's remark quoted by Mrs Humphrey Ward: 'To my mind, the beliefs and the function in the world of the historic church form just one of those obscure but all-important possibilities which the human mind is powerless effectively to dismiss from itself, and might wisely accept, in the first place, as a workable hypothesis. The supposed facts on which Christianity rests, utterly incapable as they have become of any ordinary test, seem to me matters of very much the same sort of assent we give to any assumptions, in the strict and ultimate sense, moral. The question whether those facts are real will, I think, always continue to be what I should call one of the *natural* questions of the human mind.' (*A Writer's Recollections*, p. 210.)

31. *Last Essays* (1877), p. 173.

CHAPTER VIII

1. *Christian Life, Its Course, Its Hindrances, and Its Helps*, p. viii.
2. J. Huizinga, *Erasmus of Rotterdam*, p. 103.

3. Quoted in *ibid.*, p. 110.

4. 'On First Reading Genesis', *New Yorker*, May 15, 1954, p. 144.

5. Quoted in 'Four States of Mind', *The Times Literary Supplement* (London), May 20, 1949, p. 322.

6. *Leslie Stephen*, p. 221. That Arnold, thinking in terms of polarities or opposites, thought also in terms of synthesis and reconciliation, is the theme of E. T. Campagnac's summary: 'For him art must have a meaning; poetry is the "criticism of life"; and business, organization, affairs must be illuminated by ideas. . . . What Matthew Arnold, in substance, says . . . is that . . . critics are wrong in admitting that for man there are two worlds: he seeks "humanity", the sum of those qualities which make men "humane", and in the possession and exercise of which men find "a city to dwell in", a mode of life in which manifold and varied interests are brought into harmony and order.' (*Prose Selections from Matthew Arnold* [London: Macmillan, 1928], p. xiii.)

7. H. J. Muller, 'Matthew Arnold: A Parable for Partisans', *Southern Review* (1940), 5:551. Other critics than Réville (chap. II, n. 8) have interpreted this flexibility in Arnold as an ambivalence of conservative and radical attitudes. Basil Willey sees Arnold as a 'conservative-reforming' force, and as such representative of the nineteenth-century mind at its best (*Nineteenth Century Studies*). W. S. Knickerbocker speaks of Arnold's 'oscillatory principle of attachment and withdrawals' ('Thunder in the Index', *Sewanee Review* [July–Sept., 1939], 47:439). This is an interesting comment on method; the effect of the method is happily described by Leslie Stephen, never one to spare Arnold: 'We ought to catch something of Arnold's spirit, so far as to admit, at least, that the great problem is to reconcile unflinching loyalty to truth with tenderness "infinite", if possible, for the errors which are but a grasping after truth' ('Matthew Arnold', *National Review*, in *Living Age* [Jan., 1894], 200:103).

8. E. Gilson, *God and Philosophy*, p. 117.

9. *Selected Essays*, p. 436. For an earlier criticism of the same tenor see chap. VII, n. 32. Leonard Brown vigorously rejected Eliot's view of the lineal descent from Arnold, and found Arnold's heirs rather in Hardy and Housman, trying, with the scepticism of the prevailing world-view, to see things as they really are. The late Romantics, he asserted, sought escape into Nature or the Church or sentimental humanitarianism. 'The best minds subsequent to Arnold's have been like his', a question of attitude, not of literary or philosophical influence. ('Arnold's Succession: 1850–1914', *Sewanee Review* [1934], 42:179.) Kenneth Allott offers a pertinent comment on the Eliot–Arnold relationship: 'For a generation now we have used Mr Eliot to correct Matthew Arnold. It is useful to remember that the process can run in reverse.' ('Matthew Arnold', *Writers and Their Work*, No. 60 [London: Longmans Green, 1955], p. 34.)

10. J. H. Newman, *Fifteen Sermons Preached before the University of Oxford*, p. 257. We find Newman here speaking of the 'great geniuses' in the same way that Arnold speaks of the 'sublime solitaries'.

11. *Irish Essays*, 11:415.

12. *Selected Essays*, p. 367. Mr Eliot's poison is meat to R. B. Braithwaite, Professor of Moral Philosophy. To him Arnold is 'a profound philosopher of religion' and 'that great but neglected Christian thinker' (*An Empiricist's View of the Nature of Religious Belief* [Cambridge, 1955]).

13. E. A. Burtt, *Types of Religious Philosophy*, p. 241.

14. Pfleiderer, *The Development of Theology in Germany since Kant, and Its Progress in Britain since 1825*, p. 330.

15. F. Adler, *Ethical Addresses* (17th Series; Philadelphia: American Ethical Union, 1910), p. 84.

16. *Letters*, 15:13.

17. H. H. Henson, *Retrospect of an Unimportant Life*, 2:194.

18. W. C. Brownell, *Victorian Prose Masters*, pp. 183–4. Even Frederic Harrison, recalling the 'singular mixture' of Arnold's theology, and describing it with Comtist relish as Anglicanism plus Spinozist pantheism equals Anglicanism minus Christian theism, added that this transformation of Anglicanism 'sank deep into the minds of many thinking men and women, who could neither abandon the spiritual poetry of the Bible nor resist the demonstrations of science' ('Matthew Arnold', *Nineteenth Century*, in *Living Age* [May, 1896], 209:371).

19. F. W. H. Myers, 'Matthew Arnold', *Fortnightly Review* (1888), 43:720. Arnold's already established reputation helped considerably in gaining a hearing for his religious ideas. E. E. Hale said in 1874 that when the most prominent English critic found the Bible indispensable for righteousness, 'all sorts of people' will listen, as they will not do to those they regard as 'hired advocates or prejudiced advisers' ('Literature and Dogma', *Old and New*, 8:497).

20. L. P. Jacks, *Confessions of an Octogenarian* (London: Allen and Unwin, 1942), p. 83. Professor James Moffat in September, 1929, wrote on 'Books That Have Influenced Our Epoch: Matthew Arnold's *Literature and Dogma*', *The Expository Times*, 40:534–7.

21. Percy Gardiner, *The Religious Experience of Saint Paul* (London: Williams and Norgate, 1911), p. vii. In *Faith and Conduct* (London: Macmillan, 1887), Gardiner stated that though not altogether a disciple, he felt a debt of gratitude to *Literature and Dogma*, and owed to Arnold more than to anyone else the forming of his 'views and mental habits'.

22. Percy H. Houston, 'The Modernism of Arnold', *Sewanee Review* (April, 1927), 35:196.

23. Maurice Vernes, *Mélanges de critique religieuse*, pp. 266–98. For his study of movements in religious philosophy abroad, M. Vernes, professor in the Faculty of Protestant Theology at the Sorbonne, chose 'deux des manifestations les plus distinguées': Ed. de Hartmann's *Selbstzersetzung des Christenthums und die Religion der Zukunft* (1874) and Arnold's *Literature and Dogma*, translated as *La Crise Religieuse* (1876) from the fifth English edition. The main difference to Vernes is that Hartmann sees no future for Christianity in any form; Arnold would renew it by a method of proof different from any that traditional apologetics had yet offered.

24. E. L. Hunt, 'Matthew Arnold and His Critics', *Sewanee Review*, 44:449–63. The 'curve' suggested here is easily detected by glancing over the number and nature of articles on Arnold written from the 1880's onwards. The undue depreciation of his theological work was noted even in 1904 in a review by H. S. Krans of the books on Arnold by G. W. E. Russell and W. H. Dawson (*Outlook* [1904], 78:679); the revived interest was noted by, among others, T. S. Eliot in 1930 in 'Arnold and Pater' and T. B. Shepherd in 1942 ('Matthew Arnold To-Day', *London Quarterly and Holborn Review*, 167:369).

25. We see this influence when a critic of 1897, reviewing a volume of

ethical lectures, demands, 'With our author are these sayings scientific, or are they fluid and literary?' We see it when R. F. A. Hœrnlé, in presenting his philosophy of religion in 1923, refers to 'the diverse tendencies in modern life and thought which are hostile to religion in any form in which it is more than morality tinged with emotion'. We see it even, or perhaps especially, in T. S. Eliot, whose distaste for Arnold's humanism coexists with Arnoldian values and distinctions that pervade his writing. The very structure and turn of Arnold's phrasing, with a conscious middle variation, echoes in our ears as we read of 'a state secularized, a community turned into a mob, a clerisy disintegrated'. This power to fix a thought in memorable words naturally appealed to Henry James, who found admirable and original Arnold's phrase about religion 'lighting up' morality. But James saw deeper than the æsthetic level to Arnold's seriousness about religion: 'He has cultivated urbanity almost as successfully as M. Renan, and he has cultivated reality rather more' ('Matthew Arnold', *English Illustrated Magazine* [1883–4], 1:241).

26. 'Prophet of European Unity: Matthew Arnold after 50 Years', *The Times Literary Supplement*, April 16, 1938.

27. 'Matthew Arnold', *The Times Literary Supplement*, June 28, 1941.

28. J. Llewellyn Davies gave high praise to Arnold's work as being of 'rare moral and intellectual force . . . one of the three or four leading "Gospels" of this speculative age' ('Mr Matthew Arnold's New Religion of the Bible', *Contemporary Review* [May, 1873], 21:842). H. D. Traill was satirically severe on a 'new religion' that merely furnished graceful draperies for a dying figure, though his reproach to Arnold for offering 'whipped cream to a hungry man' seems offset by another reproach four years later, when he blamed Arnold for offering too strong a meat for babes ('Neo-Christianity and Mr Matthew Arnold', *Contemporary Review* [April, 1884], 45:564 ff., and 'Matthew Arnold', *Contemporary Review*, in *Living Age* [July–Sept., 1888], 178:88 ff.).

29. J. H. Shorthouse, *Life and Letters*, 1:89. The simplicity and modesty of this little-known letter are very revealing of the real Arnold who received the warm and perceptive friendship of men like Huxley. His consciousness of intellectual purpose, and the balance of realism and idealism detected by Shorthouse, help to explain why even T. S. Eliot, having already convicted him of being a murderer in the cathedral, could yet in 1930 find him a more sympathetic writer 'to my generation' than either Carlyle or Ruskin (*Selected Essays*, p. 432), and why Paul Yvon could say in 1938, 'De ce qui nous répugne dans l'esprit victorien, il y a chez Arnold vraiment peu de chose' (*Matthew Arnold   a critique de la vie contemporaine dans sa poésie* [1849–72], p. 25).

30. 'Ardent Agnosticism', *Spectator* in *Living Age* (April–June, 1888), 177:47.

31. A. Flexner, 'Matthew Arnold's Poetry from an Ethical Standpoint', *International Journal of Ethics* (Jan., 1895), 5:215.

32. C. V. Boyer, 'Self-Expression and Happiness', *International Journal of Ethics* (April, 1923), 33:290.

33. L. E. Gates, *Three Studies in Literature*, p. 211.

CHAPTER IX

1. C. Dawson, *Religion and Culture*, p. 217.
2. A. J. Toynbee, *Civilization on Trial*, p. 262.

3. Quoted in Graham Hough, *The Last Romantics* (London: Duckworth, 1949), 155. It is interesting to find T. S. Eliot echoing this utterance of Pater, as he frequently echoes opinions and judgments from Arnold, in the quotation at the head of this chapter. He owes much to the men he attacks for their dissolving powers.

4. Karl Mannheim, *Diagnosis of Our Time*, p. 52.

5. H. J. Muller, 'Humanism in the World of Einstein', *Southern Review* (1939), 5:129.

6. Maurice Cranston, *Manchester Guardian*, June 24, 1955. Commenting on George Orwell's 'two major pre-occupations: the quest for a faith and the obsession with truthfulness', John Wain said in a review, 'Orwell, in fact, lived by Christian ethics while brushing aside the claims of Christianity to be literally "true". This explains his angry contempt for two separate kinds of people: those who did not see intuitively that Christian standards are the only ones to live by, and those who did see it but allowed themselves to become entangled with what he considered to be a lumber of obsolete beliefs.' (*Observer* [London], Jan. 2, 1955.) With a milder phrase in place of 'angry contempt', this passage could have been written about Arnold.

7. Lord Macaulay, *Speeches on Politics and Literature* (London: Dent, 1909), p. 463.

8. Broadcast discussion between Mrs Margaret Knight and Mrs Jenny Morton, published in *The Listener*, Jan. 27, 1955.

9. H. H. Henson, *Retrospect of an Unimportant Life*, 2:340.

10. John Oman, *Honest Religion*, p. 6.

11. Quoted in M. B. Reckitt, *Maurice to Temple: A Century of the Social Movement in the Church of England*, p. 230. H. S. Shelton finds the compromise positions of today hopeless. Those who need authority can go all the way to Rome. For the rest there is the position of Arnold, who 'was more modern than the moderns in that he rejected the dogmatic element absolutely'. Yet no one was surer 'not only concerning the uniqueness and essential importance of Christianity, but of the Christian Church, and, so far as possible, of an undivided Christian Church'. You cannot, the record suggests, do without a church, a communal spiritual life. But the moderns are only confused by the Church's 'irrational assertion of dogmas for which they have no sufficient authority'. Indeed, 'the best solution of our present difficulties seems to me to be to take Matthew Arnold's position as your unifying principle, and to leave it open to individuals to accept or reject this or that fragment of the remaining dogma as they think fit'. ('Matthew Arnold and the Modern Church', *Hibbert Journal* [Jan., 1946], 44:119–24.)

12. Editorial 'First Thoughts', in *The Times Literary Supplement* (London), June 17, 1949.

13. G. Santayana, *Winds of Doctrine*, p. 39.

14. T. S. Eliot, *Selected Essays*, p. 369. The dubiousness of this motive seems to have struck G. K. Clark: 'It cannot be denied that the feeling that they live in a pagan or indifferent society gives religious people a certain exhilaration, something of the moral exaltation of living in the catacombs without any of the danger' (*The English Inheritance* [London: SCM Press, 1950], p. 164).

15. *Selected Essays*, p. 387. Edmund Wilson is very suspicious of conversions among our poets: 'Eliot, in "Ash Wednesday", can move us when his weakness

and chagrin tremble into the accents of prayer; Auden, in his "Christmas Oratorio", can move us with the spectacle of his Joseph and Mary staggered by an Annunciation which seems to be breaking the news of the coming of a difficult and top-flight poet. But are such things as these religion? . . . Aren't they rather the literary devices of uncomfortable rationalists who, disgusted by the dullness of democracy, the vulgarity of revolution, have resorted for protection against them to the mythology and animism of childhood?' They appeal 'to a passion for literature which has managed to burn pure and intense through suffering and degradation. But has this much to do with the Christian cults for which the Churches are built and the parsons and priests ordained?' (*New Yorker*, Nov. 1, 1947, p. 96.)

16. *The Idea of a Christian Society*, p. 34.

17. Henri de Lubac, *The Drama of Atheist Humanism*, p. 17. The challenge, in other words, lies not in the socialist programme but in the power over minds, or souls. Another possible response than fear is shown us in *The Magic Mountain*, where the Jesuit Naphta regards the communist revolution as the necessary bloody purgation of a godless capitalism and a sterile liberalism, a revolution which will pave the way for a return to a simple Christian dualism when men find that their false gods have failed them.

18. H. D. A. Major, *Civilisation and Religious Values*, p. 108. Modernism has had its effect on Catholic teaching also, in terms of allegorizing and spiritualizing. With reference to the Fall of Man we read, 'Thus, while we are compelled to recognize that the story of Genesis is a piece of allegorical mythology, not history, we must also recognize the truth which the allegory is intended to convey' (W. L. Knox and A. R. Vidler, *The Development of Modern Catholicism*, p. 133).

19. L. E. Elliott-Binns, *Religion in the Victorian Era*, p. 277.

20. A. C. McGiffert, *The Rise of Modern Religious Ideas*, p. 142.

21. J. Needham, *The Sceptical Biologist*, p. 254.

22. C. Sherrington, *Man on His Nature*, p. 282.

23. C. A. Coulson, *Science and Christian Belief*, p. 64. Or, as Julian Huxley puts it, we believe in order to act, 'with a faith not only in the validity of our own capacity for making judgments, but also in the existence of certain outer realities' (*Religion without Revelation* [New York: Harper, 1927], p. 28).

24. H. D. Roelofs, 'The Experimental Method and Religious Beliefs', *Mind* (1929), n.s., 38:184–206.

25. C. E. Raven, *English Naturalists from Neckham to Ray*, p. 358.

26. J. M. Keynes, *Essays in Persuasion*, p. vii. Harold J. Laski believed that the problem of civilization is to achieve collective happiness through socialist economics and the mastery of nature by science. Yet he can warn against the deifying of the State, telling us that we cannot 'escape the moral responsibility of personal decision'. Deeper than our obligation to collective relations is the obligation 'to that inner self in each one of us which we can never yield to anyone's keeping without ceasing to be true to our dignity as human beings' (*Faith, Reason and Civilization*, p. 33).

27. Ruth Benedict, 'Anthropology and the Humanities', *American Anthropologist* (Oct.–Dec., 1948), 50:592.

28. E. E. Evans-Pritchard, *Social Anthropology*, p. 114.

29. Edward Glover, *Freud or Jung*, p. 17.

30. Julian Blackburn, *Psychology and the Social Pattern*, p. 114.

31. J. C. Flugel, *Man, Morals, and Society*, p. 9.

32. J. Barzun, *God's Country and Mine*, p. 38. This to T. S. Eliot is not pure but impure humanism. Humanism is valuable if properly limited: it 'makes for breadth, tolerance, equilibrium and sanity'. As such it is the mark of a small minority of cultured individuals. When it uses the language of ethics and faith and offers itself as a substitute for religion or philosophy, it becomes a dangerous and dissolvent force to both Christianity and human character. (*Selected Essays*, p. 488.)

33. J. Maritain, *True Humanism*, p. xvi. Like de Lubac, Maritain has a respect for atheist communism, whose Marxian dialectic has given socialism 'a grasp of existence and a drive' by restoring 'the values of conflict and warfare as an integral condition of the movement of history'. And like Naphta, he feels that the utopian messianism and the blood-letting are only a necessary interlude. When the absurdity of the expectations of realizing the Kingdom of God on earth becomes apparent (as an historical fact, that is) the absurdity of atheism will also become apparent, and the *new* revolution in Russia will be (already) accomplished.

34. Max C. Otto, 'Scientific Humanism', *Antioch Review* (1943), 3:534.

35. Muller, 'Humanism in the World of Einstein', p. 137. The legacy from a conflict which assigned 'facts' to science and 'values' to religion, or to humanism, is seen in the unhappy effect on education early in this century, as described by Emile Boutroux in 1909: 'This conception of things has been shown, notably in France, in the turn that college studies and philosophy have taken. Under the respective names of Sciences and Humanities, the culture of taste, of sentiment, of soul on the one side, and the knowledge of mathematics and of the laws of nature on the other, were separated and isolated.' (*Science and Religion in Contemporary Philosophy*, p. 31.)

36. H. J. Muller, *Science and Criticism*, p. 17.

37. T. S. Eliot, *After Strange Gods*, p. 30. The calm judgment of the world, St Augustine tells us, is that those who set themselves off from the rest of the world are not good.

38. Introduction to E. Durkheim, *The Rules of Sociological Method*, p. xviii.

39. E. M. Forster, *Two Cheers for Democracy*, p. 56.

40. Chapman Cohen, *God and the Universe* (London: Pioneer, n.d.), p. 101.

41. G. L. Dickinson, *The Meaning of Good: A Dialogue*, p. 128. Usually those who find tolerance inadequate as a basis for human solidarity prefer to name love, though the meaning given the word is rarely satisfactory in any practical context. Perhaps only the mystic or the artist can invest the word with moral force, the one speaking from experience and the other by imaginative sympathy with experience, and both, as Arnold insisted in defining the love that is faith in Christ, appealing to the *degree* of that experience present in everyone.

42. G. Barry, 'The Middle Way', in the *Observer* (Oct. 31, 1954).

43. Gilbert Ryle, *Dilemmas*, p. 11.

44. *Last Essays on Church and Religion* (1877), p. 164.

45. A. E. Taylor, *The Faith of a Moralist*, 1:144. The words 'we dare not believe' seem to me an admission that the religious philosopher himself, in practice, uses the 'as if' approach when he insists that man and his values

cannot be explained in merely natural terms. See chap. 1 for Martineau's line of argument.

46. Sherrington, *Man on His Nature*, p. 298.

47. P. H. Nowell-Smith, *Ethics*, p. 135.

48. Mannheim, *Diagnosis of Our Time*, p. 7. Feeling the need for a conscious formulation of a social ethics that will have authority, Mannheim speculates on the possibility, reminiscent of Comte, of establishing the basic virtues through educational and social influence, and embodying these in 'a consistent system similar to the *Summa* of St Thomas'. No new clericalism but an image of society, this system will help foresee patterns of conduct by 'religious and moral recommendations'. The problem is to reconcile this objective catholic concreteness with the Protestant conscience, and to have the theologian work with the sociologist to see whether Christian rules are viable in the modern social context. 'Official' Christianity is not experimental, but if one holds that 'the fundamental Christian attitudes have not been laid down in terms of rigid rules, but have rather been given in concrete paradigmata which only point in the direction where Right is to be sought', then every epoch may make its own creative contribution (p. 117).

49. See note 8. Referring to man's 'capacities and achievements that could never be derived from self-interest', Archbishop William Temple said, 'The image of God—the image of holiness and love—is still there, though defaced; it is the source of his aspirations; it is even—through its defacement —the occasion of his perversity' (*Christianity and Social Order*, p. 43). R. C. Cross reminds us that Plato attacked Callicles and the atheists for the 'shocking consequences' of a 'natural morality', and proceeded to set up another morality of the 'soul', also natural but of a 'different nature'. (The ultimate tradition from which Arnold's dualism derives is apparent here.) Why should we follow this higher nature? Some today find non-natural, moral facts in the universe, perceived by man's 'rational intuition' and hence natural to him, but the difficulty of decision remains. Cross would elucidate reasons for right action 'in terms of knowing how to behave. . . . Thus by training, experience, and practice we learn how to deal with situations, that is, learn how to act.' Reasons discovered thus are not mere signposts. ('Virtue and Nature', *Proceedings of the Aristotelian Society* [1949–50], n.s., 50:137.)

50. C. S. Lewis, *The Abolition of Man*, p. 33.

51. M. Ginsberg, *Moral Progress*, p. 32. The realism with which the rationalist tempers his optimism is shown in Bertrand Russell's writing. He admits that the differences with regard to rules of right action can be 'in practice a very powerful dissolvent of ethical beliefs'. Yet most differences come from asking the wrong questions: 'There is reason to hope, therefore, that a very large measure of agreement on ethical questions may be expected to result from clearer thinking; and this is probably the chief benefit to be ultimately derived from the study of ethics.' (*Philosophical Essays*, p. 57.)

52. H. J. Muller, *Science and Criticism*, p. 277, and B. Bosanquet, *The Value and Destiny of the Individual*, p. 54.

53. Graham Wallas, *The Great Society*, p. 16. S. E. Toulmin is one of today's thinkers who is willing to foresee an end to fragmentation and isolated irrelevance. Ethics is not merely applied psychology, but the two have a common ideal, 'complete knowledge of the ways in which our actions will be received

by others'. They are, he says, tunnelling under the Alps towards each other (*An Examination of the Place of Reason in Ethics*, p. 176).

54. Emile Durkheim, *Sociology and Philosophy*, p. 61. An excellent short statement of the nature and aims of a scientific sociology was given by George H. Mead: 'It is the intensive growth of social interrelations and inter-communications that alone renders possible the recognition by the individual of the import for his social life of the corporate activity of the whole com-munity. The task of intelligence is to use this growing consciousness of inter-dependence to formulate the problems of all, in the terms of the problem of every one. In so far as this can be accomplished cult values will pass over into functional values.' ('Scientific Method and Moral Sciences', *International Journal of Ethics* [April, 1923], 33:245.)

55. Sherrington, *Man on His Nature*, p. 301.

56. Karl Popper, *The Open Society and Its Enemies*, 2:258.

57. Durkheim, *Sociology and Philosophy*, pp. xxxvii–xli.

58. Muller, *Science and Criticism*, p. 275.

59. Mannheim, *Diagnosis of Our Time*, p. 148. To many this optimistic view about the possibilities of elevating the masses will seem unrealistic to the point of fantasy. Even the modern psychologist, analysing the loss of 'individual critical power and moral sensibility' that comes from the projecting of the super-ego on to group standards or ultimately disappointing leaders, implies in his description of the result the operation of a high level of intelligence and a strong moral will: 'When we can no longer project our super-ego on to our God we are compelled to re-introject it, and are to that extent more completely dependent on our own individual moral structure. In some respects, our individual super-ego, when internalized, may be more stringent in its pro-hibitions than when we could project it on to God, and rely on the divine mercy.' (Flugel, *Man, Morals, and Society*, p. 188.) Arnold created for himself such a powerful Inner Voice of Authority, as we see in the *Note-books*, but felt the need later of preserving for the many the sanctions of the Bible and the Christian Church. The Christian believes that loss of the divine authority means disintegration into moral anarchy. Flugel, naturally, is confident that the substitution of 'judgment in terms of psychological insight' for 'moral judgment' will be increasingly effective, as a science, at 'ever higher levels of the hierarchy of values'.

60. Toulmin, *The Place of Reason in Ethics*, p. 49. For a coolly rationalistic corroboration, see Amber Blanco White, *Ethics For Unbelievers* (London: Routledge and Kegan Paul, 1948), p. 149.

61. Quoted in Major, *Civilisation and Religious Values*, p. 65. Similar state-ments may be found in Taylor, *The Faith of a Moralist*, 1:69, and in William Wallace, *Lectures and Essays on Natural Theology and Ethics*, p. 461.

62. G. Tyrrell, *Through Scylla and Charybdis: The Old Theology and the New*, p. 199.

63. G. Tyrrell, *Letters*, p. 239. Tyrrell's wit can be more effective than Arnold's irony: 'As a rationalist, I should regret that Christ did not confer on His vicar the prerogative of impeccability rather than that of infallibility. It would have been a far greater stay to the Church, and refutation of her enemies, than the present unverifiable claim.' (*Ibid.*, p. 67.) And among his stray remarks is this evidence of an irrepressible nature: '*About Popes*. Could you translate *Tu es Petrus* "You're a brick"?' (*Ibid.*, p. 298.)

64. G. Tyrrell, *A Much-Abused Letter*, p. 71.

65. A. Schweitzer, *Civilization and Ethics*, p. 277.

66. Quoted in the *Observer*, July 10, 1955. In other words, the fundamental paradox of ethical idealism, that we must try to achieve the impossible, is now a matter of survival. Schweitzer's reasoning recalls that of Niebuhr (see chap. VI, n. 38). Both faith and experience are called into operation, faith as the 'imaginative reason' giving us insight into that which is best for us as human beings, experience as that selective judgment which 'verifies' and evaluates at the level of our higher or best selves. The whole process is expressed with aphoristic terseness by Arnold's favourite Platonist, John Smith: 'The conduct of life rests on an act of faith which begins as an experiment and ends as an experience' (see chap. IV, n. 27). A simple expression of Schweitzer's mystical-rational relationship is seen in Arnold's praise of Paul (see chap. IV, n. 34). Nor is the essential basis of sympathetic tolerance, attributed in this chapter to the true humanist, impossible to an orthodox theologian. The article on Chillingworth in *The Dictionary of National Biography* gives us his own words: 'My desire is to go the right way to eternal happiness; but whether this lie on the right hand, or on the left, or straightforward; whether it be by following a living guide, or by seeking my direction in a book, or by hearkening to the secret whisper of some private spirit, to me it is indifferent.'

Selected Bibliography

1. THE WRITINGS OF MATTHEW ARNOLD

A. Works, 15 vols. London: Macmillan, 1903.
B. 'The Bishop and the Philosopher', *Macmillan's* (January, 1863), 7:241–56.
'Disestablishment in Wales', *National Review* (March, 1888), 11:1–13.
Essays in Criticism, Third Series, ed. E. J. O'Brien. Boston: Ball, 1910.
Five Uncollected Essays, ed. K. Allott. University of Liverpool Press, 1953.
God and the Bible. London: Watts, 1906.
Introduction to *The Hundred Greatest Men.* London: Sampson Low, Marston, Searle, Rivington, 1879.
Isaiah of Jerusalem. London: Macmillan, 1883.
Isaiah, XL–LXVI, with the Shorter Prophecies. London: Macmillan, 1875.
Last Essays on Church and Religion. London: Smith, Elder, 1877.
Letters, ed. G. W. Russell. 2 vols. London: Macmillan, 1895.
Letters of Matthew Arnold to Arthur Hugh Clough, ed. H. F. Lowry. London: Oxford University Press, 1932.
Literature and Dogma. London: Nelson, n.d.
Note-books, ed. H. F. Lowry, Karl Young, and W. H. Dunn. Oxford University Press, 1952.
Representative Essays, ed. E. K. Brown. Toronto: Macmillan, 1940.
Study of Celtic Literature and Other Essays. London: Dent, 1919.
Unpublished Letters, ed. A. Whitridge. New Haven: Yale University Press, 1923.

2. OTHER PRIMARY SOURCES FOR CHAPTERS I–VIII

ARNOLD, Thomas. *Christian Life, Its Course, Its Hindrances, and Its Helps.* London: Fellowes, 1845.
Fragment on the Church. London: Fellowes, 1863.
Miscellaneous Works, ed. A. P. Stanley. London: Fellowes, 1845.
Sermons, Chiefly on the Interpretation of Scripture. London: Fellowes, 1845.
Sermons, Second Series. London: Reeves and Turner, 1874.
AURELIUS, Marcus. *Thoughts of the Emperor M. Aurelius Antoninus*, ed. Long. London: Bell, 1880.
BOLINGBROKE, Henry St John. *Philosophical Works*, vol. 3. London, 1754.
BRADLEY, Francis H. *Ethical Studies* [1876]. Oxford University Press, 1952.
BUTLER, Joseph. *The Analogy of Religion*, ed. Gladstone. Oxford: Clarendon Press, 1897.
Fifteen Sermons Preached at the Rolls Chapel. London: Tegg, 1841.
CHILLINGWORTH, William. *Works.* 3 vols. Oxford University Press, 1838.
CLOUGH, Arthur Hugh. *Poems and Prose Remains*, ed. by his wife. 2 vols. London: Macmillan, 1869.
COLENSO, John W. *The Pentateuch and the Book of Joshua Critically Examined.* New York: Appleton, 1863.
COLERIDGE, Samuel T. *Aids to Reflection*, ed. Fenby. Edinburgh: Grant, 1906.
Biographia Literaria, ed. Shawcross. 2 vols. Oxford: Clarendon Press, 1907.

COLERIDGE, Samuel T. *Confessions of an Inquiring Spirit.* London: Pickering, 1849.

The Friend. London: Bell and Daldy, 1873.

Literary Remains, ed. H. N. Coleridge. 4 vols. London: Pickering, 1836.

Miscellanies, Literary and Aesthetic, ed. Ashe. London: Bell, 1885.

On the Constitution of Church and State. London: Pickering, 1839.

Table Talk and Omniana, ed. Ashe. London: Bell, 1909.

EMERSON, Ralph W. *Essays, First and Second Series.* Dent, Everyman, 1906.

EPICTETUS. *Discourses*, ed. Long. New York: Hurst, n.d.

GOETHE, Wolfgang von. *The Autobiography of Goethe: Truth and Poetry from My Own Life*, tr. Oxenford. 2 vols. London: Bell, 1897.

Conversations of Goethe with Eckermann and Soret, tr. Oxenford. 2 vols. London: Smith, Elder, 1850.

HALES, John. *Golden Remains.* London: Garthwait, 1659.

'A Tract Concerning Schisms and Schismatics', *Several Tracts.* London, 1721.

HUXLEY, Thomas H. *Evolution and Ethics.* London: Macmillan, 1901.

Science and Christian Tradition. London: Macmillan, 1900.

JAMES, William. *The Varieties of Religious Experience.* New York: Longmans Green, 1917.

The Will to Believe. New York: Longmans Green, 1897.

JOUBERT, Joseph. *Pensées and Letters*, tr. H. P. Collins. London: Routledge, 1928.

KEBLE, John. *Letters of Spiritual Counsel and Guidance.* Oxford: Parker, 1870.

MARTINEAU, James. *Essays, Reviews, and Addresses.* 4 vols. London: Longmans, 1891.

Modern Materialism: Its Attitude towards Theology. London: Williams and Norgate, 1876.

MAURICE, F. D. *The Claims of the Bible and Science.* London: Macmillan, 1863.

Social Morality. London: Macmillan, 1872.

MILL, J. S. *Three Essays on Religion.* New York: Holt, 1874.

NEWMAN, F. W. *The Bigot and the Sceptic.* Ramsgate: Scott, 1869.

Phases of Faith. London: Trübner, 1881.

NEWMAN, J. H. *Apologia Pro Vita Sua.* London: Longmans Green, 1934.

Discourses Addressed to Mixed Congregations. London: Longmans Green, 1909.

Essay on the Development of Christian Doctrine. London: Longmans Green, 1891.

Essays Critical and Historical. 2 vols. London: Basil Montagu, Pickering, 1872.

Fifteen Sermons Preached before the University of Oxford. London: Longmans Green, 1892.

RENAN, Ernest. *Essais de morale et de critique.* Paris: Lévy Frères, 1859.

Saint Paul. New York: Carleton, 1869.

Vie de Jésus. 13th ed. Paris: Lévy, 1895.

SAND, George. *The George Sand–Gustave Flaubert Letters*, tr. A. L. McKenzie. New York: Boni and Liveright, 1921.

SENANCOUR, Étienne Pivert de. *Obermann*, ed. Waite. London: Rider, 1909.

SMITH, John. *Select Discourses*, ed. Williams. Cambridge University Press, 1859.

SPENCER, Herbert. *Data of Ethics.* New York: Crowell, 1879.
First Principles. London: Williams and Norgate, 1862.
SPINOZA, Benedict. *The Chief Works of Benedict Spinoza,* tr. R. H. M. Elwes. 2 vols. London: Bell, 1889.
STILLINGFLEET, Edward. *The Mischief of Separation.* London: Henry Mortlock, 1686.
STRAUSS, David F. *The Life of Jesus,* tr. G. Eliot. London: Swan Sonnenschein, 1892.
TAULER, John. *The Inner Way,* ed. A. W. Hutton. London: Methuen, 1901.
TYNDALL, John. *Fragments of Science.* 2 vols. London: Longmans, 1889.
VINET, Alexander. *Vital Christianity,* tr. R. Turnbull. Edinburgh: Clark, 1846.
WHICHCOTE, Benjamin. *Moral and Religious Aphorisms,* ed. W. R. Inge. London: Elkin Matthews and Marrott, 1930.

3. CRITICAL STUDIES AND BACKGROUND MATERIALS FOR
   CHAPTERS I—VIII

ABBOTT, E., and CAMPBELL, L. *The Life and Letters of Benjamin Jowett.* 2 vols. London: Murray, 1897.
ANNAN, Noel. *Leslie Stephen.* Cambridge, Mass.: Harvard University Press, 1952.
BROOKE, Stopford, ed. *Life, Letters, Lectures and Addresses of Frederick W. Robertson.* New York: Harper [1865],1903.
BROWN, E. K. *Matthew Arnold: A Study in Conflict.* Toronto: Ryerson, 1948.
BROWNELL, W. C. *Victorian Prose Masters.* New York: Scribner's, 1901.
BURTT, E. A. *Types of Religious Philosophy.* New York: Harper, 1939.
CAMPAGNAC, E. T. *The Cambridge Platonists.* Oxford: Clarendon Press, 1901.
CARPENTER, J. E. *The Bible in the Nineteenth Century.* London: Longmans Green, 1903.
CASSELS, W. R. *Supernatural Religion.* London: Watts, 1902.
DAWSON, W. H. *Matthew Arnold and His Relation to the Thought of Our Time.* New York: Putnam's, 1904.
DRIVER, S. R., and KIRKPATRICK, A. F. *The Higher Criticism.* London: Hodder and Stoughton, 1912.
DRUMMOND, J., and UPTON, C. B. *The Life and Letters of James Martineau.* 2 vols. London: Nisbet, 1902.
DUFF, R. A. *Spinoza's Political and Ethical Philosophy.* Glasgow: Maclehose, 1903.
ELIOT, T. S. *Selected Essays.* London: Faber and Faber, 1932.
ELLIOTT-BINNS, L. E. *Essays and Reviews.* London: Parker, 1860.
Religion in the Victorian Era. London: Lutterworth, 1936.
GATES, L. E. *Three Studies in Literature.* New York: Macmillan, 1899.
GIDE, André. *Journals,* tr. J. O'Brien. 4 vols. New York: Knopf, 1951.
GILSON, Etienne. *God and Philosophy.* New Haven: Yale University Press, 1941.
GORE, Charles, et al. *Lux Mundi.* London: Murray, 1889.
GREG, W. R. *The Creed of Christendom.* 2 vols. London: Trübner, 1875.
Enigmas of Life. London: Trübner, 1872.
GUYAU, M. J. *The Non-Religion of the Future.* New York: Holt, 1897.
HENSON, H. H. *Retrospect of an Unimportant Life.* 2 vols. Oxford University Press, 1944.

HOLLOWAY, John. *The Victorian Sage*. London: Macmillan, 1953.

HUIZINGA, Johannes. *Erasmus of Rotterdam*. London: Phaidon, 1952.

HUTTON, R. H. *Criticisms on Contemporary Thought and Thinkers*. 2 vols. London: Macmillan, 1900.

Essays on Some of the Modern Guides to English Thought in Matters of Faith. London: Macmillan, 1914.

HUTTON, W. H. *The English Church from the Accession of Charles I to the Death of Anne*. London: Macmillan, 1913.

HUXLEY, Leonard. *The Life and Letters of Thomas Henry Huxley*. 3 vols. London: Macmillan, 1913.

JACKS, L. P. *The Life and Letters of Stopford Brooke*. 2 vols. London: Murray, 1917.

LAVELEYE, Émile de. *Protestantism and Catholicism in Their Bearing upon the Liberty and Prosperity of Nations*. Toronto: Belford, 1876.

LIDGETT, J. S. *The Victorian Transformation of Theology*. London: Epworth, 1934.

LOWRY, H. F. *Matthew Arnold and the Modern Spirit*. Princeton University Press, 1941.

LYON, Thomas. *The Theory of Religious Toleration in England*. Cambridge University Press, 1937.

MANNING, H. E., et al. *Essays on Religion and Literature*. 3 vols. London: Longmans Green, 1865.

MEAD, G. H. *Movements of Thought in the Nineteenth Century*. University of Chicago Press, 1936.

MUIRHEAD, J. H. *Coleridge as Philosopher*. London: Allen and Unwin, 1930.

PAUL, H. W. *Matthew Arnold*. London: Macmillan, 1920.

PAWSON, G. P. H. *The Cambridge Platonists and Their Place in Religious Thought*. London: SPCK, 1930.

PFLEIDERER, Otto. *The Development of Theology in Germany since Kant, and Its Progress in Britain since 1825*, tr. G. Smith. London : Swan Sonnenschein, 1890.

POWICKE, F. J. *The Cambridge Platonists*. Cambridge, Mass.: Harvard University Press, 1926.

PRINGLE-PATTISON, A. S. *The Idea of God in the Light of Recent Philosophy*. Oxford: Clarendon Press, 1917.

Man's Place in the Cosmos: and Other Essays. Edinburgh: Blackwood, 1902.

PROTHERO, R. E., and BRADLEY, G. G. *Life and Correspondence of Arthur Penrhyn Stanley*. 2 vols. London: Murray, 1893.

ROBERTSON, J. M. *History of Free-Thought in the Nineteenth Century*. 2 vols. London: Watts, 1929.

SCHERER, Edmond. *Mélanges d'histoire religieuse*. Paris: Michel Lévy Frères, 1865.

SEELEY, John R. *Ecce Homo*. Boston: Roberts, 1873.

Natural Religion. Boston: Roberts, 1882.

SELWYN, E. G., ed. *Essays Catholic and Critical*. London: Macmillan, 1929.

SHERMAN, S. P. *Matthew Arnold*. New York: Peter Smith, 1932.

SHORTHOUSE, J. H. *Life and Letters*, ed. by his wife. 2 vols. London: Macmillan, 1905.

SIMPSON, J. Y. *Landmarks in the Struggle between Science and Religion*. London: Hodder and Stoughton, 1925.

STANLEY, A. P. *The Life and Correspondence of Thomas Arnold, D.D.* London: Ward, Lock, 1890.
STEWART, H. L. *A Century of Anglo-Catholicism.* London: Dent, 1929.
STORR, V. F. *The Development of English Theology in the Nineteenth Century.* London: Longmans Green, 1913.
STOUGHTON, John. *History of Religion in England from the Opening of the Long Parliament to 1850.* London: Hodder and Stoughton, 1901.
SYKES, Norman. *Church and State in England in the Eighteenth Century.* Cambridge University Press, 1934.
TRILLING, Lionel. *Matthew Arnold.* New York: Norton, 1939.
TULLOCH, John. *Movements of Religious Thought in Britain during the Nineteenth Century.* New York: Scribner's, 1901.
VERNES, Maurice. *Mélanges de critique religieuse.* Paris: Sandoz et Fischbacher, 1880.
WARD, Mrs Humphrey. *A Writer's Recollections.* London: Collins, 1918.
WHITE, A. D. *A History of the Warfare of Science with Theology.* 2 vols. New York: Appleton, 1896.
WILLEY, Basil. *Nineteenth Century Studies.* London: Chatto and Windus, 1949.
WOODWARD, E. L. *The Age of Reform.* Oxford: Clarendon Press, 1938.
YOUNG, G. M. *Victorian England.* Oxford University Press, 1936.
YVON, Paul. *Matthew Arnold et la critique de la vie contemporaine dans sa poésie (1849-72).* Caen: Imprimerie Ch. Le Tendre, 1938.

4. PRIMARY SOURCES, CRITICAL STUDIES, AND BACKGROUND MATERIAL FOR CHAPTER IX

BARZUN, Jacques. *God's Country and Mine.* London: Gollancz, 1955.
BLACKBURN, Julian. *Psychology and the Social Pattern.* London: Kegan Paul, 1945.
BOSANQUET, Bernard. *The Value and Destiny of the Individual.* London: Macmillan, 1913.
BOUTROUX, Émile. *Science and Religion in Contemporary Philosophy,* tr. J. Nield. London: Duckworth, 1909.
COULSON, C. A. *Science and Christian Belief.* Oxford University Press, 1955.
DAWSON, Christopher. *Religion and Culture.* London: Sheed and Ward, 1948.
DICKINSON, G. Lowes. *The Meaning of Good: A Dialogue.* London: Brimley Johnson, 1902.
DURKHEIM, Émile. *The Rules of Sociological Method,* tr. Salovay and Mueller. University of Chicago Press, 1938.
Sociology and Philosophy, tr. D. F. Pocock. London: Cohen and West, 1953.
ELIOT, T. S. *After Strange Gods.* London: Faber and Faber, 1934.
The Idea of a Christian Society. London: Faber and Faber, 1939.
EVANS-PRITCHARD, E. E. *Social Anthropology.* London: Cohen and West, 1951.
FLUGEL, J. C. *Man, Morals, and Society.* London: Duckworth, 1945.
FORSTER, E. M. *Two Cheers for Democracy.* London: Edward Arnold, 1951.
GINSBERG, Morris. *Moral Progress.* Glasgow: Jackson, 1944.
GLOVER, Edward. *Freud or Jung.* London: Allen and Unwin, 1950.
KEYNES, J. M. *Essays in Persuasion.* London: Hart-Davis, 1951.
KNOX, W. L., and VIDLER, A. R. *The Development of Modern Catholicism.* London: Allan, 1933.

LASKI, H. J. *Faith, Reason, and Civilization.* New York: Viking, 1944.

LEWIS, C. S. *The Abolition of Man.* London: Geoffrey Bles, 1947.

LUBAC, Henri de. *The Drama of Atheist Humanism.* London: Sheed and Ward, 1949.

McGIFFERT, A. C. *The Rise of Modern Religious Ideas.* New York: Macmillan, 1921.

MAJOR, H. D. A. *Civilization and Christian Values.* London: Allen and Unwin, 1948.

MANNHEIM, Karl. *Diagnosis of Our Time.* London: Kegan Paul, 1943.

MARITAIN, Jacques. *True Humanism,* tr. Adamson. London: Geoffrey Bles, 1938.

MULLER, H. J. *Science and Criticism.* New Haven: Yale University Press, 1943.

NEEDHAM, Joseph. *The Sceptical Biologist.* London: Chatto and Windus, 1929.

NIEBUHR, Reinhold. *The Nature and Destiny of Man: A Christian Interpretation.* 2 vols. New York: Scribner's, 1947.

NOTT, Kathleen. *The Emperor's Clothes.* London: Heinemann, 1953.

NOWELL-SMITH, P. H. *Ethics.* London: Penguin Books, 1954.

OMAN, John. *Honest Religion.* Cambridge University Press, 1941.

POPPER, Karl. *The Open Society and Its Enemies.* 2 vols. London: Routledge and Kegan Paul, 1952.

RAVEN, C. E. *English Naturalists from Neckham to Ray.* Cambridge University Press, 1947.

RECKITT, M. B. *Maurice to Temple: A Century of the Social Movement in the Church of England.* London: Faber and Faber, 1947.

RUSSELL, Bertrand. *Philosophical Essays.* London: Longmans Green, 1910.

RYLE, Gilbert. *Dilemmas.* Cambridge University Press, 1954.

SANTAYANA, George. *Winds of Doctrine.* London: Dent, 1926.

SCHWEITZER, Albert. *Civilization and Ethics.* London: A. and C. Black, 1949.

SHERRINGTON, Charles. *Man on His Nature.* London: Penguin Books, 1940.

TAYLOR, A. E. *The Faith of a Moralist.* 2 vols. London: Macmillan, 1930.

TEMPLE, William. *Christianity and Social Order.* London: Penguin Books, 1942.

TOULMIN, S. E. *An Examination of the Place of Reason in Ethics.* Cambridge University Press, 1950.

TOYNBEE, A. J. *Civilization on Trial.* Oxford University Press, 1948.

TYRRELL, George. *Letters,* ed. M. D. Petrie. London: Unwin, 1920.

A Much-Abused Letter. London: Longmans Green, 1906.

Through Scylla and Charybdis: The Old Theology and the New. London: Longmans Green, 1907.

WALLACE, William. *Lectures and Essays on Natural Theology and Ethics.* Oxford: Clarendon Press, 1898.

WALLAS, Graham. *The Great Society.* London: Macmillan, 1914.

WHITEHEAD, A. W. *Religion in the Making.* New York: Macmillan, 1927.

Index

and experience, 93; and idea of
God, 110, 113–14
Reason: ambiguity of, 226; Arnold
on, 82–3; as in Coleridge and
Cambridge Platonists, 82–4;
Hooker on, 226; J. H. Newman
and Vinet on, 81–2; as in Vau-
venargues, 225; *see also* Imagina-
tive reason
Religion: Arnold on, 28–30, 48–9;
Arnold's, 88; Arnold's criticized,
235–7; Bolingbroke on, 225; S.
Butler on, 115; crisis in, 3–5;
decline in, 185–6; Gladstone on,
6; Joubert on, 88; liberalism in,
7; Mill on, 91, 218; modern
varieties of, 171–4; and morality,
31, 134, 232; Niebuhr on, 189,
232; transition to, 28, 41, 124;
see also Religious thought; Re-
ligious writing; Science and
religion
Religion without Revelation, 239
Religious Philosophy, Types of, 171–4
Religious thought, M. Arnold's, **166–
174**; debt to Spinoza of, 64–6;
68–9; ideas owed to T. Arnold,
Bishop Butler, Coleridge, Goethe,
Platonists by, 57–60; key to, 31,
53
Religious writing: Arnold's approach
to, **73–8,** 77; Arnold's criticized,
176–8, 220, 235–7
Renan, Ernest: Arnold differs from,
168; biblical criticism of, 222;
and Christianity, 88–90; and
conduct, 133, 231; influence on
Arnold of, 61–2, 88–90, 168–9;
on Jesus, 232; quoted, 73, 151;
on St Paul, 223
'Resignation', 96
Resurrection: interpreted naturally,
54; St Paul on, 35; Spinoza on,
69, 101; Strauss on, 227
Return upon oneself, 132, **160–6,** 170
Ritschl, Albrecht: and Arnold, viii,
190, 209
Ritualism: described, 14–15; hostility
to, 4–5, 15–17

Robert Elsmere, 183
Robertson, F. W., quoted, 103, 229
Robertson, J. M.: on Arnold, viii,
220; on Coleridge and Newman,
228
Roelofs, H. D.: on science and faith,
192
'Rugby Chapel', 122
Russell, Bertrand, 172; on ethics, 241
Rutherford, Autobiography of Mark, 25

ST AUGUSTINE, 118, 183, 203, 231
St Paul: Arnold on, **32–5,** 49, 78, 177;
central idea of, 221; on idea of
God, 33; and moral emotion, 34;
and mysticism, 86; Renan on,
223; on resurrection, 35; and
return upon oneself, 160
St Paul and Protestantism: criticism of,
79, 176–7; quoted, 159
St Thomas Aquinas, 196, 197, 242
Sainte-Beuve, C. A.: influence on
Arnold of, 56, 160, 198
Sand, George: influence on Arnold
of, 62; quoted, 55
Santayana, George: on Christianity,
172, 189
Scherer, E.: and Arnold, 137; on
Vinet, 225
Schiller, F. C. S.: on idealism and
pragmatism, 139
Schleiermacher, Friedrich, 104, 173
Schweitzer, A.: ethics of, 211–12;
quoted, 182
Science: modern attitudes of, 190–4,
204–5
Science and humanism: Benedict on,
193; Boutroux on, 240; Muller
on, 184, 197–8, 207
Science and morality: Muller on,
197–8, 207; Sherrington on, 191,
205
Science and religion, 17–24, 26, 183;
Arnold on, **73–7,** 88, 159; at-
tempted reconciliation, 184; Dis-
raeli on, 6; J. Huxley on, 239;
T. Huxley and Tyndall on, 4;
Maurice on, 19; Muirhead on,
27; *Quarterly Review* on, 20; Seeley